Dameronia

JAZZ PERSPECTIVES
Eric Porter and John Szwed, Series Editors
Lewis Porter, Founding Editor

Dameronia

The Life and Music of
Tadd Dameron

Paul Combs

Foreword by Benny Golson

The University of Michigan Press
Ann Arbor

First paperback edition 2013
Copyright © by the University of Michigan 2012

Published in the United States of America by
The University of Michigan Press
Manufactured in the United States of America
♾ Printed on acid-free paper

2016   2015   2014   2013   5   4   3   2

A CIP catalog record for this book is available from the British Library.

Library of Congress Cataloging-in-Publication Data

Combs, Paul, saxophonist.
      Dameronia : the life and music of Tadd Dameron / Paul Combs.
          p.   cm.—(Jazz perspectives)
      Includes bibliographical references and index.
      ISBN 978-0-472-11413-9 (cloth : alk. paper)—ISBN 978-0-472-02881-8 (e-book)
      1. Dameron, Tadd, 1917–1965. 2. Composers—United States—Biography.
      3. Jazz musicians—United States—Biography. I. Title.
      ML410.D147C66   2012
      781.65092—dc23
      [B]   2012025920

   ISBN 978-0-472-03563-2 (pbk. : alk. paper)

This book is dedicated to the memory of Charlie Rouse, Art Blakey, Dizzy Gillespie, and Harold Vick, to whom I have kept my promise.

Contents

At Website http://www.press.umich.edu/22963/dameronia:
Further Details
Catalog of Published and Unpublished Titles
Discography
Bibliography

Foreword
Remembering Tadd Dameron

The year was 1951. I had just been hired as a saxophonist in Bull Moose Jackson's band, and when I arrived I discovered, very much to my surprise, that Bull Moose's pianist was, of all people, my hero Tadd Dameron. I had been a fan of his long before I joined Bull Moose. I marveled at the way he treated small groups of five or six musicians consisting of trumpet, a saxophone or two, piano, bass, and drums, and I longed to know how he got such a big, full sound out of such a small number of musicians. The groups I heard included Fats Navarro on trumpet, Charlie Rouse on tenor, and Tadd himself on piano.

Of course, Tadd had no idea who I was, but he immediately knew I was a fan of his. After our first rehearsal, when he had a chance to hear me play, he eagerly approached and, with a spirit of excitement, told me how impressed he was with me. Then he added, "The next time I go to Europe I'd like to take you with me if you're agreeable." If I was agreeable? I almost fell on the floor. It was then that we began our relationship, which would last until his unfortunate death in 1965. This meeting and our relationship would set the course of my career.

Tadd took me under his wing and unselfishly shared the inner workings of his exceptionally creative and perceptive mind. It seemed like he held back nothing that his mind had acquired over years of experience writing for many famous luminaries—including even Duke Ellington, who was himself a genius. He never played it close to the chest; he revealed everything he knew as I bombarded him with my endless queries of who, what, where, when, how, why. I was on an excursion full of deep musical epiphanies that were miraculously taking me to places I never knew existed.

Though he played tenor saxophone, Bull Moose Jackson had become more well-known as a singer while playing with Lucky Millinder's band. He got the name "Bull Moose" because his hands and feet were large, as well as his head. Rather than acquiring a name relating to an ape of sorts, he became Bull Moose instead. He was a lovely man with a fantastic voice, which took him to fame with a tune called "I Love You, Yes I Do." Tadd was a part of Jackson's aggregation because he and Bull Moose, whose given name was Benjamin, had been schoolmates growing up in Cleveland, Ohio. Tadd was not working at the time when "Moose" (which is what we all called him) approached him and suggested that he could join the band for a while and leave whenever he wanted to. This was the time I joined the band.

After settling into the band, it seems Bull Moose wanted to change the personnel, giving it a more up-to-date sound, something more hip yet commercial. Since Moose and his road manager, Snookie Hulbert (also a saxophonist with the group and a former member of the Jimmy Lunceford band), liked the way I played so much, they asked me if I knew a good trumpet player, bass player, and drummer. I did indeed. I suggested they call Johnny Coles, who could read anything and had a sound that could make the heart cry. Then I suggested Jymie Merit, who had played with B. B. King but was also a good jazz bassist. Then came the drummer: none other than Philly Joe Jones, who had not yet acquired the "Philly" moniker that Tadd would later give him. People will never know what a fantastic rhythm-and-blues drummer he was.

As I began absorbing the length and breadth of Tadd's knowledge, my writing began to change dramatically. I began to sound like Tadd Dameron. I remember once we were playing a town in Texas when he said, tongue-in-cheek, "What a drag! You write an arrangement and someone comes up to me and says, 'What a great arrangement, Tadd.'" Actually, he was so proud of me.

Even though we were basically a rhythm-and-blues group, the band developed two different appreciative audiences, because we were playing Tadd's and my work, as well. Some came to hear Bull Moose sing his hits, and some came to hear jazz. We realized this when we played in St. Louis, when we looked out into the audience and saw two different responses. Because of who we were, we had no problem being true to each concept.

As in most cases, the band eventually broke up, its personnel going in separate directions. But after a few months, I received a call from Tadd. He had been hired by Clarence Robinson to write and play a new show in Atlantic City for the summer of 1953. It was an entertaining show complete with a chorus line of girls, a master of ceremonies, a tap dancer, a comedy act, and a fellow who danced with a table with chairs atop, held miraculously in his teeth. Of course, Tadd called others as well: Johnny Coles, Jymie Merit, Philly Jo Jones, Clifford

Brown, Cecil Payne, Gigi Gryce, and a trombonist whose name I can't remember.

It was during this time that he recorded the album *A Study in Dameronia* for the Prestige label. The albums were ten inches in those days. Tadd, of course, went on to write and record other things, but I always felt this album was something special. Incidentally, the studio in which we recorded it was so small that Clifford's microphone was placed in front of me on my left, so that when he played his solos, his trumpet was almost resting on my left shoulder and his trumpet sound was going right into my ear. At day's end, I told him, "Brownie," which is what we all called him, "now I know everything about you." He laughed as he always did.

I will forever see Tadd Dameron as a kind and generous mentor, who was the most important part of my musical life. The thing that drew me to him, aside from how he worked so well with just a few instruments, was his sense of melody and his love for it. His melodies sang and continue to sing, as if always ready to come to center stage. Until this very day Tadd Dameron continues to sing in my mind's ear as I remember and listen. My appreciation is ineffable.

BENNY GOLSON
FRIEDRICHSHAFEN, GERMANY

Preface

I was touched by the spirit of Tadd Dameron in the early 1960s. As a fifteen-year-old boy who lived for music and wanted to compose and perform, I was profoundly inspired by Tadd's famous words, "There is enough ugliness in the world, I'm interested in beauty," reprinted in Barry Ulanov's *A History of Jazz in America*. This was not the first I had heard of Dameron; I already knew some of his writing for midsized bands, and I had already been to my first jam session, where I called "Good Bait" and nervously attempted to solo on it. But it was his words that had the greatest influence on me at the time, for they helped me to define my own aesthetic and my own sense of purpose as a musician.

Over the years Dameron's spirit, through his music and his inspiring words, stayed with me. Some time later, after writing a tune in which his influence was clearly evident, I went to the library to find a book about this man, whose words and music had made such a deep impression on me. "Surely," I thought, "there must be a book about so great a musician." I was wrong.

So, for better or worse, in 1987 I decided that if no one else would write his story, I would. Never having written a book before, I had no idea what I was in for, but as I interviewed musicians I have admired for most of my life, they all made me promise that I would see this project through.

Tadd Dameron was a very private man, and the story of his life presented here took a great deal of research. Sometimes, where there are gaps, I have had to resort to speculation. I have endeavored to be as clear about my speculations as possible, since much of what has been written about him before, speculations have been presented as fact. While some readers might criticize my efforts to come to an understanding of Dameron's state of mind at various times in his life, educated guesses are unfortunately our only recourse. Regrettably, Dameron did not keep a diary or journal, and he was vague in discussing personal matters, even with friends. My speculations are based on such information as we have and are offered as possible explanations for the man's sometimes perplexing actions or inactions.

As a composer and arranger I am particularly interested in Dameron's approach to melody, harmony, and formal structure. At times the discussion of these issues may prove a bit baffling for the general reader, but it would be irresponsible for me not to illustrate my observations. At the same time, I have endeavored to balance the technical discussions with ones of a more general nature. A great deal of the music discussed is available on recording, and it is hoped that the reader will make the effort to listen to it and in doing so will be able to understand the points made. This will be particularly important in the case of some discussions where getting permission to quote written music became impractical. Fortunately all but one of these discussions concern music that has been recorded. Regarding the music that has not been recorded as yet, it is sincerely hoped that much of it eventually will be.

The following is a brief discography of CDs released in the last dozen or so years. Some of them are currently in print and will be easy to find. Others may be out of print, but because they are CDs, you should be able to find copies in good shape with a little hunting. This listing is by no means exhaustive, and there may be items not listed here that you can find by using various search engines. The contents of some of these items overlap. In roughly chronological order:

Harlan Leonard and His Rockets—1940	Classics 670
Jimmie Lunceford and His Orchestra 1941–1945	Classics 862
Dizzy Gillespie and His Sextets and Orchestra	Musicraft 53
Georgie Auld and His Orchestra	Musicraft 56
Sarah Vaughan	Proper Box 27, Classics 958
Babs Gonzales, 1947–1949	Classics 1124
Dizzy Gillespie—	
The Complete RCA Victor Recordings	Bluebird 66528-2
Dexter Gordon—Settin' the Pace	Savoy Jazz SVY-17027
Fats Navarro—Goin' to Minton's	Savoy Jazz 92861-2
Fats Navarro Featured with	
Tadd Dameron's Band	Fresh Sound CD 171
The Complete Blue Note and Capitol Recordings	
of Fats Navarro and Tadd Dameron	Blue Note 33373
Tadd Dameron, 1947–1949	Classics 1106
Coleman Hawkins—Body and Soul	Victor Jazz 09026-68515-2

The Miles Davis/Tadd Dameron Quintet—	
In Paris Festival International de Jazz,	
May 1949	Sony Records SRCS 5695
Ted Heath—Listen to My Music, Vol. 4	Hep CD 69
Clifford Brown Memorial	
(Contains a Study in Dameronia)	Original Jazz Classics 017-2
Carmen McRae—Blue Moon	Verve 314 543 829-2
Tadd Dameron—Fontainebleau	Original Jazz Classics 055-2
Tadd Dameron—Mating Call	Prestige PRCD-30163
Blue Mitchell—Smooth as the Wind	Original Jazz Classics 871-2
Various Artists—The Lost Sessions	
(The Unreleased 12/14/61 Session)	Blue Note 21484
Tadd Dameron—The Magic Touch	Original Jazz Classics 143-2
Milt Jackson Orchestra—Big Bags	Original Jazz Classics 366-2
Sonny Stitt and the Top Brass	Collectables 6532

This book is complemented by appendices, including a complete discography, which can be found at http://www.press.umich.edu/22963/dameronia.

Acknowledgments

Books of this nature are, in a sense, the work of many people. I could not possibly have managed to write this account without the help and cooperation of others. First I want to thank, from the bottom of my heart, Valerie Wilmer, whose generous and steadfast support of this project was invaluable. Among her many important contributions to this book are her interviews, made on my behalf, with Ivor Mairants and Jack Parnell. Also due for special thanks are Don Sickler, who fits into several of the categories below and who helped me gain access to some of Dameron's music that might not have been available to me otherwise; Bertand Uberall, for his invaluable help in locating music in the Copyright Office and his great generosity of spirit; and Lewis Porter, whose support of this project was key in making possible the book in your hands and whose guidance and friendship have helped me in so many ways.

Then there are all those who have given me their time in interviews: Chris Albertson, Art Blakey, Edgar and Barbara Blakeney, Jeannie Cheatham, Buddy Crewe, Dorothy Dameron, Mia Dameron, Clem De Rosa, Gil Fuller, Benny Golson, Carl Hayse, Venus Irving-Prescott, Ron Javorsky, Hank Jones, Orin Keepnews, Stan Levey, James Moody, Dan Morgenstern, Billy Paul, Cecil Payne, Charlie Rouse, Jimmy Scott, Willie Smith, Thomas Stewart, Myron Styles, Myra Taylor, Gerald Wilson, and George Ziskind.

Many have taken the time to share with me what they could, which was often a valuable piece of information: Tony Bennett, Ray Brown, Dave Burns, Benny Carter, Emil Charlap, Caesar Dameron Jr., Denise Dameron, Frank Driggs, Dizzy Gillespie, Loraine Gordon, William P. Gottlieb, Charles Haddix, Jimmy Heath, Percy Heath, Arthur Howard, Milt Jackson, Donald Kennedy, Val Kent, Charlie Lake, Yusef Lateef, Al Liggins, Don Manning, Charlie Mariano, Neal Martin, Jackie McLean, Sam Noto, Hod O'Brien, Fr. Peter O'Brien, Sam Rivers, Max Roach, Sonny Rollins, William "Shep" Shepherd,

Floyd Standifer, Bobby Tucker, Stanley Turrentine, Paul Verrette, and Jimmy Williams.

Others gave me important references, facilitated access to interviewees, or shared their personal resources: Bob Blumenthal, Mark Cantor, Joe Ciavardone, Elaine Cohen, John Conant, Leo Curran, Peter Bodge, Dr. William Fielder, Michael Fitzgerald, Mark Gardner, Larry Glover, William Gottlieb, Hilliard Green, Maxine Harvard, Dick Johnson, Anne Kuebler, Joe Lovano, Michael Moran, Stuart Morgan, Joe Mosbrook, Ted Pease, Michael Pedecin, Harvey Pekar, Vincent Pelote, Leif Bo Petersen, Brian Priestley, Vanessa Ruben, Gray Sargent, Buddy Sullivan, Jeff Sultanof, Ray Whitehouse, and Melvin Williams.

I am also grateful to the following for specific permissions to quote from manuscripts, documents, and copyrighted material. Peter O'Brien, executive director of the Mary Lou Williams foundation, for the transcription of the "Mary Lou" piano part and for correspondence with Tadd Dameron; Frank Driggs, for quotations from arrangements written by Tadd Dameron held in the Frank Driggs Collection of Lunceford Orchestrations and for a poster from his collection; Leonard Whitcup, Inc., and Tee Pee Music Co. for the use of "Bewildered," by Teddy Powell and Leonard Whitcup; Twenty-Eighth Street Music, for the use of "A Blue Time," "Don't Forget It," "Fred's Delight," "Never Been in Love," "Pan-Dameronium," and "Sando Latino," all by Tadd Dameron; Val Wilmer, for photographs from her collection; Mia Dameron, for photographs from her collection; and the Institute of Jazz Studies, for the reproduction of a poster from its collection.

This book could not have been written without the help of the fine people at the Special Collections Department of the Library of the University of Arizona; Boston Public Library; Multnomah County Library, Portland, Oregon; Spaulding Library at the New England Conservatory of Music; the Institute of Jazz Studies at Rutgers University, Newark Campus; the library of the Western Reserve Historical Society, Cleveland; the Music Library at Yale University; the National Archives, New York; the National Museum of American History (NMAH) Archives Center of the Smithsonian Institution and the Library of Congress, Washington, DC; the New York Public Library and its branches: the Library for the Performing Arts, and the Schomburg Center for Research In Black Culture. Other institutions that helped my research are American Federation of Musicians locals 9-535 (Boston), 92 (Buffalo), 4 (Cleveland), and 7 (Los Angeles), and the Cambridge, Massachusetts, Police Department. Among the many individuals at these institutions not mentioned elsewhere are Nishani Frazier, Tad Hershhorn, Reuben Jackson, Maria Jane Loizou, Joseph Peterson, Marc Pinto, and Deborra Richardson, who were particularly helpful.

I also want to acknowledge my Internet friends at the Jazz Programmers Listing and elsewhere, among them Bob Cohen, Bobby Jackson, Paul Schomer, John Simna, Ed Trefzger, and Jim Wilke; and my friends at publishing and record companies, including Maureen Sickler of Second Floor Music, Michael Cuscuna of Mosaic Records, Judy Bell at the Richmond Organization, and Bob Curnow of Sierra Music.

In addition many musicians helped me assimilate the previously unknown music of Tadd Dameron: Jim Cameron, Bob Coviello, Jamie Dunphy, Jay Ford, Lydia Fortune, Herman Hampton, Don Hemwall, Manuel Kaufmann, Doug Leaffer, Paul Marcantonio, Mark Michaels, Wayne Mogel, Patrick Mottaz, Jim Pastore, Garo Saraydarian, Michael Shea, Tony Sumbury, and Stanley C. Swann III. After over twenty years of plugging away at this book, there are also, without doubt but with regret, people whose names have escaped me in making this list. To them I give my heartfelt thanks just the same, as well as my apologies. My apologies also go to those who gave me leads and contacts that, for various reasons, I was never able to follow up. I know this book would have been richer if I had. I would also like to acknowledge Ian MacDonald, whose groundbreaking book *Tadd—The Life and Legacy of Tadley Ewing Dameron* cleared some of the brush, as it were, for my research.

Many helped keep me on track and gave me the benefit of outside eyes. Thanks again to Val Wilmer, Jeff Sultanof, and Peter Lamson for reading, correcting, and commenting on the early draft of the book. Later drafts benefited from the observations of my peer reviewers; the former series editor, Lewis Porter; the current series editor, John Szwed; and especially my editor, Chris Hebert, whose patience and support for this project has been a wonderful gift. I realize this more and more each time I talk with another author struggling to find a publisher. I also want to thank the technical staff at the University of Michigan Press for their skill and expertise in preparing the book for publication.

Last but not least to my mother, Florence Hagedorn, who lent her eyes to policing the manuscript in its early drafts; my mother-in-law, Marie Baxter, whose hospitality made it possible for me to work in New York with freedom and frequency; and all those family and friends who have cheered me on all these years.

I

Early Days

Cleveland

Though seldom credited as such, Cleveland, Ohio, is an important city in jazz history. Although not on the scale of Chicago or New York, the list of significant players who came from and developed their skills there is diverse and impressive: Joe Alexander, Albert Ayler, Benny Bailey, Bill D'Arango, John Fedchock, Bobby Few, Jim Hall, Buster Harding, Bill Hardman, Eugene "Fats" Heard, Benjamin "Bull Moose" Jackson, Joe Lovano, "Little" Jimmy Scott, Noble Sissle, Willie "Face" Smith,[1] and Freddie Webster, among others. Cleveland was also where the Jimmie Lunceford Orchestra started out in 1929, and it was an important city in the development of the careers of Gene Harris, Artie Shaw, Johnny "Hammond" Smith, and Art Tatum.[2] Of course it was also the birthplace, incubator, and sanctuary of Tadley Ewing Dameron.

From the 1930s through the mid-1950s, Cleveland was an important stop for national touring acts, such as Duke Ellington, Benny Goodman, and Ella Fitzgerald, and it had a thriving nightlife scene of its own. For jazz, an important part of that scene was the predominantly African American neighborhood on the east side, spanning an area roughly bounded by East Twentieth Street on the west, Euclid Avenue on the north, East 105th Street on the east, and Quincy or Woodland Avenue on the south. Through the middle of this runs Cedar Avenue, a small but once bustling thoroughfare.

Hardly anything is left of the Cedar Avenue of Tadley Dameron's adult years, let alone his boyhood, just the Phyllis Wheatley House, a few churches, and a couple of stores and bars. By the time of Dameron's retreats here in the

1950s, this then-busy commercial street was home to an impressive number of live-entertainment venues. Clubs such as the Corner Tavern, the Royal Tavern, and the Rendezvous—which was owned by Tadd's brother, Caesar—featured local jazz. There were others, such as the Cedar Gardens and the Ebony, that presented floor shows with dancers and other entertainers. Jack's was one of several rhythm-and-blues bars and the only one left standing today. Some smaller places, such as the Club Celebrity, had just a pianist or organist. One could find much the same on Carnegie, Euclid, and Woodland avenues, as well as East Fifty-fifth and East 105th Streets. There were (to name just a few) the Club Congo, the Harlem Café, the Sky Bar, Café Society, the Chatterbox, Tia Juana's, and Gleason's. Today, though the clubs are almost all gone, the quiet residential areas are, superficially at least, little different from the way they were in the 1920s and '30s, the years of Dameron's childhood and adolescence. As one explores the neighborhood west of Fifty-fifth Street, one finds mostly one- and two-family frame houses. Near the railroad and on the lower numbered streets there are also a few factories. This is the neighborhood that produced Tadd Dameron and from which he was never really separated until his death in 1965.

Childhood

Tadd Dameron was born in Cleveland just weeks before the United States entered World War I, an event that would soon lead to the unprecedented growth of Cleveland's black population. Throughout the nineteenth century, a variety of European immigrants had come to Cleveland and established their neighborhoods: first Germans, then Irish, Italian, Polish, and other Eastern Europeans. Each in turn made new lives for themselves in this growing commercial and industrial center of the Midwest. Then came World War I, when immigration was cut off and large numbers of men were conscripted. Cleveland had become a major manufacturing center, with steel mills, foundries, machine shops, and the early automotive and aircraft industries. All this industry needed workers, so it turned to the large numbers of black men who were not being enlisted with the same zeal as whites. The Great Migration had begun.

However, unlike the recent arrivals, the family of Tadd's mother had been in Cleveland since the late 1890s. Ruth Olga Harris was born in 1892 or 1893 in Kosciusko, Mississippi, the daughter of Reverend Silas Caesar Harris and Sophie Tadley Harris.[3] By the time she was six, the family had moved to Cleveland, where, in 1899, her father founded St. Paul's A.M.E. Zion Church. The congregation is still active at its original location, East Fifty-fifth Street and

Quincy Avenue. Ruth had a brother, Silas Jr., who was born shortly before or after her,[4] and two sisters, Opal and Tennie, who were most likely younger.

On June 20, 1913, twenty-year-old Ruth Harris married Isaiah Peake, a porter only a year or so older than she. Given the absence of a civil marriage license on file at the city hall, it seems most likely they were married in her father's church.[5] Not much else is known about Ruth's first husband. Tadd's[6] brother, Caesar, named for his maternal grandfather, was born March 4, 1914. By August of 1914, Isaiah Peake and his young family lived at 3852 Central Avenue. By 1916, the Peakes were living at the same address as Reverend Harris.[7] By the time Tadley was born, on February 21, 1917, the family had moved to 4508 Central Avenue. Tadley was, of course, his maternal grandmother's family's name.

We know little about the Peakes' family life in those early years, but according to the petition for divorce that Ruth would file in 1924, by 1919 Ruth and Isaiah's marriage had failed. Further, the petition states that Isaiah, "ever since their marriage has failed, refused and wilfully neglected to provide plaintiff and their said children with food, clothing, shelter and the common necessaries of life, so that plaintiff has been compelled to live and care for herself and their said children, by her own labors and exertions, and upon the charity of friends and relatives." Isaiah's side of the story has not been preserved.

The years following the breakup of the Peake family appear to have been difficult ones for Ruth. She worked at different jobs and moved frequently, according to the city directory, which shows different addresses and occupations for her in the years 1922, 1923, and 1924. There may also have been tensions between Ruth and her father. After the separation, Isaiah Peake lived in a house owned by Reverend Harris, where he continued to reside for several years. One has to wonder why Reverend Harris would have rented a home to his errant son-in-law while his daughter and grandsons had to move from place to place. Another indication that there may have been a rift between Ruth and her father is the fact that her second marriage, to Adolphus Dameron, was not solemnized by Reverend Harris, but by Justice of the Peace W. J. Zoul,[8] in the neighboring town of Shaker Heights.

This must have been a difficult time for Tadd and Caesar as well, for Caesar was five when his parents gave up on their marriage and Tadd only two. In addition to the frequent moves, the failure of their parents' marriage would have meant that there was conflict not only between their mother and father, who sometimes lived on the same street, but quite likely among other members of the family. Further, conditions in their neighborhood at the time were generally difficult. The Great Migration had caused catastrophic pressure on the housing market, resulting in overcrowding and exceptionally high rents. In his autobi-

ography, *The Big Sea*, the poet Langston Hughes describes the difficult circumstances in which many East Side black families found themselves. From 1916
to 1920 Hughes attended Central High School, which Tadd would also attend
some fifteen years later. Hughes wrote of this time:

> We always lived, during my high school years, either in an attic or a basement,
> and paid quite a lot for such inconvenient quarters. White people on the east
> side of the city were moving out of their frame houses and renting them to
> Negroes at double and triple the rents they could receive from others. An eight-
> room house with one bath would be cut up into apartments and five or six
> families crowded into it, each two-room kitchenette apartment renting for what
> the whole house had rented before.[9]

Adolphus Dameron, Tadd's stepfather, was born to Cicero and Fannie Aker
Dameron in Jefferson, Georgia, in 1877 or 1878. He was living in Cleveland by
1921, and in 1923 he bought a house at 2312 Carnegie. This is where he was living
when he married Ruth on July 30, 1924. From the records, Adolphus Dameron
appears to have been a reasonably successful man. His occupation is identified
in various places as laborer, driver, and merchant, presumably of waste paper,
since that is what follows his name in the 1926 edition of the city directory. Although he changed residences every two or three years, he is usually listed as the
householder of the address listed, the exception being during the Depression
years from 1929 to 1931, when he is listed only as "resident."

Sometime after the wedding, Adolphus Dameron adopted his stepsons by
the simple common-law expedient of having them use the name "Dameron" instead of "Peake," an acceptable practice at the time. Had he formally adopted
the boys, their original birth certificates would have been sealed and new ones
with the last name "Dameron" issued. This simple adoption lends credence to
Ruth's accusation that Isaiah Peake was not terribly interested in his children,
for as their birth father he would have been able to protest the adoption if he
had wanted to.[10] In any event, one has to wonder what all this was like for Tadd
and Caesar, since Isaiah continued to live in the same neighborhood, at times in
close proximity, until at least 1932.

Many years later, Tadd told the British author and photographer Val Wilmer that around the time of his mother's remarriage, when he was seven years
old, he and his brother had the opportunity to play with Bessie Smith. Since
some of the other things he said to Wilmer at the time have been shown to be
questionable or even untrue, one does not know what to make of this. However,
other things he said in his interview with Wilmer are true, and it is quite likely

that Adolphus Dameron was a man of some substance in his community. As such, he may well have entertained the great singer in his home. A case for the level of Adolphus Dameron's place in black Cleveland society could be made by examining the divorce papers filed by Ruth Harris Peake. In her suit for divorce from Isaiah Peake, Ruth was represented by the lawyer, politician, and early civil rights activist Chester Gillespie, who had already begun his distinguished political career. Given Ruth's likely poverty at the time, it is worth considering that Adolphus Dameron arranged for Gillespie to represent her.

Just as it is reasonable to assume that the years from 1919 to 1924 were difficult ones for Tadd, his mother, and his brother, one can infer that Ruth's second marriage brought stability to the boys' lives. Tadd never discussed these matters in public, but he did talk about music in his childhood. In a 1952 interview, he said he became interested in music at "four years old." He went on to say, "Everybody in my family played music, my mother played piano, my father played piano and sang, my brother plays alto, my cousins and my aunts, they all play. My uncle plays guitar and bass. . . . My mother [taught] me piano, not to read but by heart, by memory."[11] Indeed, Dameron's uncle Silas and aunt Carrie were known to be musical; the same was true of his aunts Tennie and Opal. His cousin Eddie Harris was a trumpet player who worked in the Cleveland area.[12]

Tadd's claim to have become interested in music at the age of four is most likely accurate, and later in his life Tadd claimed, "I've played [piano] since I was five."[13] It is clear from his later development that he possessed an unusually high degree of musical aptitude, and it is not uncommon for such individuals to show a strong interest in music at an early age. Nonetheless, we have to wonder if Ruth could have afforded to have a piano moved every year or so. There may have been others among family or neighbors who had pianos she could play and use to introduce her younger son to the instrument, when time permitted. Tadd also said that his mother played piano for the silent movies. Perhaps the theaters provided the necessary access to a piano. After Ruth's marriage to Adolphus there almost certainly would have been a piano in the house, so we can be fairly certain that Tadd's instruction, however informal, would have started no later than age seven or eight.

Some time in 1924 or 1925 the Damerons moved to 2115 East Seventy-seventh Street and then in 1926 to 2186 East Eighty-ninth. At the time Silas Harris, Tadd's guitar-playing uncle, also lived at the latter address. Then, in 1928, the family moved to 2273 East Ninety-fifth. This address connects with a story told by a former playmate of Tadd's, Myron Styles, who lived across the street. "I took [piano] lessons at the Cleveland Institute of Music," recalled Styles. "I don't know where Tadd took lessons. There were a lot of teachers around the neighborhood, however." Some days, when Tadd was more interested in playing baseball than piano, he would ignore his mother's calls to come practice, and she would come out of the house to bring him in. Styles remembered that "Mrs. Dameron used to come up Ninety-sixth Street with that double-sided strop and stop Tadd from playin' baseball."[14]

The radio was an important source of music for Tadd Dameron in his childhood. "I was always listening to the radio [and] records," Dameron noted, "way back in Louis Armstrong's day, when he was real great [the mid- to late 1920s]."[15] This was also the time of Duke Ellington's early masterpieces, such as "East St. Louis Toodle-oo" and "Black and Tan Fantasy," which were recorded in 1927. As we will see when we examine Dameron's earliest recorded work, Ellington had a profound influence on the young composer. Dameron also enjoyed listening to Fletcher Henderson and the Casa Loma Band, whose arrangements he admired.[16] The year 1927 was also when sound was first synchronized with film and the famous Al Jolson movie *The Jazz Singer* was released.

Within the next couple of years, the "talkies" became more sophisticated. Tadd was around eleven years old in 1928, and he may well have been able to explore his neighborhood a bit on his own. "I used to go and see the musicals— when the talkies came in. And my mother used to have to come and get me out of the theater . . . I used to stay there all day," he recalled. There were three movie theaters in the 105th and Euclid "second downtown" vicinity, the closest of them only about eight or nine blocks from his home in 1928. After the family moved to Eighty-third Street in 1929, he would have been around the corner from the Quincy Theater and just nine blocks from the Cedar Theater. The motion picture musicals also introduced Dameron to the later songs of George Gershwin, a composer he cited as an influence more than once. Gershwin's first work for film dates from 1930, though Dameron may well have been aware of his earlier work. "When I heard George Gershwin, then I said, 'This is really it.' Gershwin was beautiful. Gershwin and Duke Ellington—always Duke Ellington."

By the end of 1932, around the time Tadd would have entered Central High School, the Damerons owned their home again, this time at 2159 East Seventy-third Street. Tadd's uncle Silas and aunt Carrie lived on the next block, and his aunts Opal and Tennie were also in the vicinity, listed as Mrs. William Johnson and Mrs. John Steele, respectively. Also living in the immediate neighborhood, on Seventy-second Street, was the young trumpeter Freddie Webster, and Tadd and Freddie's friendship certainly dates from this time, if not earlier. As Dameron said later, "We were raised together."[17] They also attended Central High School together and probably graduated in the same class.

Tadd and Freddie probably shared in a Central High custom as well. Many of their contemporaries recalled that musically inclined Central High students regularly cut school on Fridays to go hear the bands playing at the Palace Theater, spending the mornings or even the entire day. While no one has specifically mentioned Dameron or Webster in this regard, one would expect them to have done this as well.[18] The Ellington band first played the Palace for a week starting on July 4, 1931, returning to the theater for another week on June 11, 1932, and again for the week of March 22, 1935. Lunceford, Fletcher Henderson, McKinney's Cotton Pickers with Don Redman, and other great bands of the time played there as well.

Because of the school district's confidentiality policy, Dameron's high school transcript is unavailable. Tadd himself said that he did not do well in his music classes, implying to Ira Gitler that he read books on harmony on his own. He claimed to have failed the courses that were offered because he found them boring, saying, "Everything they were teaching me, I knew already."[19] This may or may not be the case; however, it is most likely that he learned the fundamentals of jazz from his older brother, Caesar. According to Gitler and some other sources, Tadd learned more advanced harmony and how to write for larger groups from another Cleveland musician, Louis Bolden, who either co-led or was a member of Ceasar's band in the mid- to late 1930s. Bassist Jimmy Williams, who played in Caesar's band in the late 1930s, remembered rehearsing with them at Bolden's home at 6101 Hawthorn Avenue.[20] Near the very end of Dameron's life, his wife Mia recalled him receiving a long letter from Bolden. She identified him as the man "who helped [Tadd] with his harmonies back in 1936."[21]

Early Career

The beginning of Tadd Dameron's career cannot be cataloged with much accuracy—too much time has passed, and we were never able to get an accurate recollection from the man himself. However, by cross-referencing various accounts regarding not only Dameron but other related musicians, it is still possible to to construct a likely picture of his early professional life. One thing is certain: Tadd Dameron did not attend Oberlin College to prepare for a career in medicine, as has been reported in various sources. Nor did he study premedicine anywhere else. Unfortunately, Dameron was the source of this falsehood, having first said it to Barry Ulanov in an interview for *Metronome* in 1947.[22]

At the time Dameron graduated high school, in 1935, Cleveland was beginning its slow climb out of the Depression. Prohibition had ended in 1933, making a legal and somewhat saner nightlife possible, and jobs provided by the Civil

Works Administration and Works Progress Administration were beginning to put some cash back into the local economy. A perusal of 1934 issues of the *Call and Post*, the black community's newspaper, gives some idea of the entertainment in the neighborhood. We find advertisements for the Musicians and Entertainers Club, Little Harlem, Val's- in-the-Alley,[23] Tucker's Tea Room, the Cedar Gardens, and Ye Rhythm Club. The Cleveland Cotton Club, which was located on East Fifty-fifth, off of Cedar, opened in September with Don Redman's Band. Fletcher Henderson would play there later in the year. It claimed to be the only establishment presenting black entertainers in a grand style between the Cotton Club in New York and the Grand Terrace in Chicago. At the close of the year, the Log Cabin Bar & Grille, which would often have entertainment in the coming years, opened. In later years, we know, many more places offered entertainment than those advertising in the *Call and Post*, and it is not unreasonable to assume the same for the mid-1930s. Other establishments presenting music in the neighborhood, and known to be operating in the mid-1930s, include the Columbus Nightclub, where Tadd is said to have first sat in with Leroy "Snake" White; the Turf Club, down the street from the Cedar Gardens; and the Furnace Room (later known as the Heatwave and the Rose Room), in the appropriately named Majestic Hotel, which was in the very heart of the neighborhood. It was into this world that Tadd Dameron graduated in 1935, and not to the college a short drive to the west, in Oberlin.

Dameron may well have started picking up little jobs here and there, including working with his saxophonist and bandleader brother, Caesar, who was already well established. Caesar would go on to have a career as a popular local musician, Musicians Union official, and club owner.[24] Tadd may also have been backing up singers in some of the smaller rooms and playing and singing himself with the kid bands of his contemporaries, such as Freddie Webster and others from the fine music program at Central High. In an article for the February 1948 issue of *Record Changer*, Dameron dated the beginning of his professional career as 1938, but this seems unlikely. Perhaps he was not quite able to support himself by playing music until then and did not consider himself completely professional until he could do so. In any event, Dameron stated that in 1938 he subbed for Clyde Hart in the band of Blanche Calloway (older sister of Cab Calloway, the famous bandleader), when Hart became too ill to work. If this is true, it would have to have been in late 1935 or early 1936, since Hart had left Calloway by May of 1936[25] and was in New York working with Stuff Smith no later than the beginning of 1937.[26] Jimmy Scott recalls that Tadd worked with Blanche Calloway "right out of high school" and that he was also involved with Cab around the same time,[27] though in what capacity is not clear.

If Dameron worked with Blanche Calloway in 1935 or 1936, we would assume that the still very young Tadd must have had an exciting few weeks. This was a typical big band for the time, with three trumpets, two trombones, four saxes—two altos, a tenor, and a baritone—and a four-piece rhythm section. Imagine being a young pianist with aspirations of becoming an arranger, sitting in the midst of all of those instruments. The band was made up of very good players and was capable of both ensemble precision and solid swing, as can be heard in the instrumental "Line-A-Jive," recorded at the end of 1935. It is strange, however, that Dameron never discussed this experience in any detailed way. Surely it would have been impressive, educational, and inspiring for so young a musician. Ultimately, his silence might be the most convincing evidence that his brief time with the band did not come until 1938, when Calloway was most likely leading a smaller band.

Between 1935 and 1939, Tadd was also associated with the bands of Marion Sears and Zack Whyte. Marion Sears may not have been maintaining a consistent band by the time Tadd worked with him. Albert McCarthy's research indicates that the band for which Sears was known came together in 1930 and broke up some time in 1936.[28] In 1933 alto saxophonist Earle Warren joined the band, staying until the spring of 1935, when he went west to work with Eddie Barefield in California. Warren rejoined Sears briefly in 1936 and said later that by then Sears was no longer getting good bookings. Freddie Webster, who had already been playing professionally while still in high school, also worked with Sears at the Cedar Gardens, although the precise dates are unknown. All this would suggest that the house band Marion Sears led at the Cedar Gardens was a smaller combo, probably of five or six musicians at the most. Interviews with musicians active in Cleveland at the time suggest that Sears did not "own" the job at the Gardens, and it is also likely that he led combos at other venues in Cleveland and the surrounding cities. Under these conditions, Sears would have been calling on available musicians, and Tadd could well have been one of them. For instance, we know that Marion Sears was booked at the Hotel Ambassador in January of 1937.[29]

Just as Marion Sears's business was in a state of decline by the time Dameron was beginning his career, so was the working situation of Zack Whyte's band, the Chocolate Beau Brummels. Still, Dameron's involvement with Whyte would have been important in his development. For one thing, Sy Oliver, one of Dameron's admitted models, did his seminal arranging for this band, which was very highly regarded in its time. Dameron later claimed to have replaced Oliver in Whyte's band, but Oliver joined Lunceford late in 1933, when Tadd was still a sophomore in high school. Dameron probably did have a chance to hear

Oliver's charts, given that the Chocolate Beau Brummels were a local band. He may even have played them, if he worked with the band soon after graduating Central High.[30] Other musicians who worked with Zack Whyte in the 1930s were trombonist Vic Dickenson (with whom Tadd may have worked while with Blanche Calloway) and bassist Truck Parham, who would become a good friend of Dameron's in the 1940s. Trumpeter Leroy "Snake" White, who had already figured in Tadd's story, also played with the Beau Brummels. Unfortunately, Zack Whyte's orchestra remains obscure to us today because it was never well recorded.

Another reason for Dameron to give 1938 as the beginning of his professional activities is that, as he himself stated, he contributed an arrangement to the Jeter-Pillars band that year. Formed in 1933 or '34 by James Jeter and Hayes Pillars, the band played some of its earliest engagements in Cleveland, at the Hollywood Café and the Magnolia Hotel Creole Bar. They went on to become the house orchestra at the Plantation Club in St. Louis, and several important players worked in this band on their way to later fame, including Harry Edison, Jimmy Blanton, Charlie Christian, Sid Catlett, and Kenny Clarke. Dameron recalled, "Everything was wrong with it [an arrangement of 'I Let a Song Go Out of My Heart']. Good ideas, but no voicings or anything like that."[31] Given the quality of his work that would be recorded just two years later, Dameron may have been too hard on himself about his voicings. He may have contributed other charts to the Jeter-Pillars book as well. In any event, Tadd continued writing whenever possible and was known to be trying to sell charts to other band leaders at the time. George Hoefer, writing in *Down Beat* in 1961, suggests that "he sent scores on a free-lance basis to [Andy] Kirk, Lucky Millinder, and Basie"[32] around this time.

The year 1938 was also about the time that Freddie Webster assembled his big band. Chick Chaiken, a veteran Cleveland pianist, recalled Webster touring with a fourteen-piece band in northern Ohio in 1938 and '39 and Dameron being in it.[33] Another member of the band was the recent Central High graduate Benjamin Clarence Jackson. Jackson was a saxophonist who would go on to work with Lucky Millinder. As "Bull Moose" Jackson, he would become a rhythm-and-blues star in the late 1940s, employing Dameron as a pianist and arranger in the early 1950s. Just when in 1938 Webster started the band is not clear, and it is quite possible that the band was already formed in 1937, for Webster was on a recording session with Earl Hines in the summer of 1938.[34] According to various accounts, Tadd played piano and sang in Webster's band and wrote arrangements for it as well. At some point during this period, while Webster was with Hines, Dameron had one of his early arrangements played by the Hines band. According to Budd Johnson, "We took Freddie [Webster]. We put Freddie in the band. Freddie, Tadd Dameron—he was included in that . . . one of his first arrangements I brought in and played in Earl's band. It was 'Sweet Georgia Brown.'"[35]

In Ira Gitler's *Swing to Bop*, a collection of oral histories regarding the transitional period of the late 1930s and early 1940s, there is a passage in which Trummy Young recalls working with Dameron in the late 1930s. Young asserts that Dameron wrote for Lunceford "before he left Ohio." Young goes on to say:

> In fact Tadd was the one instrumental in getting Snooky Young and Gerald Wilson to come with Lunceford. He had a band there. He had Scatman Crothers in the band. He had Scatman singing and everything, and Snooky and Gerald—a wonderful little band. And Tadd had written "Good Bait" way back then. And this is the thirties, man![36]

How much of this is true remains unclear. Gerald Wilson, who replaced Sy Oliver in 1939, reported that he didn't meet Tadd until he joined the Lunceford band.[37] Wilson went on to say that Dameron joined Lunceford sometime late in 1941 and stayed on after he left to join the navy in April of 1942. However, there is considerable anecdotal evidence supporting the claim that Dameron wrote "Good Bait" in the late 1930s. Further, Eugene "Snookie" Young was an Ohioan, and Benjamin "Scatman" Crothers was known to be active as a musician in the Midwest from some time in the 1930s. It is possible that Snooky, Scatman, Trummy, and Tadd played together at some time in the late 1930s.

As difficult as it is to piece together Tadd Dameron's early career, it is even more difficult to know about his personal life in these years. The Cleveland city directory shows him as living at his mother's house into 1940. Those who remember him all agree that he was a man of few words, and those few words were generally reserved for music. But we do know that sometime in 1939 he either married or entered into common-law marriage with a woman whose identity is something of a mystery. She receives credit as "Marguerite Dameron" on one of Tadd's early copyrighted songs, recorded in 1940. Myra Taylor, who sang the song, recalled that Marguerite was a dancer, an attractive woman, and that she came from Buffalo, New York.[38] The couple may well have met when Dameron played there with Freddie Webster. Long-time friends Buddy Crewe and Myron Styles also had a vague recollection of her, but all they could say was that she was not anyone they knew from Cleveland. Tadd may have had children with Marguerite. According to one's source of information, Tadd seems to have had two or possibly three children, although this, like so much of his private life, is shrouded in mystery. Marguerite moved with Tadd to Kansas City in 1940, and if she was the mother of two of these possible children, she also seems to have become a source of some distraction to Dameron later on.

Whatever the exact sequence of events in these early years of Tadd Dameron's career, it is clear that he was getting around and becoming known as a young fellow to watch. At some point in August or September of 1939 he went to Chicago again and took a job as staff arranger and pianist for a new band formed by tenor saxophonist Vido Musso, who had come to prominence with the bands of Benny Goodman and Gene Krupa.[39] This was the second of Musso's three attempts to start and lead a big band. According to Dameron, he met Musso in Chicago, and after submitting some arrangements, he was hired. When the band got to New York, there were money problems, and although the band played a seven-week engagement at Roseland, Musso could not keep it together and took an offer from Harry James. According to *Down Beat*, "Vido explained that working with Harry, plus the rosy offer James made him, was too much temptation to resist."[40]

In the stress of all this effort and failure, there may have been a falling-out between Musso and Dameron. In one source Tadd says, "It was in Chicago. I made arrangements for him and he liked them. Then we came to Roseland in Brooklyn, and he fired me. I don't know why."[41] In another he says, "I got a job arranging for Vido Musso's band in Chicago and came to New York with him. I was still learning and still had a lot to learn; Musso fired me because my voicing wasn't good enough."[42] In any event, Dameron was left out of work and possibly demoralized in New York. However, his first big break was about to come as a result of a chance meeting with bandleader Harlan Leonard.

2

The Early 1940s—Kansas City

Harlan Leonard's Rockets, an offshoot of the original Benny Moten Band,[1] was one of the premiere bands in Kansas City, after those of Count Basie and Andy Kirk. The Rockets had a long history in Kansas City, but not until late 1939 did they—and the Jay McShannn band—begin to be known outside of the Southwest. Much of the Rockets' growing visibility came thanks to some good press in *Down Beat*. In the October 15 issue, George Avakian wrote favorably of the band, and in the following issue, the magazine announced that Leonard had signed with Music Corporation of America (MCA). The promotion people at MCA went right to work, with Harlan Leonard's picture showing up in the December 1 issue of *Down Beat* and a "Season's Greetings" ad in Leonard's name in the December 15 issue. On January 11, 1940, the Rockets made their first recordings for RCA Victor's Bluebird label in Chicago.

From early February to late March, Leonard and the Rockets were in New York for an extended engagement at the newly opened Golden Gate Ballroom. This is where they crossed paths with Dameron. As Leonard recalled, "One day I ran into Tadd Dameron at the Woodside Hotel. He was broke and looking for work. I took him along with me to Kansas City and for awhile he played piano in the band as well as writing a lot of our arrangements."[2] Leonard was going to need fresh material for the tours and recordings that he was anticipating, now that the Rockets were signed with MCA and Bluebird, and the eager young arranger was likely just the man he was looking for. With his next big job lined up, Tadd went back to Cleveland and worked with his brother for a few weeks.

On their way back to Kansas City, the Rockets picked up Dameron in Cleveland.[3] By the first of April 1940, Tadd, along with Marguerite, had taken up residency in Kansas City, where he lived for the next few months and wrote his first recorded work. His even briefer tenure as pianist must have taken place in June, for the *Kansas City Call* reported that he was introduced to Rockets' fans on June 9. Since William Smith is in the piano chair on all of the Rockets' recordings before and after that time, we are left to assume that he was unavailable for those few weeks, and Dameron sat in for him.

Tadd also met Charlie Parker while he was in Kansas City. Later, he recalled his first meeting with Bird:

> Bird was cleaning up the club. I never knew he played horn until one jam session he pulls out this raggedy alto with this pipe tone he had then. I couldn't hear anyone but him because I could hear his message. So we got together and we were playing "Lady Be Good" and there's some changes I played in the middle where he just stopped playing and ran over and kissed me on the cheek. He said, "That's what I've been hearing all my life, but nobody plays those changes." So we got to be very good friends—he used to come over to my house everyday and blow. . . . And my wife would cook. And the people used to knock on the door, and I'd say, "Oh, I'm sorry we're making so much noise." "No" they'd say, "we want you to leave the door open" because he was playing *so* pretty.[4]

Another friend Dameron made while in Kansas City was Mary Lou Williams, the brilliant and often overlooked pianist, composer, and arranger who was, in a way, the heart and soul of the Andy Kirk band. Williams felt that, "though very young, [Dameron] had ideas even then that were 'way ahead of his time.'"[5] Suggestions of these ideas can be heard in the arrangements recorded by the Kansas City Rockets. In the collection of Mary Lou Williams's papers,[6] there is a piano part for Dameron's "Rock and Ride," which shows moderate signs of wear and has a revised ending with the original crossed out in pencil. One has to wonder just how this got into Mary Lou's possession. Was it from the original parts for Leonard, or was it from parts for another band? It has been said that Dameron was under contract to Leonard, which would have made his writing for other bands unlikely. However, his relationship with Leonard was probably more open.

Jay McShann recalled to Stanley Dance that "Tadd Dameron heard us play an arrangement he'd written for Harlan Leonard, and he liked the way we played it better."[7] McShann explained this in more detail to Chuck Haddix:

> One day Tadd came over to my rehearsal with some music and said, "Play this." We put the number down, and the cats played it. He said, "Man, this sounds

like a completely different number the way you phrase, so much different than Harlan. I like the way you all phrase.... Look, I will give you this number. I got another number, just let me hear so many bars." We played a few measures of that and he said, "I'll give that number to you."[8]

McShann did not have enough money to pay Dameron at the time, but they seem to have worked out an agreement, for McShann went on to say, "I got a chance to get a lot of stuff from him during that time."

From Dameron's words to McShann, and from other sources, it would appear that Tadd's arrangements were at first difficult for the Rockets. On June 23, 1940, the Cab Calloway band was in Kansas City. Their guitarist Danny Barker recalled:

> The band seemed annoyed at a passage he wanted played. So he went to the piano and played the sequence slowly, and after a while the band played his arrangement. This arrangement seemed difficult to them, and as he looked at the leader and the silent sidemen, a trumpet player fingering his horn said, "This fingering is funny and tricky; I'll get it, but it'll take me time." The piano player was a serious young arranger, Tadd Dameron. He did not say anything, but the wrinkle on his brow spoke: "What's wrong, can't they hear?"[9]

The band did get Dameron's charts down in the end. Just three weeks after Danny Barker heard them in rehearsal, the Rockets recorded four of Tadd's new arrangements for Victor's Bluebird label.[10] Tadd's work in rehearsal seems to have improved the overall ensemble sound of the band, as well. In his book *The Swing Era*, Gunther Schuller notes the shaky intonation and other ensemble problems in the earlier recorded performances of the Rockets.[11] This is most painfully evident in "Snaky Feeling," recorded in January, and to a lesser degree in "Ride My Blues Away," recorded in March. Many years later Myra Taylor and the Rockets' drummer, Jesse Price, recalled Dameron's positive influence on the band in a radio interview with Ken Borgers on KLON, Los Angeles. Bassist Ron Javorsky heard the broadcast and recalled:

> The female singer and drummer from [The Rockets] were saying how when Tadd joined the band everything was knocked up a notch, and everything was harder. They both said that Tadd decided that the band was going to have a rehearsal every day. They rehearsed at noon, and at 1:00 or 2:00 on Sundays. Things got difficult, but they said that everyone became a better musician as a result of Tadd's discipline and difficult music.[12]

While one could make a case for the role of the recordings themselves in this improvement—any musician worthy of the name benefits from hearing a recording of his performance—it is clear that Tadd Dameron was a coach who insisted that musicians attend carefully to all the details of the music at hand in rehearsal. Later in his life Dameron told Ira Gitler, "I like to direct the band, I like to rehearse a band. I like to supervise a date, to bring out the beautiful things that are happening."[13]

It is a notable that four of the six selections recorded in Chicago on July 15 were Dameron's work, an impressive debut for an unknown composer and arranger. Although Harlan Leonard shares the composer credit on all of these titles, it is unlikely he had a hand in composing them. Myra Taylor explained that she discovered many years later that Harlan Leonard had put his name on everything that everyone in the band had written, a common practice in those days. She recalled that "he brought the copyright forms into the rooms where we were, for us to sign. When he took them out, there was all kinds of space in there for him to write his own name."[14]

The four Dameron compositions recorded at the July 15 Bluebird session were "Rock and Ride," "400 Swing," "My Dream," and "A-La Bridges" (credited as a collaboration with tenor saxophonist Henry Bridges). The first two are medium up-tempo swingers, and the last two are for slower dancing. All four numbers were released by Victor on the Bluebird label[15] and are remarkable in that they hold up well next to the pieces the Rockets recorded by more experienced writers, such as Eddie Durham and Buster Smith.[16] One has to question Dameron's self-deprecating comments on his release from the Vido Musso band for "weak voicings." Even though he had been a working musician for probably five years by now, and had been arranging professionally for only two or three, when one listens to these recordings, one does not question the maturity of the arranger.

While the influence of others, including Jimmie Lunceford's arrangers, Duke Ellington, and the Kansas City collective style, can be heard clearly, Dameron is—at twenty-three—already undeniably his own man. His accomplishments during this early period point to a high level of native musical aptitude, and the sophistication of his compositions and harmonic concepts suggests that Dameron had already been experimenting with harmony and composition while still an adolescent.

Saxophonist Andy Anderson, who played with Marion Sears's band in Cleveland in the 1930s, recalled his first encounter with young Tadley in 1934 or 1935, when Caesar Dameron brought his brother to the Columbus Nightclub to sit in with Snake White's band. According to Anderson, "He's got ten fingers, and all of them went down just like this (on the piano keys) and all of them were on different notes. He had been playing and studying all the time, and I said 'Gee Whiz, with kids like that who stay in and study!' You don't expect to hear anything that good [from a youngster]."[18]

"Rock and Ride," "400 Swing"

Of the four Dameron compositions recorded at the July 15 session, the up-tempo numbers illustrate his formal and harmonic concepts most clearly. Luckily, the copy of the piano part to "Rock and Ride" found among Mary Lou Williams's papers provides critical information about the composer's own designated harmonies, as well as his suggested bass line.[17]

Most of the basic elements of Dameron's emerging style are present in "Rock and Ride": harmonic sophistication, a command of variation techniques, and an awareness of the expressive potential of musical form. "Rock and Ride" is, at its core, a thirty-two-bar riff-based dance tune in AABA form. Harmonically it is very simple, with the A sections based on a fundamental I-vi-ii-V turn-around formula and the bridge built on the often-used V7 of IV, VI, V7 of V, V7 sequence, which we will call the "common bridge." This was a well established genre by 1940; good examples of it include the Lunceford band's "'T'aint What You Do," Basie's "Shorty George," and Mary Lou Williams's "Bearcat Shuffle."

Of particular interest in "Rock and Ride" is Dameron's exploration of both chromatic and whole-tone root motion—most often descending and most often targeted on the V7 chord.[19] The piece, which is in the key of Bb, begins with an eight-bar introduction, an outline of Bb6 harmony over an F pedal, which concludes with a cadence of B7, substituting for the more conventional F7, to Bb7 and a quick turn-around of F#7 to F7. The effect is slightly mysterious and serves to draw the listener in. The first turn-around in the tune itself is harmonized:

Bb Gmi | G7 F#7 F7|

Note the three descending chromatic steps. After the opening chorus there is a four-bar interlude that sets up the solos. Here, Dameron extends the progression beyond the targeted F7: Ab7-G7-F#7-F7-E7-F7. He would use this kind of parallel chord progression in many different guises in the coming years.

Form is also an important consideration for Dameron. Although it is common in jazz to view composing a basic melody and arranging a melody as two separate processes, this is far from an accurate description. Arrangements themselves are compositions, and the writer is concerned with the same issues of proportion and overall melodic, harmonic, and rhythmic integrity. There is the basic tune "Rock and Ride," notated in the thirty-two bars of melody filed with the Copyright Office, and then there is the development of this tune into a larger musical structure, as performed by the Kansas City Rockets. The introduction, with its quiet tension of anticipation ending in a brief explosion of densely voiced chords, which hold the germ of an idea of their own, is followed by the tune itself with its two themes and then a four-measure fanfare for the soloists that develops the chromatic germ from the introduction. The first solo is split between two trumpeters, alternating every eight bars, accompanied by a suave but harmonically straightforward riff from the saxophones. The written piano part shows a one-chorus piano solo next, although there is no piano solo on the recording, which goes directly into the tenor saxophone solo, again shared by two players, but with the chorus divided in half, each player playing for sixteen bars. The brass backgrounds now incorporate some of the chromatic chord movement, heightening the tension. Then comes the out-chorus ensemble, built up in layers of riffs assigned to the three orchestral voices, saxes, trumpets, and trombones. This is a proven swing era technique, but Dameron subtly reorganizes these riffs in each of the three A sections. At first listen they all seem the same, but as one listens more carefully, one discovers the variety. Finally the opening A theme of the tune is reprised by the saxes, who have been hinting at it in the riffs they played in the previous chorus, and the piece concludes with the coda.

While not quite as intricately structured as "Rock and Ride," "400 Swing" still contains a subtle and continuous development of ideas from beginning to end. The basic form of the thirty-two-measure tune is ABAC—another form popular with songwriters of the time—which can be thought of as an enlargement of the very common melody-with-two-endings. Harmonically, "400 Swing" is straightforward, but there are interesting formal subtleties. The introduction of eight bars is in two parts, the first a high trumpet fanfare, the second a somewhat quieter passage using the suspension of tonic over a dominant bass, along the same harmonic lines as the introduction to "Rock and Ride." In the first chorus, the saxes carry the bulk of the melody, with rhythmic punctuations in the brass. In the second A, Dameron introduces a rhythmic variation, much as most jazz players would if presenting the melody solo. Two measures before the expected end of the chorus, there is an interlude to introduce the next chorus. But where one would normally expect an interlude passage of four or eight measures, Dameron gives us only three. Later, the interlude that precedes the final chorus is five measures long, as if to subtly make up for the shortened first interlude. The effect of the first, shortened passage is a little startling and perhaps not entirely successful. Indeed, Dameron does not use this device again in any of the music we have available to us.

"My Dream," "A-La Bridges"

In Dameron's up-tempo arrangements and compositions we find that he has more in common with the work of Lunceford's arrangers Sy Oliver and Willie Smith, and his Kansas City colleagues, such as Roselle Claxton, Eddie Durham, and Mary Lou Williams, than he does with another of his heros, Duke Ellington.[20] However, in his ballads, especially those written while he was working for Leonard, the Ellington influence is quite clear. For instance, Ellington and another of Dameron's acknowledged influences, George Gershwin, both employ pentatonic scales in a variety of ways.[21]

The most striking similarity between Dameron's and Ellington's melodic construction is the use of the sixth, the seventh, the ninth, and other "upper tensions" over the prevailing harmonic root. Often these notes are organized melodically in pentatonic scales and are used prominently, placed on strong beats or stressed in some other way. Dameron employs this use of upper tensions throughout his work and appears to have several different ways of arriving at the use of these intervals, some of which are distinct from Duke Ellington's. "My Dream," however, shows the Ellington influence very clearly, especially in the opening phrases.[22]

An interesting feature of the arrangement of "My Dream" is the restraint Dameron shows in not overusing the pungent, descending diminished arpeggio played by the trumpets in cup mutes at measure four of the melody, which Dameron has the good judgment not to repeat at measure twelve, where the chord returns. He is also careful not to overuse E♭7 as a substitute for C7, saving it only for the second measure of the A section of the tune. Also worth noting is the ensemble variation on the A section at the beginning of the second chorus. The melodic line of this ensemble (fig. 2.1) is centered around the note G, the ninth of the tonic F chord, before it comes to rest on D, the sixth of F chord. This choice of notes, and the block-chord voicing, foreshadows his writing for smaller ensembles in the late 1940s.

In the instrumental ballad "A-La Bridges," Dameron again uses a dominant seventh chord built on the flatted seventh degree of the key, A♭7 in the key of B♭. However, this time he uses it in the last bar of the first A section as a turn-

Fig. 2.1. Ensemble line from the beginning of the second chorus of Dameron's arrangement of his own "My Dream," written for Harlan Leonard.

around. Then, in the bridge, the A♭7 takes on the function usually assigned to the subdominant, E♭ in this case. Dameron also stresses the sixth over the root of the prevailing harmony in "A-La Bridges," only here he stays with it as the melody's concluding note, where in the other song he uses it as a kind of dissonance that gets resolved in the end.

At the end of the bridge in the deposited lead sheet of "A-La Bridges," we also find the seeds of "bop" harmonic/melodic practice. Because Henry Bridges alters the melody slightly here, treating it more in the manner of the swing era player that he was, this is not evident in the recording. In figure 2.2 we see that the original melody uses the ♯11 (B natural) in addition to the augmented fifth (D flat) and the ♯9 and ♭9. When the melody is played this way, it sounds more like the sort of melody that would later be found in the mid- to late 1940s.

"It Couldn't Be," another Dameron song from this time, also has an Ellingtonian feel to it. An arrangement of this song was recorded at the next Rockets recording session in November but has never been released. While we thus cannot discuss the arrangement, the lead sheet is available, and it reveals a feature that shows up frequently in Dameron's work, the use of the arpeggio as a melodic element. All of the sections of this melody, which is in ABAC form, open with an arpeggio: the As with an upward E♭Ma9 arpeggio and the B and C with a downward A♭Ma6 chord. It is part of Dameron's genius here, as in most cases,

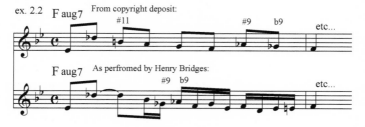

Fig. 2.2. Last measure of the bridge (bar 24) of "A-La Bridges," comparing the way Dameron wrote the melody at that point and the way saxophonist Henry Bridges played it.

that this technique is not obvious to the listener; the melodic line is heard as just that, a strong melodic line, and not the outlining of the underlying harmony.

November 13 Bluebird Session

On November 13, 1940, the Rockets made their final commercial recordings. For this session Dameron contributed at least five of the charts, although there is some confusion regarding which work is his on this session. His own "Dameron Stomp," "Society Steps Out (Rachmaninoff Jumps)," "Take 'Um" (another collaboration with Henry Bridges), "Keep Rockin'" (probably by trumpeter William H. Smith),[23] and "Dig It" (most likely by Myra Taylor) all sound like his arrangements and have been credited to him in one source or another. The unreleased "It Couldn't Be" is credited to Dameron and Darwin Jones, with the arrangement credited to Jones.[24] Regarding the authorship of "Dig It," Myra Taylor insists, "I wrote 'Dig It,' and I did 'Dig It' with Harlan Leonard. . . . He took my name off of the tune and he put his name, Tadd Dameron's name and Tadd Dameron's *wife's* name on the record. *I* wrote 'Dig It!'"[25] In any event, "Dig It" sounds so unlike any other Dameron tune that Myra Taylor's case is compelling. It should be noted that only "Keep Rockin'" and "Dig It" were issued on 78-rpm records. "Dameron Stomp," "Society Steps Out," and "Take 'Um" were released many years later on LP, after Dameron's death.

"Dameron Stomp," in the key of F and in AABA form, could be considered a harmonic paraphrase of "Honeysuckle Rose." Tadd is again exploring chromatic root motion descending to the dominant. In the A sections he moves from the V7 to the ♭VI7 and back again. In the bridge he reverses the motion as he approaches the IV chord. It is probably easier to understand what happens here by laying out the essential harmonic structure of the tune (fig. 2.3).

For the introduction, Dameron takes the four chords (*) at the end of the bridge and rhythmically augments the sequence to eight bars. In this way he introduces one of the elements of the tune itself in a developmental way (the introduction will also return as an interlude before the final chorus). This is a compositional device Dameron would use to a greater extent in his through-composed works, such as "Fontainebleau." Dameron varies the treatment of each of the four choruses comprising the entire piece. For instance, in the final full chorus the saxes play a variation on the first four measures of the A theme, answered by a solo trombone improvisation. The final bridge is an improvised solo by one of the trumpeters, and there is a final statement of the A theme with a four-bar coda tagged onto its last two measures.

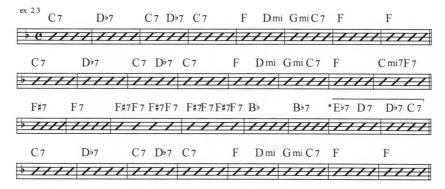

Fig. 2.3. Chord progression of Dameron's "Dameron Stomp."

"Rachmaninoff Jumps," the alternate title for "Society Steps Out," leads one to expect a swing treatment of a theme by the Russian composer and pianist. Indeed, Sergei Rachmaninoff's "Prelude in C-sharp Minor" caught the ear of various jazz musicians, from the Casa Loma Orchestra to Charles Mingus. Usually a substantial portion of the beginning of the work is quoted, but in "Society Steps Out" Dameron makes only a motivic reference to Rachmaninoff's Prelude in the introduction before presenting a thirty-two-bar AABA tune that hovers between C minor and its relative E♭ major. The overall arrangement is as solid and well crafted as the others Dameron wrote for these sessions. It is an exciting piece of music taken at a Lindy-hop tempo, around 250 to 260 beats per minute, and to say it is an arrangement of a thirty-two-bar tune is to miss the point of its overall compositional structure.

As in Dameron's other works in this set (and in much of the best writing of the swing era), there is continual variation and development in "Society," only here it could be said to be more extensive. After the introduction, with its "tip of the hat" to Rachmaninoff, there is the thirty-two-bar "tune." The first eight measures (the A theme) are as written in the deposit, but the second eight are a variation, and after the bridge, the last eight measures are yet another variation, the last two measures tagged with a four-bar interlude that modulates up a step to D minor/F major. The next chorus features a muted trumpet solo accompanied by a legato line in the saxophones, which clearly outlines the song's AABA form. Henry Bridges's tenor saxophone solo begins in the next chorus, accompanied solely by the rhythm section, and continues into the chorus following, with the addition of background figures in the brass and an abrupt change of key to B♭ minor/D♭ major. After a four-bar interlude that modulates back to the

home key, the last chorus develops the original melodic material further by presenting the chorus as one continuously unfolding ensemble. An eight-measure
coda is tagged on to the last chorus.

"Take 'Um," another flag-waver, is a twelve-bar blues feature for saxophonist Henry Bridges, who shares in the composer credit. The recorded melodic
content has nothing to do with the music deposited under this title with the
Copyright Office, except for the twelve-bar blues form. The entire piece is constructed of a series of riff choruses, twelve in all, bracketed by an introduction
and coda. It is another of Dameron's studies in thoughtful and well-structured
overall composition. The entire piece can be seen as divided into two large over-
lapping sections. The first has Bridges improvising over the first two choruses of
ensemble and the band continuing without him for the next three. The second
section begins—and the first concludes—with Bridges's reentry over the sixth
riff and a reordering of some of the melodic material from the first section. The
whole form of the piece looks like this, the numbers indicating the twelve-bar
choruses:

    0. Twelve-bar fanfare-like introduction
    1. Riff 1.   Bridges solos
    2. Riff 2.   Bridges solos
    3. Riff 3.   Ensemble only
    4. Riff 4   Ensemble only
    5. Riff 5   Ensemble only
    6. Riff 6   Bridges solos
    7. Rhythm section only   Bridges solos
    8. Rhythm section only   Bridges solos
    9. Riff 1.   Bridges solos
  10. Riff 2.   Bridges solos
  11. Riff 6   Bridges solos
  12. Riff 4   Bridges solos
    + Coda at half tempo, Bridges leading the ensemble

"Keep Rockin'" and "Dig It" are taken at a medium tempo, indicated by
Dameron as a "bounce" in the scores that he wrote in this period. Like "400
Swing," "Keep Rockin'" is a "Honeysuckle Rose" type of tune, and in arranging it
Dameron again stresses development of the melodic content, giving it the same
close attention he would give one of his own melodies. The introduction brings
the listener's attention to the note C above middle C, which is the first note of
the melody, in a way that makes its arrival in the first full chorus sound inevi-

table. Smith's melody, in the key of F, is built tightly around a two-bar phrase that has at its heart the minor-third interval between C and the A below it (fig. 2.4a). In the last eight bars of the first chorus Dameron reduces the phrase to just this interval (fig 2.4b).

In the bridge Smith takes this motif up a fourth instead of creating a second theme. However, in the course of the bridge either Smith or Dameron introduces the minor 6 chord:

Fig. 2.4. Comparison of two two-bar segments from Dameron's arrangement of "Keep Rockin.'"

Cmi7 F7 |Cmi7 F7 |Cmi7 F7 |Cmi7 F7 |

B♭ |B♭mi6 |B♭mi6 |B♭mi6 |

Dameron then uses this sonority in reharmonizing the background for the soloists in the next two choruses, replacing the Gmin7 chord in the A sections with a B♭mi6,[26] which includes the note D♭. This gives Dameron the opportunity to exploit the chromatic descent from D♭ to C. As we have seen, he likes this movement of the flatted sixth degree of the scale to the fifth or dominant.

In the interlude to the final chorus, a blues-based fanfare (fig. 2.5a) sets up another harmonic variation on the essentially dominant harmony of the first four bars of the "Honeysuckle Rose" type of progression. The next chorus involves a four-bar exchange between the ensemble and the trumpet soloist in the A sections of the melody. The line in the ensemble (fig. 2.5b) outlines a B♭Maj7 chord and is harmonized in the brass and reeds accordingly. The bass line underneath it (fig. 2.5c) rises in a sequential figure from G to arrive, appropriately, at F in the fifth measure. Here Dameron is superimposing subdominant harmony on an essentially dominant bass line, creating a rich sonority that still has the same general function as the ii-V harmonic motion of the opening chorus. While there certainly are precedents for this harmonic device, the use of it in jazz was innovative and forward looking in 1940. Also note the two-eights-quarter-note figure (*). In figure 2.5a, the quarter note falls on the stronger third and first beats of the measure. At the beginning of figure 2.5b, the eighth-notes

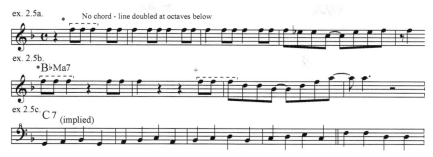

Fig. 2.5. Analytic reductions of elements from Dameron's arrangement of "Keep Rockin."

are on the strong beats, adding to the rhythmic tension, which is resolved in the third measure (+), where the figure resolves into the longer eighth-note line. This technique of playing with small rhythmic motifs is something Dameron will use significantly in his through-composed works, such as "Nearness," "Soulphony in Three Hearts," and "Fontainebleau."

Regardless of whether Tadd Dameron or Myra Taylor wrote the song itself, Dameron's arrangement for "Dig It" is a solid as the others written for the Rockets. The song is kind of advertisement for the Rockets, with Myra Taylor singing the praises of the band. A brief four-measure introduction gets our attention with wide-voiced, harmonically dense chords. Then Taylor sings over a soft saxophone section background that parallels her melody. Punchy brass interjections respond to her phrases. The saxes, joined by a muted trumpet obligato, continue their gentle support in the bridge of the song, which is in AABA form. A four-bar interlude leads to sixteen measures of patter using the first half of the song's form, and another four-bar interlude, in the form of a drum solo, leads to the next complete chorus. Here the A sections are presented as three interlocking riffs, with Myra Taylor singing the lead riff and a unison trumpet variation on the bridge. Another eight measures of patter from Taylor precedes the out-going chorus, in which Dameron paraphrases part of the last chorus of his own "Rock and Ride." There is a very full-voiced ensemble in the last statement of the bridge, which is recalled in the coda. Always attentive to detail, even in this innocuous novelty number, Dameron uses the elements of the arrangement carefully to give it cohesion.

There is one more copyrighted melody from Dameron's tenure with Harlan Leonard that was never recorded, "Conversation," a melody in AABA form. Like the other copyright deposits filed by Leonard, this one has only a melody, and a curious melody it is. The A sections present a theme that consists of a string of quarter notes. While the chords are not specified, the author has settled on a progression, which has proven quite satisfactory in performance and is, no doubt, close to the progression Dameron had in mind:

C6 Cdim7| A♭mi7 D♭7| C6 Cdim7| A♭mi7 D♭7|

C6 Cdim7| A♭mi7 D♭7| C6 | Dmi7 G7 |

Here we have a very early example of Dameron's use of the I♭II7 relationship as a compositional device, which would become more common in the mid- to late 1940s in the work of both Dameron and his friend Thelonious Monk. "Conversation" is also interesting from the standpoint of melodic design. The A sections build a certain kind of tension in their continuous succession of quarter notes, as well as the extra-diatonic harmony. The harmonic tension does get a resolution with a pentatonic line in measures seven and eight of the section, but the rhythmic tension is only relieved by the swinging, syncopated rhythmic nature of the bridge. The bridge's harmonic structure, with a descending succession of "ii7-V7s," as assumed by the author, also anticipates the harmonic thinking of the later 1940s. We have no way of knowing whether this tune was arranged for the Rockets, but given that it was copyrighted by Leonard, we cannot rule out the possibility that it was.[27]

"Conversation," along with all of the original compositions recorded by the Rockets, was published by Bregman, Vocco and Conn (BVC). Dameron would have a long relationship with this company, as well as with one of its partners, Jack Bregman. Although several companies published Tadd's work over the years, only BVC[28] held the rights to work from all the stages of his career. It is worth considering that the publishing deal with BVC was part of Leonard's agreement with MCA and that there may have been behind-the-scenes help from Count Basie, whose working relationships with both companies began in the late 1930s. This would support the claim that Basie and Dameron's relationship started as early as 1940 or even 1939. There is a studio photo of the young Tadd Dameron in the August 1, 1940, issue of *Down Beat*, which had to have come from either MCA or BVC. The caption reads:

> Promising arranger whose work has been causing much talk in colored jazz circles is Tad Dameron, 23-year-old Cleveland boy now under full-time contract to Harlan Leonard, the Kansas City band leader. Dameron started with the ill-fated Vido Musso band, went to New York and scored for Kirk, Millinder,

Basie and others, and last week watched Leonard's band cut four of his originals for Bluebird.[29]

There seems to be no surviving evidence of any early work Dameron did for Kirk, Millinder, or Basie. However, there are at least two surviving arrangements for Basie from later in the 1940s, as well as indications that Dameron wrote for Millinder (also later in the 1940s) and work that suggests he may have written for Kirk. The question of Dameron's early associations with these three band leaders may never be answered, but it does seem clear that insiders in the musical community, especially the black musical community, were aware of this talented young man and were watching his progress.

Leaving Kansas City

The Kansas City Rockets entered a period of decline after their last recording session.[30] Contemporary publications often reported on the increasing stress on the big-band business, which had experienced a boom in the late '30s. While the Rockets had a long engagement at Kansas City's College Inn that lasted through the end of April 1941, the band had shrunk to four brass, three reeds, and four rhythm by the end of August of that year. By this time, Harlan Leonard had lost several of his key players, including Henry Bridges and drummer Jesse Price. The extraordinary trombonist Fred Beckett had already left to join Lionel Hampton before the November 1940 recording session, and Dameron probably left before the end of 1940.

Although Dameron later said, "I spent a year in Kansas City with Harlan Leonard,"[31] he also spoke of spending a year working in a defense industry plant. This led Ira Gitler to write, "After war was declared, Tadd went into war-plant work in Chicago and Lima, Ohio. 'There was no music for me,' he said."[32] America did not enter World War II until a month or two after Dameron started working for Lunceford. Of course, the war had begun already in Europe in 1939, and the conscription of American soldiers began in 1940. There were thirteen months between the last of Harlan Leonard's recording sessions for Bluebird and the first recording of a Dameron arrangement for Jimmie Lunceford, his next known employer, and there are two periods in the 1940s for which we have no documents regarding Dameron's activities, neither recording dates nor copyright registrations, one from November 13, 1940, to December 23, 1941, the other the period of the AFM recording ban,[33] from mid-1942 to the spring of 1944. We do have anecdotal evidence of his being in New York during the ban, but we have nothing for the first period, which would be the only time when Dameron could have worked in a defense-related factory.

With the institution of the draft, it seems most likely that Dameron was about to be called or was indeed called in the later months of 1940. His uncle Silas Harris was a machinist by trade and may have had the connections to get his nephew a highly prized machinist job, which would have exempted him from military service.[34] We do not know what became of Tadd's "wife," Marguerite, but she may have left Kansas City with him, although no one has any recollection of her (at least by name) after Tadd's time with Harlan Leonard.

3

The Early 1940s—New York

At some point in the fall of 1941, Dameron became a staff arranger for Jimmie Lunceford. Gerald Wilson remembers him being with Lunceford late in the year, after they picked him up in Ohio.[1] In the 1930s, Tadd had listened with great delight and interest to Lunceford's band. "As a boy, I was always most interested in Duke Ellington and the Lunceford band, because they were trying to do things differently than anybody else," said Dameron.[2] However, while Tadd may have found inspiration in the music of the Lunceford band, the reality of working for Lunceford was far from glamourous. While the band toured, Dameron worked out of the office of Lunceford's manager Harold Oxley in New York, only occasionally joining the band on the road to rehearse new material. Dameron's greatest disappointment seems to have been the lack of recordings of the music he arranged for Lunceford. Asserting that he had written many arrangements for the band, he told Ira Gitler, "Lunceford didn't record them. That's been the story of my life. The very good arrangements I'd make for the band, nobody recorded. I made 'I Dream a Lot about You,' things for the vocal group.... Then I quit Lunceford."[3]

Actually two or probably three of Dameron's arrangements were recorded by Jimmie Lunceford: "I'm Losing My Mind Because of You," "It Had to Be You," and "I Dream a Lot about You." Further, his disappointment did not keep Dameron from continuing to write arrangements for Lunceford on a freelance basis, some of them as late as 1945 or 1946.

Among the recorded arrangements, there is some uncertainty about Dameron's authorship of the arrangement of "I'm Losing My Mind Because of You"[4] (recorded Dec. 23, 1941). It seems highly probable that the arrangement is his, because in this piece we find many of the same strengths that made Dameron's work for the Rockets noteworthy. The arrangement is full of interesting details and ideas. "[My] ideas [were] much better than now," Dameron said of this period in his 1952 radio interview with Harry Frost. "As you write, you settle down. . . . I was real ambitious then." This highly detailed arrangement certainly seems to be the work of an ambitious young writer.

The introduction to "I'm Losing My Mind Because of You" begins with four measures of dominant harmony, G7, during which a little chromatic figure is introduced—first played by muted trumpets then by saxophones—that will be employed as a structural device. The introduction continues with a statement of the first eight measures of the melody in the key of C major, followed by a sudden modulation in the turn-around that takes us to D major,[5] the key of the main body of the arrangement. There is a particularly attractive cascading trumpet passage in the turn-around at the end of the first A, and in the final turn-around, muted brass return to set up a reprise of the first two bars of the introduction, which now introduce Willie Smith's sixteen-bar clarinet solo. Joe Thomas's tenor sax solo comes in the bridge, at the end of which the turn-around is extended by a development of the opening chromatic figure. Vocalist Dan Grisom finishes out the chorus, this time with a tag. The band then plays a final eight-bar coda built on the tag harmonies. The first four measures are dominated by intense high trumpet notes, the last with subdued saxes, as if a final scream of anguish has been replaced by resignation. Indeed, it is "tone painting" that stands out in this arrangement. The subject of the lyric has been jilted and has lost not only his heart but his mind as well. The arrangement presents an alternate expression of the lyric in the orchestration, and this sort of "tone painting" shows up in several of Dameron's vocal arrangements.

In his treatment of "It Had to Be You," by Gus Kahn and Isham Jones, recorded April 14, 1942, Dameron employs two of the band's stylistic trademarks, the light two-beat feel and the elegantly arranged vocal trio. The introduction has two parts, one instrumental and one vocal, making it a subtle reduction of the entire piece. We can hear suggestions of Dameron's evolving style in the punctuations behind the vocalists. After an interlude, Dameron sings in his own voice through a sophisticated instrumental chorus. This passage is full of the sixths and ninths above the chord root that were becoming a hallmark of his line-writing and compositional style: "boppish" rhythmic surprises and skillful, almost symphonic use of the instrumental colors of the band. The out-going vocal chorus reprises the song from the middle with a coda that rhythmically augments the last phrase of the song.

On July 14, 1942, the Lunceford orchestra recorded "I Dream a Lot about

You," by trombonist Trummy Young. This song gets a noticeably more conservative treatment than the previous two recorded arrangements. After a "curtain-raising" introduction that reminds this writer that Tadd loved movie musicals as a youngster, the song is presented in two choruses. The first is a complete vocal chorus, with a nicely scored accompaniment. The second chorus has an eight-bar sax ensemble statement of the melody, followed by an eight-bar solo by Willie Smith. The vocalist returns to reprise the second sixteen measures of the song, and the arrangement ends simply, with just an additional measure from the band.

There are at least another eight Dameron arrangements listed in the Frank Driggs Collection of Jimmie Lunceford Orchestrations, held by the National Museum of American History at the Smithsonian Institution in Washington, DC. The information in the finding aid[6] reveals something of Tadd's ongoing relationship with the Lunceford organization even after he left the staff. It also brings to light some hitherto unknown Dameron compositions. There are most likely other scores that Dameron wrote for Lunceford, since the three recorded arrangements are not present in the collection, and other known works, such as Gerald Wilson's arrangements, are also missing.[7]

The finding aid for the Driggs Collection shows the following Dameron arrangements:

"*Bewildered*" (Powell and Whitcup), 1941, parts only
"*Frolic at Five*" (Dameron), 1945, parts only
"*Good Bait*" (Dameron), 1945, parts only
"*Moo-See-Ka*" (Dameron), 1946, parts only
"[*The*] *One I Love*" (composer not indicated, but it is the song by Kahn and Jones), no date, parts only
"*You Do Something to Me*" (most likely written in the 1950s for Ed Wilcox) no date, score only[8]
"*Zakat*" (Dameron), 1946, parts only

The dates given for these arrangements are educated guesses, based on a number of factors. After careful study, it seems clear that "Bewildered" and "The One I Love" date from Dameron's tenure with Lunceford, 1941–42, and the rest are from a later period, around 1945, when Dameron was working freelance. "The One I Love" and "Bewildered"—in spite of some radical reharmonization—are very close in style to the three pieces that were recorded at the earlier time. "Good Bait," "Frolic at Five," "Moo-See-Ka," and "Zakat," the later of which foreshadows Tadd's late-1940s writing for smaller bands, all reflect the changes starting to take place in Dameron's post-AFM-ban big-band writing. In addition, Gerald Wilson recalled an arrangement of "Fine and Dandy" that Dameron wrote for Lunceford.[9] This is also in the Driggs Collection, and while it is credited to Ed Wilcox, it sounds very clearly like Dameron's work from the 1945 period. Further study of this collection may uncover still more of Tadd's charts.

The two arrangements that date from the 1941–42 period show the next stage of Dameron's stylistic development. Gus Kahn and Isham Jones's "The One I Love (Belongs to Somebody Else)" gets a straightforward dance chart treatment, without space for improvised solos. However, there are some details here that are worth noting. There is Dameron's introduction of chromatic passing chords that further develop his practice of approaching a dominant seventh chord with another of the same species from a half-step above. "The One I Love," in the key of G, has secondary dominant chords, the V7 of V (A7) and the V7 of II (E7). Dameron approaches these with B♭9 and F9 chords, respectively.

In the second chorus of this arrangement, Dameron modulates to the key of E♭ for further ensemble development of the song: a sixteen-bar sax soli; an eight-bar alto sax solo, with brass accompaniment; and the final eight bars, with the full ensemble with a false coda. After this the second half of the tune is suddenly reprised in the key of G♭, with a stylistically forward-looking coda, ending in the kind of chromatic cadence that would become a cliché, albeit an effective one, in the 1950s—a decade after this was written (fig. 3.1).

The other 1942 arrangement held at the Smithsonian, "Bewildered," is an AABA-form ballad by Leonard Whitcup and Teddy Powell. The arrangement is for female voice and full band. Here Dameron is more extravagant in his reharmonizations. A comparison of the eight measures before the bridge from the original with the same eight from the arrangement (fig. 3.2) should be enough to make the point. Where the original harmonic sequence follows a very standard I-vi-ii-V pattern, Dameron's reharmonization starts to depart from the expected sequence in the third bar, with the highly altered C dominant-seventh chord in place of the C minor seventh. The next four bars take the melodic cadence to G♭, with the melody note, E♭, as a sixth against the major seventh of the chord, called for in the piano part and present in the second alto saxophone. One should also note the A9 chord (only present in the piano part) in the fifth measure of the example. The ninth, B, of that chord creates a dissonance with the B♭ in the melody, which is resolved in the next measure as the harmony moves to a Cmi7 and the B to a B♭, the seventh of the Cmi chord. As striking as these dissonances seem in description, the effect in performance is lush and lyrical.

The arrangement is also beautifully detailed, with subtle solo lines inside

ex. 3.1

Fig. 3.1. Coda from Dameron's arrangement of "The One I Love."

the saxophone background that support the vocalist. After the first vocal chorus there is an ensemble passage that reprises the song from the bridge. However, Dameron puts this statement of the bridge up a major third, into the key of G. The key returns to E♭ for the vocalist's return with the final segment of the song and the coda. The overall effect is grand and highly romantic. This arrangement is one of the clearest examples of the influence of George Gershwin on Dameron.

While the extant arrangements from 1941 and 1942 are of "standards," there are also copyrights of Dameron tunes registered by New Era Music (a publishing company closely associated with Lunceford) in those years that were probably intended for the Lunceford book. Dameron's lyric for one of these, "Hey

ex. 3.2

Fig. 3.2. Second eight-measure section of "Bewildered," by Powell and Whitcup, shown twice to compare the composer's harmonies with Dameron's substitutions. © 1939, Leonard Whitcup, Inc., and Tee Pee Music Co.

Messy!" mentions not only Lunceford but several members of the band. The last of Dameron's tunes to be registered by New Era was filed in December 1942, around the time Dameron most likely left Lunceford.

At first hearing, these eight melodies are conventional for their time. Still, among them we find elements of Dameron's evolving approach to harmony, in which parallel chord progressions play an important role. "What about You?," written with Jack Reynolds, was composed in Kansas City. It was copyrighted first by the composers early in 1941[10] and again by New Era, with slight rhythmic alterations, in March of 1942. The earlier copyright deposit shows another early instance of Dameron's use of the ♭II7 as more than a substitute for the V7—the melody line actually calls for this harmony. By the end of the 1940s, it would not be surprising to find the turn-around figure iii7-vi7-ii7-V7 replaced with iii7-♭iii7-ii7-♭II7, and in "The Seventh Chord Affair"—which has no lyric and would seem to be intended as a medium-tempo "bounce" tune—Dameron uses this progression both harmonically and melodically. He also indicates the cadencial progression ii7-♭ii7-I, or Cmi7-Bmi7-B♭. The use of a minor-seventh chord on the lowered second degree instead of a dominant seventh is an interesting variation on the chromatic progression ♭II7-I, a progression not uncommon a few years after this was written. However, Dameron does not return to this particular use of a minor-seventh species in place of dominant again in any of the written music available to us. "Dig These Riffs," written with Charles White,[11] also employs the ♭II7, and since it may well have been written in Kansas City, it could be another instance of Dameron working with this chord in 1940. In "Don't Forget It," the ♭VI7 chord plays a more prominent role than it did in Dameron's work from a couple of years earlier. We find it used harmonically and melodically in the fifth measure of the A section (fig. 3.3a). In the bridge we also find the harmonic/melodic use of the ♭II 7 (fig. 3.3b).[12]

Fig. 3.3. First eight bars and first four bars of the bridge of Dameron's "Don't Forget It." © 1978, Twenty-Eighth Street Music.

As for the remaining four of the known New Era compositions, "Do You Remember Now?," written with Jack Reynolds, is more diatonic harmonically but an attractive melody just the same; "Buy Bonds Right Away!" and "Hey Messy!" are not particularly noteworthy in their musical character; and "The Hepster's Glide" presents a melody that is not entirely clear in its harmonic implications.

Recently, six more titles from Dameron's time with Lunceford have come to light in assignment documents, "Dim Out," "For All Fans," "Harlem Express," "My Heart for Two," "Stuck Up," and "Thirty Two Bar Leape" [*sic*]. Unfortunately, they were never accompanied by deposited manuscripts and were never recorded. Undoubtedly, there were other arrangements that Dameron wrote for the band, and probably some of these were of his own tunes. How many there were and what became of them is anyone's guess.

"Mary Lou"

Some time early in 1942, while working for Lunceford, Dameron composed a piece intended to be performed by Mary Lou Williams. It is not a song or melody in the conventional sense, but rather a setting for Mary Lou Williams's piano improvisation, and can be seen as another example of Duke Ellington's influence. Although the parts were found among Mary Lou Williams's papers, it is quite clear that this was written for her to play with Andy Kirk's Clouds of Joy, and the existence of these parts may be evidence of a working relationship between Dameron and Kirk, as well. The three trumpet parts are named "Big Jim," "Harold," and "McGee" [sic], and the alto saxophone part is labeled "Ben." The other parts are labeled with the name of the instrument they are written for. "Big Jim" was the nickname of Harry Lawson, who played with Kirk from the band's early days with T. Holder, until dental problems forced his retirement from music in 1956. "Harold" is, of course, Harold "Shorty" Baker, who left Kirk shortly after his beloved Mary Lou, and "McGee" is Howard McGhee. These were the three trumpets in the Kirk band at the beginning of 1942. "Ben" is Ben Smith, an alto saxophonist who was also in the Clouds of Joy at that time.

This piece of music was never heard during Dameron's lifetime. Obviously Mary Lou's departure from the Clouds was one factor. However, even if she had stayed a while longer with Kirk, it is highly unlikely that so uncommercial a piece would have received anything more than a reading at a rehearsal. One imagines that this gift was met with a mix of pleasure and sadness, as there was little for Williams to do but put it away for safekeeping. Fortunately she did so, and it now documents Dameron's interest, at the time, in producing something more than reasonably conventional commercial arrangements and songs in the popular style of the day. It also indicates Dameron's continued contact with Mary Lou Williams after his move to New York.[13]

"Mary Lou" consists of a twenty-four-measure ABA form with a ten-measure introduction; a twelve-measure interlude that introduces a trumpet solo chorus, with ensemble background; and another solo chorus for piano, with rhythm only. The piece concludes with a final twenty-four-bar ensemble and a five-measure coda. There is no tune as such, but a motif on the progression F-F#7 (chromatic root motion between I and bII7 again) that generates the composition through a series of contrasting responses and associated transformations. "Mary Lou" also explores another of Dameron's emerging interests and another connection with Ellington, the integration of improvisation into an overall composition beyond just giving a particular player some solo space. The entire piece is cast as a conversation between the ensemble and the soloists, primarily the pianist.[14]

As stated elsewhere in this book, Tadd Dameron returned to Cleveland with some regularity. At the end of the summer of 1942, after Mary Lou Williams and Shorty Baker formed a six-piece band, he is mentioned as being in the audience at Mason's Farm, where they played their one successful engagement, from August into October.[15] Others mention seeing and hearing Tadd in Cleveland in the early 1940s. Saxophonist and educator Andy Goodrich recalls hearing him at Lindsay's Sky Bar,[16] and trumpeter Benny Bailey, a fellow Clevelander, remembered Dameron writing arrangements for the small band of Tommy Enoch around this time. As Bailey recalled, "Oh, [Enoch] was beautiful. He used to play in a nightclub [in Cleveland] for a floor show. And after the floor show, they would play dance music, but very hip arrangements. I think they had a trumpet and tenor, I believe, maybe a trombone or so, very small group."[17]

Regarding the Williams/Baker band, Linda Dahl, in her biography of Williams, maintains that "Dameron gave her some of his arrangements to try out as well."[18] While it is entirely possible that he did so, nothing in his hand seems to have survived from the sextet's book. After an unsuccessful engagement at Kelly's Stable in New York—without Baker and with only a group of very young players—Mary Lou disbanded the group. At the same time, she also had a falling out with the band's drummer, Art Blakey. As a result, he took part of the book and went back to Pittsburgh.[19] It is possible that somewhere, either among the items in Blakey's estate or hiding in an attic somewhere, there are those charts, among them some by Dameron.

After Lunceford

It would appear that during his time on staff with Lunceford, Dameron was employed mainly for his arranging and rehearsing skills. This naturally would have been frustrating to a musician who not only considered himself primarily a composer but had already enjoyed a situation where his original work was recorded. Although he may have regarded Oxley's office as a home base for working Tin Pan Alley, the imposition of the recording ban, along with the shellac rationing required by the war effort, severely diminished the odds for success in the popular song market. It was time for Tadd to move on. We have no documentation of Tadley Dameron's activities for the year of 1943, but we do have his recollections, as well as those of some of his associates. In several of Dameron's interviews, he says he went from Lunceford to Basie, but to Ira Gitler he said, "Then I quit Lunceford and I was just writing for different bands—Benny Carter, Teddy Hill."[20] Even though Carter maintained that Dameron never wrote for him,[21] this account of freelancing (with Basie as one of his clients) is probably closer to the truth than Dameron's more commonly stated litany of full employment with a succession of bands.

That Tadd worked for the Count is irrefutable, but the details of his involvement with the Basie band are not clear. There is no mention of his working with the band in any of the three biographical books on Basie, and the only corroboration of Tadd's association with the Count is the three known arrangements they recorded,[22] Basie's credit as coauthor of "Good Bait," and a comment by Babs

Gonzales. While Dameron told Orrin Keepnews, "After Lunceford I worked with Count Basie,"[23] he did not specifically say this was full-time employment. Tadd was probably either on Basie's staff or on call, as a copyist and rehearsal coach. Dameron's success in improving the Rockets' level of ensemble precision would almost certainly have come to Basie's attention, and it was probably in this second capacity that he was most valuable to the band. As Willie Smith, Cleveland-based saxophonist, arranger, and Dameron's long-time friend, said, "Tadd, he knew how to get guys together and play his things—play period, you know. I mean he knew how to rehearse a group, and to get the musicians honed in on what they were trying to play. He was good at that."[24]

Dameron was also known to be on the progressive scene in New York, and he probably started going up to the jam sessions at Minton's Playhouse in Harlem as soon as he arrived in town. Just how often Dameron took part in the Harlem jam sessions is not known, but clearly he left an impression. Kenny Clarke, who would have a close working relationship with him later on, remembered hearing Dameron using chords with flatted fifths in the early 1940s.[25] Clarke went on to say, "It sounded very odd to me at first. Tadd was one of the first men I heard playing eighth-note sequences in the new legato manner, too."

Bassist Charles "Truck" Parham had joined the Lunceford band by the April 14, 1942, recording session, as had Tadd's childhood friend Freddie Webster. Parham, who had been introduced to Dameron by Webster, lived down the hall from Dameron, at the Braddock Hotel. They became good friends, and Parham recalled that they would spend much of their free time together, often trying out Tadd's arrangements along with other musicians. Parham went on to say, "We'd go down to Minton's every night where Monk was playing. We were all buddies, we were all down there every night; stayed down there 'till broad daylight, jammin' [with] Monk and Kenny Clarke."[26]

In 1943, Leonard Gaskin was bassist in the house band at Monroe's Uptown House,[27] along with Duke Jordan on piano and Max Roach on drums. He recalls Dameron being there: "Tadd didn't play too much in those days but I saw him quite often in Monroe's and at most of the other 52nd Street clubs when I went there to jam. He had only just come to New York but he was already becoming quite well known on the local scene."[28]

In his 1952 radio interview with Harry Frost, Dameron placed his introduction to Dizzy Gillespie at Minton's, and in "The Case for Modern Music" he recalls his first meeting with the trumpeter: "I walked into a jam session and, while waiting around, sat down at the piano and played a few chords. 'Are you going to play like that?,' he asked me, and when I told him I was, he just said, 'Man, you're a life-saver. I've been looking all over for a guy like you.'"[29] This meeting probably took place in late 1943, after Gillespie left Earl Hines's band and was working around New York. After living in hotels on the road for several years, Dizzy and his wife took an apartment, and he started holding court in his home. Budd Johnson recalled Dameron as one of Gillespie's visitors in early 1944:

> Tadd Dameron at that time was one of Dizzy's students. Tadd would say, "Well, Dizzy, I'm making an arrangement for so-and-so and look . . . and I'm doing this." Dizzy would say, "Look, don't use these chords. Lemme show you what to do." And Tadd would get up from the piano. And Dizzy would sit at the piano and show him the changes. Actually, Tadd would have never been able to write the way he did if it hadn't been for Dizzy Gillespie.[30]

Although Gillespie's influence on Dameron's writing is overstated, it is likely that the perception of Tadd as Dizzy's "disciple" started from this time period. It is also likely that Johnson was not well acquainted with Dameron's arrangements for Harlan Leonard, some of which already show signs of the work that would make him famous, or the already "boppish" reharmonization that Tadd did of "Bewildered" for Lunceford. Given the difference in the temperament between Tadd and Dizzy—Tadd was quiet and soft-spoken, Dizzy demonstrative and outspoken—it would be easy to misinterpret their relationship.

There is also documentation of Dameron and Gillespie's collaboration during the 1940s. On the copyright deposits of two of Dameron's more daring compositions, "Nearness" and "Soulphony in Three Hearts," he credits John Birks Gillespie as coauthor. However, both of the manuscripts are in Dameron's own hand, and Dizzy introduced "Soulphony" publicly as Tadd's work in a concert recorded at Cornell University. Gillespie's name also appears on the copyright deposits of two other compositions generally referred to as Dameron's: "Cool Breeze" and "Stay On It." "Cool Breeze" appears to be, without doubt, a collaborative work, as it is based on part of Coleman Hawkins's "Disorder at the Border," to which Gillespie made a substantial contribution (see chap. 4). Gillespie's coauthorship of "Stay On It" is, most likely, a courtesy on the part of Dameron.

It seems likely that one of Gilespie's influences on Dameron may have been to get him to start taking solos when performing publicly. Prior to one night late in 1943 or early 1944, all indications are that Tadd's professional performing consisted mainly of accompanying singers and playing as part of a big-band rhythm section. As Dameron recalled later:

> Dizzy was playing at the Onyx club with Max Roach, Oscar Pettiford, Don

Byas and George Wallington. I had met him at Minton's with Monk and Kenny
Clarke. So one night George had to go somewhere, so Don said, "Why don't you
come down and just chord for us?" and I said, "I don't take any solos," and he
said, "Come on, come on, you know the changes to all the tunes." So I'm sitting
there playing, and all of a sudden, Dizzy says, "You got it." So I started playing.
But I never wanted to play.[31]

In September of 1943, Decca met the Musicians' Union's demands for royalties
and better pay, and by the beginning of 1944, the smaller record labels started to
settle with the AFM, too. Bands were starting to record again, and Tadd Dameron would emerge as a real presence on the jazz scene.

4

The Architect of Bop

1944

There is a subtle but quite noticeable change in the overall sound of big-band arrangements in general between 1940 and 1944. This change is apparent, for instance, if one compares the recordings of Count Basie from the late 1930s with those from the mid-1940s. It can already be heard in Dameron's work between the Harlan Leonard charts and the Lunceford charts. While the instrumenation differs, there is also a smoother, more legato quality to the melodic lines. The music of the 1930s tends to have more staccato articulation in the ensemble lines, and a more emphatic statement of the beat in the rhythm section as compared with the music of the 1940s. These changes in writing and playing surely took place gradually, but because of the nearly two-year recording hiatus, their effect is striking when we get to the music recorded in 1944.

Count Basie and his band were under contract to Columbia records, and Columbia, along with RCA Victor, was not willing to settle with the AFM until the fall of 1944. However, the smaller Savoy company had met with union demands earlier in the year, and in April, Earle Warren and His Orchestra—actually the Count Basie band, with Clyde Hart sitting in for the Count—recorded an arrangement of Warren's own "Poor Little Plaything."[1] This was the first commercial recording of a Tadd Dameron arrangement since the summer of 1942. There are also notations in some discographies that Dameron directed the band at this session, which would fit with the most likely scenario of his activities in the first half of 1944.[2] This arrangement, with its bright, bold, exuberant brass passages, as well as the new suavity of rhythm and articulation, represents an obvious stylistic evolution from the 1941–42 writing heard in the Lunceford recordings.

Warren's song, in ABAC form, has a phrase structure that invites a call-and-response treatment from the arranger. In these two-measure spaces, as well as elsewhere in the chart, Dameron unleashes the power of the brass, creating a mood that might be best expressed as "heroic." Musically, these bold brass lines make an attractive contrast with Warren's cool baritone voice,[3] although this device seems a bit of a non sequitur in relation to the lyric. Dameron continues this element of contrast between the "heat" of the brass and the "cool" of the soloist by having Lester Young take his eight-bar solo, after eight bars of the full ensemble, with only the rhythm section for accompaniment. Dynamic contrasts like these would be an important element in some of his most memorable arrangements during this period.

Another Dameron chart recorded in the spring of 1944 also documents his writing for a band other than Basie's or Lunceford's. On March 29, the Sabby Lewis[4] Orchestra was recorded in an air-check from the Club Zanzibar in New York City, and one of the selections was Tadd's arrangement of George and Ira Gershwin's "Embraceable You."[5] Tadd's good friend Freddie Webster was in the band for this recording, and Webster's friendship with Dameron may have had something to do with the presence of this arrangement in Sabby's book. There may have been more that were not recorded.

Dameron's arrangement of "Embraceable You" comprises two choruses, one instrumental and the other vocal. The introduction is just a brief four-measure fanfare to set up the first chorus, but Tadd does make a strong statement of his own in the eight bars that introduce the vocal chorus, making something grand out of the modulation from the key of F major to that of Eb major. The Lewis band was a very good one, the same size as Harlan Leonard's, but without a guitar. However, the trumpet section's precise intonation and the presence of a baritone saxophone result in a fuller-sounding ensemble. It seems that Dameron was intent on giving the musicians something to emphasize the beauty of their music making, particularly the trumpet of Freddy Webster and the voice of Evelyn White.

The Billy Eckstine Orchestra

In "The Case for Modern Music" Dameron says, "I left Basie and in 1944 . . . I went with the Billy Eckstine Band. There for the first time I could not only use my own ideas but had musicians who wanted to and were able to play them."[6]

Billy Eckstine had established himself nationally as a singer with Earl Hines's early-1940s band, regarded as one of the incubators of the bop movement because of the generally free hand that Hines gave his younger musicians.[7] Eckstine left Hines in the fall of 1943, working solo on Fifty-second Street. He also probably did odd guest spots with various bands, such as his appearance with Georgie Auld at the Laurel Garden in Newark on April 1, 1944.[8] For a few weeks early in 1944, Dizzy Gillespie shared the bill with Eckstine at the Yacht Club, on Fifty-second Street, both men working with Billy Shaw of the William Morris Agency. Over the next couple of months, these three men—Eckstine, Gillespie, and Shaw—developed the idea for the Billy Eckstine Orchestra, and by June of 1944 the band started to perform publicly. The band's personnel included several musicians who had been with Hines, most notably Charlie Parker, Dizzy Gillespie, Gerry Valentine, and Sarah Vaughan. The saxophone section included Lucky Thompson, Leo Parker, and Charlie Rouse, who would all emerge as important players in the coming years. On drums, Eckstine hired Shadow Wilson, one of the most progressive musicians of the time, but Wilson was drafted just as the band was forming.[9] For the first several weeks, before they could find a replacement, Eckstine played drums on the ballads while Gillespie and others took turns on the fast numbers.

The band went on the road very quickly. Even though they had some arrangements by Gillespie and Valentine, as well as a dance book generously provided by Count Basie[10] and some charts from Boyd Raeburn, they had no copyist and had to work up head arrangements to get through the one-nighters booked in June and July. After a tour of the South and Southwest the band opened briefly at the Club Plantation in St. Louis, where they were joined by Tadd Dameron and Art Blakey, who would become their permanent drummer. Later Blakey recalled an incident that tells us something of the radical and rebellious spirit of the young musicians who made up this band. It may seem humorous today, but it must have been a bit frightening at the time:

We were playing in a prejudiced club [the Plantation Club]: [Sarah Vaughan], Billy Eckstine, Bird, Dizzy. The man told us all to come in through the back door, and these damn fools, they got together and they came in the front door. The guy wigged. They all come in the front door havin' a ball. He said, "I don't want you to fraternize with the customers." When Charlie got to the intermission, they all sat at the tables and the guy was about to wig. He told someone, "You gotta get this band the hell outta here." The guys were carrying on something fierce despite the fact that gangsters were walking around with big guns on their hips. They didn't scare Bird or anyone. Tadd Dameron was drinking a glass of water, out of one of the beautiful glasses they had to serve the custom-ers. Bird walked over to him saying, "Did you drink out of this, Tadd?" Tadd says, "Yeah." Bam! He [Parker] smashes it, "It's contaminated. Did you drink out of this, Tadd?" "Yeah," Tadd says. Bam! "It's contaminated." He broke about two dozen glasses. A guy was glaring at Bird: he just looked back coolly. "What do you want? Am I bothering you?" Bird asks him. "Are you crazy?" the guy asks. "Well if you want to call me crazy," Bird replies. Then once again he turns to Tadd, "Did you drink out of this glass?" Bam! "It's contaminated." They put us out. They sent Jeter-Pillars in our place at the Plantation and they sent us to the Riviera, which was a colored club. There the band started, and we went from there to Chicago.[11]

During the band's two-week stay at the Riviera, across the river in East St. Louis, Illinois, Billy Eckstine, Dizzy Gillespie, Gerry Valentine, and Tadd Dam-eron were finally able to pull the band together. Eckstine recalled that Dam-eron had come from Kansas City to join the band. It seems most likely that Dameron had been on the road with Basie, since the Count and his band were booked into the Tower Theater in Kansas City from Friday, July 21, through the following Thursday, July 27. After that they were off to the West Coast for an extended stay. The Eckstine band was due in Chicago to open at the Regal Theater on Friday, August 18. Dameron did not stay very long, most likely four to six weeks, but during this time he contributed several arrangements to the book and rehearsed the band. The arrangements Dameron wrote for Eckstine included Billy's own "I Want to Talk about You"[12] and some of his own compo-sitions that would end up in the Gillespie book in 1946, when Dizzy started his second big band.

"I Want to Talk about You" provides a fully realized statement of Dameron's "heroic" approach to the ballad. Taken at a very slow tempo, somewhere around 63 beats per minute,[13] the entire performance consists of only one thirty-two-bar chorus, with ten measures of introduction. Much has been said about the social dimensions of Eckstine's work in the 1940s, when racial discrimination was still very much a part of American life: from the "Jim Crow" laws of the South, to subtle taboos in even the most liberal areas of the North. While there were black male singers of romantic songs before Eckstine, there was about him an assertiveness that was more in tune with the mood of the black artists and intellectuals coming to the fore in the 1940s—quite noticeable in the work of writers like Richard Wright—and it can be argued that he was the first black male entertainer to present himself to the general public as a romantic figure and to be accepted as such. Dameron, not surprisingly, is in complete accord expressively and politically with Eckstine in this unapologetically romantic arrangement. The slow tempo of this song and its lush, full orchestration encourage a more intimate sort of dancing. The bold brass exclamations and richly voiced saxophone lines are of a piece with the singer's sincerity and romantic ardor. Dameron's arrangement of "I Want to Talk about You" was recorded three times: for Delux (Dec. 5, 1945), for Armed Forces Radio (Jan. 1945), and in the movie *Rhythm in a Riff* (July 1946).[14]

"Cool Breeze," an elaborate composition/arrangement (it is difficult to separate the two in this case) based in the twelve-bar blues, is a collaborative effort on the part of Dameron, Dizzy Gillespie, and Billy Eckstine. Gillespie's obvious contribution is the first two choruses, which are taken from the first two choruses of his solo on Colman Hawkins's "Disorder at the Border." Eckstine's contribution is not so clear, but since he was not in the habit of taking composer credit for new work written for his band—as many other band leaders did—it seems likely that he really did have creative input here. The overall arrangement and orchestration were probably Dameron's work, and ten years later Billy Eckstine would connect Dameron alone to "Cool Breeze."[15] The introduction and the counterline in the trombones under the first full chorus of the piece sound very much like Dameron's writing, as does the modulatory interlude setting up the tenor sax soloist. The background behind the trombone's second chorus sounds more like Gillespie but could have been written by Dameron as well. The background for the tenor sax solo is the line that becomes Dameron's "The Squirrel."

"Cool Breeze"[16] was played often in the 1940s, and Dameron wrote a substantially different arrangement for Buddy Rich just after the drummer formed his first big band. Although Rich never recorded the chart commercially, he played it at least twice in transcribed live performances, and one would assume it was an active number in the band's book. Dizzy Gillespie had the original chart in his book, and he, too, played it often, recording it commercially for Victor and playing it in several radio broadcasts. In the live performances one hears an additional saxophone solo chorus with a background figure that becomes the basis for an obscure Dameron tune, "Pan-Dameronium," which was written for and played by Gillespie's band around the same time. The figure sounds very much like something Dizzy would have come up with, so it is hard to know if it was part of the original arrangement or something Gillespie added and Dameron elaborated on. Dizzy Gillespie would revive the arrangement of "Cool Breeze" in the mid-1950s, adding more backgrounds and using it, in concert, as an effective marathon blues jam.

The next of the five Dameron arrangements for Eckstine to be recorded are two vocals written for Sarah Vaughan,[17] Ahlert and Roy's "Mean to Me" and "Don't Blame Me," by Fields and McHugh. These were recorded in the winter or spring of 1945, when Vaughan, who had left the band, made guest appearances in these Armed Forces Radio Service (AFRS) transcriptions. "Mean to Me" is in two choruses, the first a slow ballad tempo of about 66 beats per minute, the second a nice "bounce" at double the speed. The arrangement is more subdued than Eckstine's "I Want to Talk About You," especially in the first, slow chorus, but it allows Vaughan to play with the line of the melody. In the slow chorus there is a nice touch of tone painting as Dameron underlines the words "you always scold me, whenever someone is near" with ominous-sounding chords. "Don't Blame Me" is taken at the same slow ballad tempo as the first chorus of "Mean to Me" and is a bit more fully orchestrated. On the recording it sounds as if there were a cut in the score for the sake of timing for the program. After Vaughan sings one chorus, the band opens up with an instrumental statement that sounds like the beginning of a second chorus, but it turns out to be a reprise of the last eight bars. The singer comes back in with the very last phrase of the song. The author's suspicion is that there was originally an eight-measure ensemble passage, followed by a second eight-measure solo by one of the instrumentalists. After this the singer would have come back at the bridge and sung the song out from there. As it is recorded here, the arrangement sounds uncharacteristically ill proportioned.

The last of the set of arrangements recorded by the Eckstine band is Dameron's own "Our Delight," one of his best-known melodies and one of the pieces that Eckstine shared with Gillespie, who was actually the first to record it. As in his arrangement/compositions for Harlan Leonard, Dameron develops his theme through variation from beginning to end, in parallel with the improvisations of the soloists. The most complete reading of the score is in the live recordings of Dizzy's orchestra. The Musicraft release by Gillespie and the movie version by Eckstine both have been cut because of overall time restrictions; a twelve-bar interlude is omitted in the latter and the interlude and a whole chorus from the former. The thirty-two-bar AABA melody from which the arrangement is developed has an unusually narrow compass for a Dameron melody. We will return to further analysis of this melody later.[18]

There is no clear record of Dameron's activities for the rest of 1944. Some of the literature on Charlie Parker tells us that Tadd left the Eckstine band with Bird, in early September, after the Regal engagement. The only likely date we can establish for him in the rest of 1944 is the week of Friday, December 15, to Thursday, December 21,[19] when he was at a marathon jam session at the Majestic Hotel in Cleveland. Dizzy Gillespie was still with Eckstine at this time. Trumpeter Benny Bailey was there as well and recalled, "About two or three bands were in town at the same time. . . . Probably Eckstine [because of Gillespie's presence] and Cootie Williams was in town. Bud Powell and Eddie Vinson, who was then playing fantastic alto in the style of Charlie Parker, were playing with Cootie Williams. And Tadd Dameron happened to be in town."[20] While we do not know if Dameron was in Cleveland on one of his frequent visits home or there with Eckstine, it is certainly plausible that he continued to work with the Eckstine band off and on after his initial stay with them.

The presence of Parker and Gillespie, and the writing of Dameron, Gillespie, Budd Johnson, and Gerry Valentine, are good reasons for acknowledging Eckstine's band as the "first bebop big band." However, these individuals were not alone in the evolution of a clearly modern style in 1944. Boyd Raeburn and His Orchestra were simultaneously moving in same direction, and Tadd Dameron contributed to their book, as well. Raeburn had been leading a "sweet" band since the mid-1930s, but in 1939 or '40 he changed his book completely to swing. By 1942 the band was ready to go into the Arcadia Ballroom, in New York, with arrangements written largely by Budd Johnson and Gerry Valentine. At the end of 1943 Raeburn reformed the band, hiring several young musicians who would later be associated with the bop movement, including Sonny Berman (briefly), Don Lamond, Marky Markowitz, Earl Swope,[21] and Hal McKusick.

On August 13, 1944, the Raeburn band lost all of its music in a disastrous fire that consumed the Palisades Park Casino. According to Boyd Raeburn's son Bruce, Billy Eckstine "returned charts earlier lent to him plus forty more."[22] It seems quite likely that some of Tadd's charts were among these and that Dameron then continued to write for Raeburn. By the summer of 1945, tenor saxophonist Frank Socolow had joined Raeburn. He recalled that "at the time it was a wonderful musical organization. It was less commercial than any band I had been with, and the arrangements were great because a lot of them were Tadd Dameron arrangements."[23] As of this writing no scores or parts for any of Dameron's arrangements for Raeburn have come to light, although Dameron would mention later that they had played a chart of "Our Delight"[24]—possibly among those provided by Eckstine. There is also a title, "Boydstown," listed in a 1964 copyright-assignment document, and we must consider the likelihood that Dameron contributed to the Raeburn book throughout the life of the band. Saxophonist Hal McKusick remembered Dameron and Gillespie visiting the band at New York's Lincoln Hotel in the winter or spring of 1944. According to McKusick, "Dizzy used to come into the Blue Room [at the Lincoln] a lot with composer-arranger Tadd Dameron." Four years later, Mel Lewis, who played drums with Raeburn for several months in 1948, found that "the scores by George Handy, Tadd Dameron, Johnny Richards and Tiny [Kahn] made work each night a pleasure."[25]

1945—*Spring*

On January 9, Dizzy Gillespie made the first recording of "Good Bait," one of Dameron's best-known compositions. Given the close association between Tadd and Dizzy at this time, Dameron was probably involved in the session. This sextet arrangement uses some of the lines found in the one written for Count Basie and may be derived from the one Tadd said he wrote for his brother in 1939. This thirty-two-bar AABA melody is constructed of eight-bar sections using the "rhythm changes" A section, with the same progression stated a fourth higher for the bridge. One of the challenges in writing an effective jazz composition is to present something with enough structure and character to shape the work of the soloist, but not so much complexity as to prove unwieldy. If we were to put good jazz compositions on a scale from simple to complex, we might find Duke Ellington's "C-Jam Blues" at the extremely simple end and something like Clare Fischer's "Pensativa" or Antonio Carlos Jobim's "Chega De Saudade" at the complex end. "Good Bait," with its almost folk-song simplicity, balanced with its chromatic sophistication, provides an ideal framework for the improvisor, and its popularity with jazz musicians to this day bears this out.

"Good Bait" is the first instance of Dameron's use of an "open bridge," where the melody is not specified for the B section of the tune and must be improvised by one of the players. He made at least seven treatments of this tune:[26] for Gillespie's sextet, for Basie, for Lunceford, for Gillespie's big band, for Buddy Rich, for his own small groups, and the published stage-band arrangement. In only the Basie, the Rich, and the published arrangements does he move the melody up a fourth for the bridge.[27] In the other cases someone improvises over the chords at the bridge. In the mid- to late 1940s, Dameron would often use this device as a way of integrating improvisation with his composed melody, as would Charlie Parker and Dizzy Gillespie on occasion. What is interesting here is that Dameron was clearly using this device in 1945, while Gillespie only hinted at it at this time, and Parker had not yet entered the period of his career when he was composing frequently. While this is not a revolutionary practice, it was previously used primarily only in the latter choruses of an arrangement. Dameron would soon write melodies in which a section of improvisation is clearly required.

Most musicians play only the melody of the opening chorus of "Good Bait,"

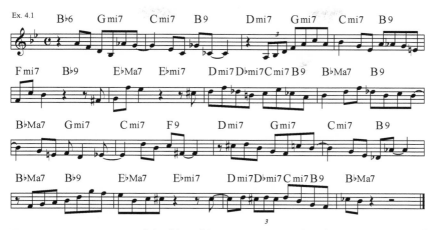

Fig. 4.1. Approximation of the "shout" line Dameron used in his arrangements of "Good Bait."

even though all but one of Dameron's treatments include a sixteen-bar "shout" for the first half of the final chorus.[28] This line, shown without embellishments in figure 4.1, is always recognizable, but each version is different. Sometimes the differences are small, sometimes considerable, but elements of this "shout" melody are always present. The one exception to the length and placement of this second theme would be the Basie version, in which only part of the line is used in a saxophone ensemble over the bridge of the second full chorus. The version for Basie was probably the first of these, as suggested by Basie's cocomposer credit, the copyright date of 1944, and the general sound of the chart. It should be noted that Basie's name appearing on "Good Bait" does not necessarily mean that he had a hand in composing this tune. Indeed, there is good reason to believe Dameron's claim that he wrote it in Cleveland in the late 1930s— trumpeter and educator Thomas Stewart recalled Caesar Dameron confirming this to him in 1962.[29]

Not long after Gillespie's January recording session, he and Charlie Parker began working together in various settings leading to their historic stand at the Three Deuces in March and the "Diz and Bird" recordings made in May, which included "Hot House," Dameron's famous contrafact of "What Is This Thing Called Love." This is one of the defining records of the bebop era, and melodically it is Dameron's most radical composition. The melodic complexity of "Hot House" contrasts strongly with the simplicity of "Good Bait": the compass of the melody is more than two octaves, and the melody regularly employs dissonant upper tensions of the prevailing harmonies: flatted ninths, fifths, and thirteenths. While the harmonic structure, borrowed from Cole Porter's "What Is This Thing Called Love," defines two identical eight-measure periods in the first half of the chorus, Dameron creates a sixteen-bar melody for the first half. There is a contrast between the two eight-bar periods: the first has mostly stepwise motion; the next is distinguished by dramatic arpeggios, with flatted ninths and fifths. The dissonant arpeggio-based construction continues in the bridge, and the last eight measures repeat the opening eight. The entire melody describes a dramatic arch, boldly stated.

While this has become a well-known melody today, it must have been quite startling when it was first released in 1945. "Hot House" is so full of melodic dissonance that it is unique in Dameron's body of work. Only the previously unknown "Conversation" is quite so confrontational in its attitude, and even there the bridge has a lyrical quality that contrasts with the ominous tone of the A sections. However, in its careful construction and graceful proportions, "Hot House" is consistent with the best of Dameron's work.

Stan Levey, the drummer for the Three Deuces engagement, remembered Dameron being at a rehearsal one day and making a very important contribution to the sound of the band:

> The rhythm section was Al Haig, Curly Russell and myself. Al was a very good piano player, you know, he got around the keyboard, but his comping wasn't exactly what Dizzy liked. So, we're rehearsing in the 3 Duces, before we opened, and Tadd is, of course, there listening and everything. And Dizzy says, "Tadd, come on up here and show Al how you comp," which Tadd did; and Al picked right up on it and then sat down and played.[30]

Not surprisingly, Levey knew Dameron socially as well. Levey had moved to New York in the summer of 1944, and shared lodgings at the Schuyler Hotel with Ellis Tolin, another young drummer from Philadelphia. Tolin recalled:

> Our apartment at the Schuyler became a gathering place. The guys with the big bands dropped by after finishing work in the theaters or hotels. So did the 52nd Street players. When the clubs closed, Stanley and I would grab a bite to eat, go back to the apartment, play and listen to music, and talk to the guys about this and that until well after daylight. Bird, Max, Vic Coulsen—the trumpet player—and Tadd Dameron were around a lot.[31]

Dameron also recommended Levey for a job with Georgie Auld in the spring of 1945. Tadd was working for Auld in the first half of 1945, and Stan—who is on Auld's May 24 session, which included Dameron's arrangement of "Honey"—said that Dameron traveled with the band on the bus.[32] Georgie Auld was already something of a star player, having become popular while working with Benny Goodman and Artie Shaw in the late 1930s and early 1940s. In September 1943, Auld returned to civilian life after a short stay in the army and formed a band that would eventually blend commercial sensibility with the emerging modern jazz. A March 1944 review in *Metronome* shows that the band included some young musicians who would go on to establish themselves on the jazz scene in the coming years, including trumpeter Al Porcino, saxophonists/arrangers Al Cohn and Manny Albam, and pianist Harry Biss. Sonny Berman also played in this band after his brief stint with Raeburn. In addition to "Honey," Auld would record two more Dameron charts in October 1945, as well as another pair in 1946.

The song "Honey"[33] is simple and a bit old-fashioned, and Dameron dresses it up with strings of ii-V sequences that flesh out the relatively slow-moving chord changes, as well as a restless sequence of modulations. There is an introduction, in A♭, with four bars of piano, followed by six more of the band in a sequence that sounds as if it is getting ready to move to another key but does not. This leads to the first full chorus, scored for the full orchestra, the first half in A♭, the second in C. Then there is an interlude that changes the key to D, and Auld sings a chorus. Another interlude brings everyone back to C for the last chorus, which features Auld's tenor sax. The whole chart is wrapped up with a smoothly boppish coda that would not have been out of place in something Dameron might have written for Eckstine.

Dameron also wrote some small-band arrangements for Sarah Vaughan to record in the spring of 1945. Tadd's association with Sarah, which began in the Eckstine band, would continue into 1946, and he may also have been coaching her around this time.[34] He had certainly established a friendship with her that would yield some of the best of her early recordings. Dameron, along with others in what we might call the progressive circle at the time, was very impressed with the young singer and was interested in helping her along her way. Mary Lou Williams recalled, "I met her while she was touring with Earl Hines. . . . Tadd Dameron later brought Sarah to the house and we became great friends."[35]

Further evidence of the closeness of this circle of progressive New York–based musicians is found in a recording of Sarah Vaughan and Her Octet, made for Continental on Friday, May 25, two weeks after the session that produced "Hot House." Here we have Tadd, Dizzy, Bird, and Sarah working together, with Flip Phillips, Nat Jaffe, Bill DeArango,[36] Curly Russell, and Max Roach.

On this date, they recorded "Mean to Me"; "What More Can a Woman Do," by Dave Barbour and Peggy Lee; and a Dameron arrangement of "I'd Rather Have a Memory Than a Dream," with Dameron at the piano. It is a simple score for trumpet, alto sax, tenor sax, and rhythm section: a four-measure introduction, followed by the horns providing a simple background for the singer. The trumpet leads the ensemble, and this type of small-group arrangement would become fairly standard for Dameron's small-group vocal settings in the later 1940s. It is Sarah's singing that carries the day here, for the ensemble performance is rather ragged, despite the star power of its members—Gillespie, Parker, and Flip Phillips. It seems likely that this arrangement was a last-minute addition to the session; Dameron might possibly have written it at the session, and the song could even be his, since no author is known.[37] This would explain his presence at the piano, even though the very capable Nat Jaffe had been engaged to play piano, as he does on the other two numbers recorded at this session.[38] Dameron was still shy about his piano playing in 1945, but as we can hear on this recording, he could produce a beautiful tone and was musically eloquent when playing at slower tempos.

Count Basie recorded a tune called "San José" for V-Disc around this same time (May 14, 1945) that had to have been arranged by Tadd Dameron. Some have speculated that the melody's similarity to "Our Delight" suggests that it was written by Dameron, but the tune is credited to Bryan and Edwards in the V-Disc logs.[39] "San José" begins with the chord progression V7 of V-♭vii7-♭II7-I, the same as Dameron's "Our Delight," only it proceeds differently. It is impossible to know which chart came first, and there are subtle similarities in the two. For instance, in the fourth measure of the bridge in the opening statement of "San José," the saxes play the figure in figure 4.2, which is heard prominently in the introduction to the "Our Delight" arrangement written for Eckstine. There is also a paraphrase of "Our Delight," in the last eight bars of the closing chorus. At the beginning of this final chorus there is an exchange between the trumpet section and Basie, in which the trumpets play a Gillespie-like line. This is probably the sort of thing (remember this is 1945) that Dameron was referring to when he said, "[Basie] felt [my arrangements] were too far out of line to be used on his recordings."[40] Fortunately, Basie made an exception for this V-Disc date.

ex.4.2.

Fig. 4.2. Figure found in background parts of arrangements of both Dameron's "Our Delight" and the uncredited arrangement of "San José."

1945—Fall

We do not know where Dameron was in the summer of 1945, but it is likely that he was in New York in the fall. Woody Herman, who had a regular radio show, picked up a new sponsor, Wildroot Cream Oil, on October 13. He would broadcast with their support for some eighteen weeks, during which time Tadd wrote a jingle for the company's hair tonic, called "Cream Oil Charlie."[41] Tadd may well have written other things for Woody in late 1945; there are titles attributed to Dameron held by companies associated with Herman, who did record two Dameron compositions later, in 1949 and 1958.

On October 23, 1945, Georgie Auld recorded Dameron arrangements of "It Had to Be You" and "Airmail Special."[42] The first is a joyous romp, full of Dameron's heroic brass outbursts, the sensual singing of Lynne Stevens, and a very fine half-chorus solo by Auld on tenor. The introduction sets up the singer by playing on the rhythm of the opening motif of the song. There is an interlude to introduce Auld's tenor saxophone solo, and the second half of the second chorus gives us Dameron's take on the song in a breezy ensemble. Lynne Stevens returns for a reprise of the second half of the song, and the band goes out with an ecstatic coda.

Contrary to the assumption of some authors, Tadd Dameron did not write the arrangement of "Airmail Special" for Eckstine; Budd Johnson did.[43] While Dameron did paraphrase Johnson's opening chorus in his opening chorus for Auld, the introduction, the interludes, the modulation, and the final shout chorus are all different from the Johnson chart. What has confused people is the presence of the same descending line in the brass against the saxophones playing the melody. However, both men use this line differently. In the A section, Johnson uses the line continually, while Dameron uses it only in the second four measures. This line has so much character that the casual listener might think both were the same arrangement. Besides the obvious differences, it is quite easy to hear each arranger's voice in the respective charts. This is particularly true in the saxophone voicings and in many of the lines. Dameron and Johnson were contemporaries in that they were writing at the same time and involved with several of the same bands, so there are similarities, but there are certainly things in the Eckstine chart that Tadd Dameron never would have written. Likewise, there are things in the Auld chart that would have been unlikely for Johnson to write.

It seems likely that, as a freelancer, Dameron was still writing for Lunceford in the fall of 1945, but dating this later work for the Harlem Express is a matter of making educated guesses, since none of it was recorded. Between the estimates made by Deborra Richardson and Annie Kuebler in preparing the finding aid for the collection of arrangements from the Lunceford band held at the Smithsonian Institution, and the stylistic elements of these arrangements, the author's guess is that "Frolic at Five" and "Moo-See-Ka" were written sometime in 1944, "Fine and Dandy" and "Good Bait" probably in early 1945, and "Zakat" in late 1945 or early 1946. It is a pity that these were never recorded and have remained unknown since Lunceford's death,[44] because they give us another window into the transition from swing to bop and Dameron's thinking on this transition.

"Frolic at Five" and "Moo-See-Ka" are, without doubt, intended for general dancing. Technical considerations in each indicate that a tempo above 138 beats per minute would be difficult to achieve and sound awkward. More to the point, at a moderate tempo they make one feel like dancing. At the same time, they incorporate elements of Dameron's sophisticated approach to harmony and formal design. In the case of "Frolic," he deconstructs the AABA form of the initial tune, creating a larger form; functionally, the result has some resemblance to the classical *sonata allegro* form, in which two or more themes are presented and then developed in a variety of ways, depending on the size of the work and the possibilities that interest the composer. It is the sort of sophistication of design implicit in "Mary Lou," to which Dameron would return in compositions such as "Nearness," "Soulphony in Three Hearts," "Lyonia," and "Fontainebleau."

In "Frolic," the first full chorus of the AABA tune in E♭ presents the two contrasting ideas that make up the song-form melody. An eight-bar interlude that sounds like an alternate bridge modulates to B♭. The form seems to remain intact for one more chorus. There is a trumpet solo, with saxophone background, over the first sixteen bars of the tune's chord progression—the first two As—which is abstracted and simplified. As expected, the B harmonies follow, here with a piano solo. The final A of the form begins an exploration of this part of the original song-form melody and its harmonies. The saxes, which continued to provide background in the bridge for the pianist, now present an ensemble of sixteen bars, or two more A sections, before modulating to D♭ and continuing to provide a background for a trumpet ensemble over another A section with considerably modified but still recognizable chord changes. This is followed by one more A, with a tutti ensemble played very softly. Finally we hear the bridge again, in a trombone solo over a saxophone background, which modulates suddenly back to the original key of E♭. The piece concludes with two more statements of the original A theme and a coda.

One could see this arch form in many arrangements that return to the open-

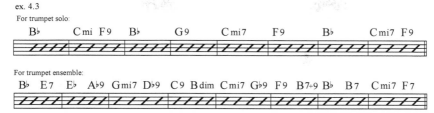

ex. 4.3

Fig. 4.3. Comparison of the harmonies Dameron used in the first eight bars of the opening chorus of "Frolic at Five" and the harmonies used for a corresponding eight bars later in the piece.

ing theme. What distinguishes this one is the departure from the strophic repetition of the AABA form of the initial melody. Dameron takes the first theme of the opening tune and develops it separately, which is most unusual in this idiom. The extent of the modification of the harmonic progression in the trumpet ensemble can be seen easily by comparing it to the simplified progression used for the earlier trumpet solo. To make this easier to understand, both versions are shown in the key of B♭, even though the second is in D♭ (fig. 4.3).

Although "Moo-See-Ka" does not have quite the same complexity as "Frolic at Five," it too seems to have a larger compositional design. The tune starts with a six-measure introduction featuring a cascade of dominant-seventh chords that set the key, B♭. The root motion of the cascade is very interesting, with chord roots progressing in alternating diminished and perfect fifths—A♭7 D7 G7 D♭7|G♭7 C7 F7 B7| B♭maj7 B7|—which can be seen as an extension of the concept of approaching dominant and secondary dominant chords from a half-step above. This leads to an AABA tune that is only played once. The A section of the melody consists of two two-bar phrases, each with two bars of melodic silence, inviting and receiving a response. In the last of these "holes," at the end of the third A, there is a simple two-chord modulation to the key of E♭. The form and the changes for the bridge remain the same, but the A sections are now harmonized with a series of clearly identifiable "rhythm" variants—the original melody would not fit well with any of these progressions. However, the consistency of harmonic language, the consistent harmonic sequence in the bridge, and the fact that each of these A sections is harmonically different make everything sound of a piece. The last chorus is cast as a big "shout chorus," with each A section outdoing the previous one. These three joyously melodramatic outbursts are tempered by a piano solo over the bridge. The last A becomes a high-strutting fifteen-bar coda.

The arrangement of "Good Bait" is unique and quite different from the one for Basie that would have been written perhaps a year earlier. The Basie chart has an unusual first chorus, in which one of the As is left out, giving that one chorus the same structure as "Mary Lou." The Lunceford chart is more open, with very little background writing for the soloists—more akin, in this regard, to the small-band Gillespie treatment—but with an interlude and a short but very interesting coda. The interlude that sets up the first solo starts in a manner similar to the one used in the Eckstine/Gillespie big-band chart but comes to a very different conclusion. The coda written for Lunceford repeats the eight-bar theme of the tune one more time and has five measures tagged on to the end. The music here moves through this chord progression (the first double bar marks the beginning of the coda): B♭6 || Cmin7 | F♯7 | A♭7 | D♭9(♭5) | D♭9(♭5) ||. This wild sequence of chords is held together by a melody line that develops the opening motif of the tune. The effect is startling and yet quite logical (fig. 4.4).

In "Fine and Dandy," the extensive use of chromatic substitutions in the turn-arounds (fig. 4.5a) and the boppish trumpet lines (fig. 4.5b) in some of the transitional passages suggest that this arrangement would likely have come from 1945. The "Fine and Dandy" chart is also built around two full-chorus solos—one for second trumpet, the other for first tenor—that could be easily opened up for additional choruses, another feature shared with the two later arrangements, but not with the earlier ones. While it seems unlikely that this arrangement was written in 1942, given its style, if this arrangement dates from Dameron's earlier tenure with Lunceford, as posited by Eddy Determeyer in *Rhythm Is Our Business*,[45] then it certainly gives considerable weight to Tadd's statement that he started writing in the modern idiom "when I started writing for Jimmie Lunceford's band."[46] We have already seen Dameron's creative use of chromatic harmony in "Bewildered."

"Zakat,"[47] like "Good Bait," is structured more along the lines of the smaller-band arrangements Dameron would be writing a couple of years later. Like those small-band arrangements, "Zakat" is easy to open up for extended solos, and it does not seem to be as well suited for dancing, with its musically sound but oddly placed rhythmic accents. In AABA form, the chord progression of the A is closely related to Dameron's ballad "We're Through," which Sarah Vaughan would soon record. Dameron again employs a melodically open bridge. The arrangement of this tune has another thing in common with the Lunceford version of "Good Bait," an ending on a chord outside of the key. In this case the chart is set in the key of F, and it ends with a D♭ major seventh chord, with the sixth and sharp eleventh added as well. The distribution of the notes, or voicing, is quite wide, with the notes in close intervals in the center and more open

ex. 4.4

Fig. 4.4. Coda of Dameron's arrangement of "Good Bait" for Lunceford.

ex. 4.5a - turnaround at mm.14 & 15 of the opening chorus:

ex 4.5b last three bars of interlude before first solo chorus:

Fig. 4.5. From Dameron's arrangement of "Fine and Dandy" for Lunceford, the turn-around harmonies at measures 14–15 of the opening chorus and the last three bars of the first interlude.

ex. 4.6

Fig. 4.6. Voicing of the final chord from Dameron's arrangement of "Zakat."

intervals, mostly fifths and fourths, on the bottom and top, and it produces a massive sound (fig. 4.6).[48] Dameron uses this type of voicing later to get a big sound from a small number of winds.

1946

The year 1946 got off to a good start for Tadd Dameron. *Esquire* magazine, which was in the midst of a brief three- or four-year flirtation with jazz journalism, held a poll of prominent musicians. One of the categories in the poll was the "New Stars Band," and Tadd placed second, behind Ralph Burns as arranger. The number of individuals polled was small, requiring only three votes for the honor. Still, we may be able to get an idea of the extent to which he was known in the jazz community by this time, by considering the three who voted for him: Coleman Hawkins, well-known supporter of and participant in the new developments in jazz; bassist Jimmy Butts (born the same year as Dameron, he had played with the swing bands of Les Hite, Chris Columbus, and Don Redman and, at the time of the voting, played for the pre-swing veteran Noble Sissle); and trumpeter and violinist Ray Nance. Nance, born in 1913, was just four years older than Dameron and had started his career in the earlier days of the swing era. He had gone to work with Ellington in 1940 and had just left Duke's orchestra to work as a single.[49] In the same poll, repeated at the end of the year, Tadd would finish first. Dameron is also well represented on record in 1946. Billy Eckstine, Georgie Auld, Dizzy Gillespie, and Sarah Vaughan all made commercial recordings of his arrangements and compositions. Dameron's work is also represented on an unreleased commercial recording by Basie, an informal recording of Don Redman's European tour orchestra, and AFRS recordings by Buddy Rich.

Dameron was writing for the new Buddy Rich band at the end of 1945 and the beginning of 1946. After a controversial departure from Tommy Dorsey, and with financial help from Frank Sinatra, Rich and his new orchestra went into rehearsal in November of 1945. On Christmas Eve, at the Valley Forge, Pennsylvania, General Hospital, the Rich band played in public for the first time. If the record that is claimed to have been recorded on that date is correctly labeled, it documents the presence of an arrangement of "Cool Breeze" by Dameron—a stripped-down version of the one written for Eckstine—in the Rich book before the end of 1945. Another Dameron arrangement known to be in the Buddy Rich book around this time is "Just You, Just Me," recorded for AFRS in March or April of 1946. There is also an arrangement of "Good Bait" recorded by Rich and company for V-Disc in 1948, which was never released by AFRS and has become available only recently.[50] It is not known whether this was in the book earlier or if Dameron wrote other charts for Rich. Buddy seems to have liked both "Cool Breeze" and "Just You" since he used them more than once in broadcasts and AFRS transcriptions.

In the case of "Just You, Just Me,"[51] Dameron wrote arrangements for both Buddy Rich and Georgie Auld. Although the two charts share some of the same lines, they are quite different, especially in their character, which matches that of their respective bands and leaders. Both arrangements take joyous advantage of the power of the four trumpets and three trombones, but there is a sense of restraint in the Auld version, in contrast with thick, dissonant brass and tutti voicings in the Rich.

In the Auld version, a trumpet solos first in the second chorus, and then Auld is given the bridge for a brief alto solo. In the next chorus, he is featured on tenor—Auld distinguished himself as an excellent soloist on all the saxophones. The whole affair is assertive but gentlemanly. In the arrangement for Rich, Dameron sets up several "holes" for Buddy to fill throughout the arrangement. These are usually preceded by the same sort of colossal-sounding chords that start the arrangement, giving the drummer a good reason to use all of his considerable power. While the Auld version is certainly memorable, the one written for Rich has to be one of Dameron's most exciting and extroverted arrangements. As always, Tadd Dameron has a sense of balance. The Auld chart stays at the same general full dynamic level right up to the end. The Rich version is more of a study in contrasts, with the double forte outbursts and the full-throttle third chorus offset by passages of cool nonchalance and an ending with a gradual decrescendo into a final sly, muted trumpet figure that would not be out of place in an arrangement written twenty or more years later.

Neither of the other two known Dameron charts for Rich has the same exceptional quality, although they are perfectly good arrangements. "Cool Breeze" is closely related to the original, but without the multiple backgrounds, inter-ludes, or key changes. In "Good Bait"[52] Dameron gives Rich several more oppor-tunities for his dynamic fills. He also plays with the overall structure relative to the other arrangements of this tune. Here the second full chorus has the second A section omitted, as in the first chorus of the Basie version. The arrangement for Rich also has an unusually long coda, which sets up a closing three-bar fill for the drummer, essentially giving Buddy "the last word." The shout chorus for the trumpets is quite different from the one in the two Gillespie versions, the Dameron small-band version, and the published arrangement. However, as noted before, it has recognizable elements shared with the other shout choruses.

Sarah Vaughan

On April 30, 1946, at the same session that yielded "Just You, Just Me," Georgie Auld recorded Dameron's arrangement of "One Hundred Years from Today," a vocal feature for Sarah Vaughan. The song is taken at a leisurely tempo some-where in the 70-beats-per-minute range and consists of a sixteen-measure intro-duction and one sung chorus with a tag ending. The introduction incorporates the first three phrases of the melody and features the saxophone section led by Auld's soprano. In the 1940s there were very few players using the soprano, and Dameron takes advantage of this opportunity to create an introduction that is quite striking even today. As in the arrangements he wrote for Vaughan to sing with Billy Eckstine's band, Dameron gives her plenty of room here, trusting in her skill and presence to carry the song. The band mainly supplies smooth har-monic support for the singer.

Tadd Dameron's other collaborations with Sarah Vaughan from the spring of 1946 are noteworthy on several accounts. First is the quality of the writing, second the variety of settings, and third the fact that these would be the last signs of any direct professional contact between the two. The first recording was made on March 21, when trombonist Dickie Wells recorded with a sep-tet for the Hot Record Society (HRS).[53] The Wells group included trumpeter George Treadwell—who would marry Sarah in September of that year—as well as Budd Johnson on tenor sax, Cecil Scott on baritone sax, Jimmy Jones on piano, Al McKibbon on bass, and Jimmy Crawford on drums.[54] For this date, Tadd arranged a song of his own, "We're Through," with words by Anne Greer. The melody is built on an ascending harmonic progression, reminiscent—as noted before—of the one employed in "Zakat," with the bridge beginning with this same sequence a fourth higher. In contrast to the Continental session a year earlier, there seems to have been more rehearsal for this date—HRS, although small, was known for the high quality of its sessions. This arrangement, although still understated, is more detailed in its lines than the one for "I'd Rather Have a Memory Than a Dream." In spite of the quality of the ensemble and singer, and proper rehearsal, this recording has slipped into obscurity; "We're Through" is one in a long line of Dameron's romantic ballads that never seem to have caught on.

One of the interesting features of the arrangement for "We're Through" is Dameron's use of bowed bass. He is trying to create a contrapuntal web of melodic lines behind the singer, and it almost works. Unfortunately, the result is ponderous and muddy, not for lack of skill on anyone's part but because Dameron lacks the instrumental forces to present his ideas. In his next outing with Sarah Vaughan he seems to have everything he needs, and the results are outstanding. The four songs recorded by Musicraft on May 7, 1946, "If You Could See Me Now," "I Can Make You Love Me," "You're Not the Kind" and "My Kinda Love," helped establish Vaughan as an artist in her own right. Other than the 1945 date for Continental, these are Vaughan's first recordings under her own name. Previously she was just the singer with someone else's band. These discs are labeled "Sarah Vaughan, with orchestra under the direction of Tad Dameron." As Sarah Vaughan rose to international stardom, these recordings were often included in compilation LPs of her early work.

This is a particularly significant recording session for Tadd Dameron as well. Dameron wrote the arrangements—which are his first recorded orchestrations for strings; contracted and directed the orchestra; and contributed the song "If You Could See Me Now," with lyrics by Carl Sigman. Between the beauty of this song and the strength of Vaughan's performance, it has become one of Dameron's best-known and most-recorded compositions.

The orchestra consists of nine bowed strings, trumpet, alto sax, baritone sax, bass clarinet, piano, bass, and drums. One of the reed players doubles on flute. With this instrumentation Dameron creates a luxuriant setting for Vaughan's voice, in a way establishing the tone for some of her pop hits of the following decades. The string writing is idiomatically perfect, even though Dameron had never written for strings before, as far as we know. Melodic lines that speak well on winds do not necessarily do so on bowed strings, and it is not uncommon for perfectly good band arrangers to get less-than-happy results in their first string arrangements. We do not know whether Dameron prepared for this project by doing some research or if he had simply acquired a sense of what would be appropriate from listening to the excellent string writing of the film composers of the day. He also makes clever use of the four winds to suggest a still-larger ensemble, skillfully balancing the winds with the strings and using the baritone sax and bass clarinet as cellos, as well as winds.

Dameron was also careful in his choice of musicians. Pianist Bud Powell plays beautiful, flowing obligato lines in the background, subtly thickening the overall sound of the ensemble and even rewarding close listening, if one can set aside the vocal charms of Sarah Vaughan. Powell also gets a brief-but-elegant solo on "I Can Make You Love Me." Then there are the exquisite tone and phrasing of trumpeter Freddie Webster and the rich baritone saxophone of Leo Parker, who solos on "My Kinda Love." Webster is heard prominently in the introductions to "If You Could See Me Now" and "I Can Make You Love Me," and he gets a solo on "You're Not the Kind." Freddie Webster had the ability to play with great projection even in the lower register of the trumpet, and Dameron makes use of this skill, most notably in the introduction to "I Can Make You Love Me." This low register forte is a unique timbre, and Webster was exceptional in his ability to produce it. These four recordings certainly rank among Dameron's masterpieces.

Even though this session marks the end of Vaughn and Dameron's professional association, "If You Could See Me Now" and "You're Not the Kind" remained in Sarah's repertoire for the rest of her life, and she even retained a curious detail from one of the arrangements. Dameron gave "You're Not the Kind" an unusual tag ending, in which the song, sung in the key of B♭, finally ends in the key of G—another ending a third away from the home key, as in the Lunceford "Good Bait" and "Zakat" charts. In recordings of this song made later in her career, Sarah retains this delightfully off-center coda, most notably on the December 1954 Emarcy date with Clifford Brown.

The Dizzy Gillespie Orchestra

Dizzy Gillespie's first big band, the one that went on the "Hep-sations" tour, lasted only until the end of September 1945. After that Gillespie returned to playing around New York with small groups and made his historic stand with Parker at Billy Berg's in Los Angeles. By June of 1946 he had assembled another orchestra, one that would last until early in 1950. Gil Fuller, who served as Gillespie's music director, recalled later, "Tadd never sat down and wrote an arrangement for Dizzy [in 1946] because Tadd wanted to get paid, and we had no money. They weren't giving [Dizzy] money to get a book."[55] However, Gillespie was able to add some of the Dameron charts from the Eckstine book to his repertoire, and while Tadd may not have written for the Dizzy Gillespie Orchestra in 1946, it seems he was rehearsing the band. Dave Burns joined the band early on, in time for the June 10 session for Musicraft. When Burns came to audition, Dameron was rehearsing the band in an arrangement of "How High the Moon." Burns started by playing the third trumpet part, but then Dameron asked him to play lead,[56] and Dave Burns continued to lead the Gillespie trumpet section until he left the band early in 1949.

Cecil Payne, who joined Gillespie late in 1946, also remembered Tadd's involvement with the band. "Tadd would come to the rehearsals to get the band to play his charts just the way he wanted," he said. Payne also credited Dameron's careful rehearsing of the band, along with similar coaching by Gil Fuller and, later, George Russell, for the very high quality of its performances.[57] Ray Brown and James Moody also remembered Dameron's rehearsals from this general period of time.

Soon after the new Gillespie band was formed, they recorded Dameron's "Our Delight" for Musicraft. They also broadcast performances of "Our Delight" and "Cool Breeze" from the Spotlite Club on Fifty-second Street, which were recorded off the air. "Stay On It," another Dameron composition, may have entered the Gillespie repertoire around this time. Basie recorded it for Columbia on July 31, 1946, but it was never released,[58] and a comparison of this recording—issued much later by French CBS—with the Gillespie recordings of the same title reveals that Gillespie had the very same chart. This arrangement and the two arrangements Eckstine gave to Gillespie are the only recorded instances of two different bands recording the same Dameron arrangement.[59]

Apparently, Tadd felt that "Stay On It" did not fit Dizzy's band and said as much: "I'm walkin' down the street, the score under my arm, and Dizzy comes along and snatches it out, and he says, 'Oh, I got another arrangement.'"[60] While this may be so, it seems a bit fanciful. Both Basie and Gillespie have acknowledged that "Rock-a-Bye Basie," a big hit for the Count, grew out of a riff Gillespie played with Teddy Hill, known as the "Dizzy Crawl." Gillespie never received any credit or royalty for this, and in 1946 he was still struggling to establish his big band. It would seem more likely that, having decided not to release "Stay On It," Basie gave the chart to Gillespie as a gesture of thanks.[61]

"Stay On It," "Good Bait," and the unrecorded (and possibly never performed) "Jumpin' in Society" were submitted for copyright at the same time (early in 1945) and are all variations on the "rhythm changes" format. Since they all have some connection with Basie, they—at least arrangements of them—were likely written around the same time. When taken together, they seem to be part of an ongoing process of working out variations on this venerable form that extends through Tadd's Lunceford and Basie work. Dameron would return to the "rhythm" template at various times, even as late as "Swift as the Wind," from 1962.

A week or so before the Gillespie band broadcast from the Spotlight, the Billy Eckstine Orchestra made a thirty-minute "featurette" that included performances of "Our Delight" and Dameron's arrangement of "I Want to Talk about You."[62] Following the success of "Caldonia," a similar promotional film made by Louis Jordan and His Tympani Five, Eckstine's *Rhythm in a Riff* was intended for distribution in movie theaters in predominantly black neighborhoods and as a preview in theaters where the Eckstine Orchestra would soon be appearing.[63] Footage from this little movie is included in various jazz videos and presents some of the finest performances of the band that have been preserved.

Also during that summer, the pioneering arranger, saxophonist, and bandleader Don Redman put together a tour of Europe, with the help of Danish expatriate Timme Rosenkrantz. For this tour—the first by American jazz musicians since the end of the war—Redman assembled a big band of three trumpets, three trombones, five saxes, piano, bass, and drums. An informal recording made in Copenhagen by Rosenkrantz on the opening night of the tour bears witness to the strength of this band. The musicians represented all the generations of jazz musicians: pioneers such as Redman himself; transitional players such as Don Byas; and youngsters such as trumpeter Alan Jeffries, saxophonist Ray Abrams, and pianist Billy Taylor. Likewise, the book represented music from the whole of big-band jazz: from Redman's "Chant of the Weed" to a number titled "Oo-Ba-Ba-Le-Ba," which quotes the bop anthem "Anthropology," and a composition from Tadd Dameron, wryly titled "For Europeans Only," written as a feature for tenor saxophonist Don Byas.

By the middle of 1945 Tadd Dameron was well established on the New York scene and had made significant contributions to the development of modern jazz, contributions that grew out of his own unique perspective on harmony and melody and his sense of overall composition. By the fall of 1946, his music was being heard on radios and jukeboxes in America, on American military bases overseas, and by European audiences. Dameron was also beginning to work as a smallgroup pianist, as a member of Babs Gonzales's band, and possibly as a sideman with others on Fifty-second Street and elsewhere around New York. In the mid-1940s Tadd Dameron came to musical maturity, and the range of his writing preserved from the 1944–46 period is impressive, although his small-band writing does not yet have the clarity that would make it important in the coming years. The skill and subtlety that he demonstrated at the beginning of the decade had developed into an ability to create exceptionally sympathetic settings for various individual performers and bands, whether complimenting the musical and extra-musical qualities of someone like Billy Eckstine or adjusting to the personalities and musical needs of different band leaders, as in the case of his arrangements for Auld and Rich. As the year drew to a close, he was on the verge of the most successful stage of his career.

5

1947—Into the Limelight

Big-Band Arrangements

The days of the big band as a practical, commercially viable musical ensemble were drawing to a close. Among the many to turn to other ways of working in the music business were Georgie Auld, who gave up his big band in the summer of 1946, and Billy Eckstine, who would disband his orchestra the following spring or summer. Jimmie Lunceford himself died of a heart attack in the summer of 1947, and his band would not last much longer. Boyd Raeburn and Buddy Rich staggered on into 1948 before disbanding, and by 1950 Dizzy Gillespie had thrown in the towel—even Count Basie had to cut down to as few as six pieces.[1]

In spite of the contraction of the big-band business after World War II, Dameron would continue to write scores for large ensembles in the late 1940s. Anecdotal evidence strongly suggests that there were many Dameron arrangements from this time that have been lost.[2] Among those that we do know of, most were his own compositions, although a few were written by others. Sometime late in 1946, or at the very beginning of 1947, he wrote two charts for a big-band date featuring tenor saxophonist Illinois Jacquet: a second version of "For Europeans Only" and Jacquet's own "You Left Me All Alone." This particular big band was assembled for this date only, since Jacquet's working groups were eight or nine pieces at most, when he was not touring with Jazz at the Philharmonic.[3]

For the ballad "You Left Me All Alone" Dameron wrote another of his lush, heroic settings. This arrangement allows Jacquet, who was best known for his altissimo screaming, to demonstrate the actual depth of his musicianship. The tune's harmonic structure shows that Jacquet, like Dameron, was interested in the expressive possibilities of chromatic root motion. The bridge of "You Left Me," in the key of G, has this harmonic sequence:

D-7 G7 | E♭-7 A♭7 | E-7 A7| E-7 A7|

E-7 A7 | F-7 B♭7 | E-7 A7 | E♭-7 A♭7 || G

The double bar marks the return to the A strain of the melody. The entire arrangement is one and a half choruses, with a reprise from the bridge. Dameron takes advantage of the A♭7, the ♭II7 of G, to take the final strain of the melody to the key of D♭ for a dramatic conclusion. The coda is a series of chords over which Jacquet plays a cadenza, concluding with a strikingly dissonant chord (especially for big-band writing in 1947) that could be described as D♭ma7 ♯9 ♯11 13 or as a D♭ major chord with a C7 superimposed over it—a beautifully dissonant expression of the abandonment implied in the title.

The version of "For Europeans Only" composed in the summer of 1946 for Don Redman's historic tour of Europe would remain unknown to Americans until 1953, when it was recorded by Louie Bellson, with Redman's addition of a fourth trumpet and trombone. As in the case of the "Just You" arrangements made for Auld and Rich, Jacquet's "Europeans" is substantially different from the one written for Redman. What is the same is that the arrangement is a tenor saxophone feature. The melody, thirty-two bars in AABA form, is written over "rhythm changes" in the A sections and the "common bridge" formula. This familiar harmonic sequence, which was favored by many jazz musicians— including Duke Ellington—shows up in several Dameron melodies, providing a comfortable setting for the soloist.

In the tune's original version, the recording of which was finally released on the Danish Steplechase label in 1983,[4] the soloist is Don Byas. However, in the out-going chorus, brief solos spots are written in for trumpeter Alan Jeffries and pianist Billy Taylor. In the Jacquet version the corresponding "holes" are filled by Jacquet himself. In the Redman version there is also an eight-bar interlude,[5] signaling a transition from the extended, three-chorus tenor sax solo section to the final chorus. There is no corresponding interlude in the Jacquet score, which seems appropriate since Jacquet is given solo space right out to the end of the arrangement. While both arrangements share some secondary lines, the background figures behind the soloist are different in the two versions.

The Bellson performance is taken at a faster tempo than the Redman, and there is a better recorded balance between the sections of the band, as would be expected from a studio recording. However, although the Bellson performance is well executed, it is missing some of the dynamic subtleties of the Redman band's performance. This suggests that Dameron himself rehearsed the Redman band, since there are no dynamic indications in the score. If this assumption is correct, Dameron had the musicians pencil the dynamics in their parts in rehearsal.

New Music for Gillespie

Of course, Tadd was now writing for Dizzy's big band, as well as rehearsing it. In addition to "Good Bait" and "Stay On It," the Gillespie Orchestra would introduce, either on record or in broadcast, six more Dameron compositions in 1947 and 1948, and there is evidence of others that he may have arranged for Gillespie at this time that were never recorded. These works range in character from the open-for-blowing blues "The Squirrel" to the completely notated "Nearness" and "Soulphony in Three Hearts." As far as we can tell, none of these charts were in the set copied from the Eckstine book. Exactly when Tadd provided these charts to Dizzy and under what terms we can only guess, but these recordings do give us definite dates by which the band was performing them.

On January 22, 1947, Dizzy Gillespie and His Orchestra broadcast from the Apollo Theater and recorded off the air. Included in the program was an arrangement of Dameron's "Lady Bird," the first known recording of this tune. Although the arrangement may have been written for Eckstine, this was most likely a new arrangement for the Gillespie band. The copyright was registered on February 3, 1947, and the lead sheet appears to have been written by Gil Fuller, who was not only deeply involved with the Gillespie Orchestra but was publishing some of Tadd's music at the time. "Lady Bird"[6] is a particularly important Dameron composition, not only because of its popularity over the years but because of its then-unusual form. Only sixteen bars long, half the length of most popular melodies, it does not resolve to the tonic at the end but continually turns back on itself. However, in the opening statement of the melody in this arrangement, Dameron makes the tune sound as if it has a thirty-two-bar ABAB form by resolving it into an interlude beginning at the fifteenth bar of the second statement—the only time, on record at least, that Dameron or anyone else presents the melody this way.[7] Sixteen-bar melodies of this type are often played twice at the beginning of a performance and are ambiguous by their very nature. Still, in Dameron's own 1948 recording for Blue Note, he does not repeat the sixteen bars at the beginning of the performance, setting up the expectation of a sixteen-bar rather than a thirty-two-bar strophe. Whatever his original intention, "Lady Bird" establishes a sixteen-bar form that would be used afterward by many musicians, starting with Miles Davis in "Half Nelson,"[8] which he wrote to the changes to "Lady Bird" and recorded for Savoy in August of 1947. "Lady Bird" is another tune that Dameron claimed to have written before 1940. As with "Good Bait," there has been plausible but secondhand corroboration of this.

Unlike the other tune-based arrangements, Dameron treats the "Lady Bird" arrangement recorded by Gillespie as a complete composition. The tune that was copyrighted appears only at the beginning and is followed by the ten-measure interlude mentioned above. He then keeps with this thirty-two-bar strophe of two nearly identical sixteen-bar sequences for another sixty-four measures, plus a coda. These are ostensibly sections for a soloist, but the soloist has to work around very strong backgrounds.[9] That Gillespie does not open up this chart for extra choruses in the other recorded live performances (July 1947 and Oct. 9, 1948) supports the perception that Dameron intended this treatment of "Lady Bird" to stand as a fixed composition.

Clearly the up-tempo "Hot House" is intended to be opened up for extra solo choruses. It is a more expansive affair than "Lady Bird," six choruses in all, starting with an introduction that is so dissonant that the melody itself sounds quite lyrical when it enters. As heard in the air-check from the Downbeat Club (Aug. 1947) there are two two-chorus solos, one by Gillespie, the other by baritone saxophonist Cecil Payne. However, in the performance recorded on September 29, 1947, at Carnegie Hall, Payne gets an extra chorus with just the rhythm section. The out-chorus is written as an exchange between the band and Gillespie. While Dameron does not seem to be as concerned with the precise proportions of this arrangement as he was with "Lady Bird," he takes full advantage of the backgrounds provided for the solo choruses to keep spinning out a stream of variations on his theme.

For "The Squirrel" Dameron took one of his backgrounds from "Cool Breeze" and gave it a life of its own as his most popular twelve-bar blues tune. He recorded it first in a small-band arrangement for Blue Note at his own September 29, 1947, session. The Gillespie Orchestra recorded the big-band version for the first time in the summer of 1948 for Armed Forces Radio. There is no introduction to this arrangement; it starts with the trombones playing the basic "Squirrel" riff with a response from the saxes, an integral part of all of Dameron's treatments.[10] Then the full band plays the riff, and alto saxophonist Ernie Henry gives an improvised response, effectively beginning his solo. After a chorus with just the rhythm section, Henry is accompanied by an ensemble

Ex. 5.1.

Fig. 5.1. First four bars of Dameron's "Pan-Dameronium." © 1978, Twenty-Eighth Street Music.

background riff based on the flatted fifth of the tonic chord, which repeats for a second chorus an octave higher. Henry, who also played on the small-band recording, is the soloist in all three of the Gillespie recordings, and it is likely that this arrangement was written with him in mind. Gillespie's solo spot begins with two choruses of four-bar exchanges with the band. The next two choruses have a relatively subdued ensemble background before Gillespie gets one more chorus with a much more aggressive accompaniment from the band. There is a one-chorus ensemble "shout" before the two choruses of the theme return, but in reverse order, giving the arrangement the feeling of an arc.

"Pan-Dameronium" gives separate life to another background riff from "Cool Breeze," the one that follows the "Squirrel" riff in the uncut chart heard in the live performances (see chap. 4). This time, however, Dameron uses the riff as the opening three phrases of a "Sweet Georgia Brown" contrafact. The riff is built on a chromatic decent from the thirteenth to the flatted fifth of the accompanying chord (fig. 5.1).

As one would expect from the title, "Pan-Dameronium" is another barn-burner like "Hot House." The only existing example of this piece is from the end of a broadcast from the Downbeat Club, recorded in August of 1947, and the performance is cut short. After an eight-bar introduction and the opening chorus, the first soloist, Cecil Payne, follows without an interlude and gets a background accompaniment. The next two choruses feature Gillespie, the first with just the rhythm section, the second cast as an exchange of four-measure phrases with the ensemble. After vibraphonist Milt Jackson gets a chorus with just the rhythm section, the announcer says they will have to end the program, and the band goes into what might be the final chorus, consisting of the first sixteen measures of the tune, answered by another sixteen of Dizzy soloing.

The remaining two compositions for the Gillespie Orchestra are through-composed pieces closely related in character to Dameron's better-known "Fontainebleau." "Nearness" first appeared as a piano solo, copyrighted, but not published, by Bregman, Voco and Conn early in 1945 and attributed to Dameron and Gillespie. Two recordings exist from 1947 concerts at Carnegie Hall and Cornell University.[11] The core of the piece is fifty-two measures long, with an opening melodic segment of twelve bars, followed by five more eight-bar segments. The orchestrated version has an eight-bar introduction and a six-bar coda not found in the piano version. The entire piece lasts over four minutes since it is performed at a slow 60 beats per minute. After the introduction, with its dramatic opening featuring a high solo trombone, the melody is carried, for the first three segments or twenty-eight measures, by a solo alto saxophone—the featured instrument. The fourth segment is dramatically led by Dizzy's trumpet, but in the fifth, the alto returns to answer a quiet passage played by the trombones. In the seventh segment the ensemble caries the melody, but the ends of the phrases are filled out by cadenza-like flourishes from the alto. The alto leads in the final segment and has a cadenza in the six-measure coda.

The entire piece is held together by subtle redeployment of various melodic elements: phrase rhythms, harmonic movement, and phrase structure. These elements are continuously recombined in a process that spins an evolving, coherent melody across the entire length of the piece. The strongest example of this is the sequential connection between the second and fourth sections of the composition. The melody of the second section returns, albeit in altered form, a step lower in the fourth segment. Melodically, the second phrase of this melody in the fifth section is an almost perfect sequential mate to its counterpart in the third section. Another unifying element is found in the first phrases of all the sections, save the first. These end with a dotted-quarter/eighth/half-note rhythm, creating something like an internal rhyme in a poem.

The same process is at work in "Soulphony in Three Hearts," from 1948. However, this is a more complicated piece of music, with shifts of time-feel, tempo, mood, and even meter, this last feature being unique among all of Dameron's known compositions. The overall kaleidoscopic effect foreshadows some of Charles Mingus's music of the next decade, particularly those pieces written to accompany modern dance. Unlike "Nearness," where most of the entire piece is present in the copyrighted piano version, the copyright deposit for "Soulphony" shows only the melody line. In the recorded performance, there is a twelve-bar introduction not shown in the deposit, followed by Gillespie playing either his own interpretation or a later version of the melody in the first eight measures. In the next eight, the remainder of the first "heart," he seems to be improvising, no doubt as Dameron intended.

The second "heart" continues at the same slow tempo, around 60 beats per minute, for ten measures. Then, after a *molto ritardando* in the eleventh bar, this section concludes with eight measures in 3/4 at 144 beats per minute, with a hold on the last measure. "Heart" number three begins in 4/4 again at about 170 beats per minute. After sixteen measures the tempo is cut to around 72. After another eight measures there is another *ritardando*, followed by another eight measures at 72, and then the tempo abruptly jumps to a very fast tempo, around 240 to 250 beats per minute, for the next twenty measures or five four-bar phrases. Another abrupt change brings the music back to the previous tempo, maybe a little slower, and there is a gradual slowing down for the remaining ten measures of the piece. The piece is through-composed, but as in "Nearness," there are all sorts of subtle connections between the various melodic phrases. Among them, the fourth measure of the second "heart" has a boldly stated two-eighths-and-a-quarter-note rising fourth figure that recalls the beginning of the introduction. The first four measures of the passage in 3/4 have a contour similar to that of the previous two 4/4 measures. The intervals are different, but the resemblance is strong enough for it to sound clearly connected. There is a descending fourth motif that begins the very fast section near the end of the piece that can be traced back to two measures before the 3/4 passage. The leap of a fourth also figures prominently in the very opening of the piece, only there it is ascending.

In an interview with English jazz critic Max Jones for *Melody Maker* just a few months after the premier of the piece, Dameron indicated that "Soulphony [as a concept] is a cross between bop and symphony."[12] The idea of drawing on both jazz and "classical" techniques in the same piece had been developing throughout the 1940s: Igor Stravinsky's "Ebony Concerto" collaboration with Woody Herman, Mary Lou Williams's "Zodiac Suite," and of course Ellington's suites are among the works that come to mind in this regard. All the same, Dameron's approach to embracing concert music[13] concepts and techniques is quite personal and varied. Along with the variety, we find his abiding interest in structure—whether in unifying one long melodic invention as in "Nearness" and "Soulphony" or in altering common formal structures as in "Mary Lou," or "Frolic at Five."

Pianist and Bandleader

Tadd's career as a New York–based, small-band pianist started with his collaboration with Lee Brown, better known as Babs Gonzales. Babs was viewed by some critics as just a hustler from a poor family in Newark, New Jersey. However, he clearly had musical talent and had attended Newark Arts High

School along with Sarah Vaughan and saxophonist Ike Quebec.[14] He played a little piano and drums, wrote songs, and was a credible singer. Gonzales sang, briefly, with the bands of Charlie Barnet and Lionel Hampton, and it was as a singer that he had a musical career under his own name in the late 1940s and early 1950s.

Of course, Tadd Dameron had been playing in small combos and backing singers since the beginning of his professional career. But other than jam sessions and the occasional fill-in, he is not reported to have been playing in New York until 1946, when he joined Gonzales's band, sometime after the May 7 Sarah Vaughan session. Gonzales recalled that "for the next year we gigged up and down the East Coast from Boston to Washington with occasional locations in Newark and New Haven. Finally, Alfred Lion heard us and gave us our long awaited first record date."[15] Lion recorded Bab's "Three Bips and a Bop" for his Blue Note label twice in 1947.

At the time of this writing, Gonzales has long since slipped into obscurity, and he was always something of an underground figure. However, the recordings he made with Dameron are much more substantial than the novelties that some critics have thought them to be—indeed, Babs would always record interesting music with accomplished musicians. Bop vocalization was in vogue at the time: Mary Lou Williams's "In the Land of Oo-Bla-Dee" and Dizzy Gillespie's "Oop Bop Sh' Bam" and "Ool-Ya-Koo" come to mind, as well as Charlie Ventura's Bop For the People band, with Jackie Cain and Roy Kral. Gillespie recorded Gonzales's "Oo-Pop-A-Da" less than four months after the composer did. As Bob Bach put it, in the May 1947 issue of *Metronome*, "You'll hear a chorus by Babs Gonzales . . . in that strange new musical language of his; it's almost all vowels—oo-Eee-e-oo uh-uh—the one and only way that other people, like Chubby Jackson and Buddy Rich and Ella Fitzgerald, have found to transmit the Gillespie style from one person to another."[16] If Gonzales was "out there," he at least had some company.

In the same article, Bach supports the likelihood that Babs's "Three Bips and a Bop" had been active around New York for several months before the recording session, giving us his impressions of Tadd Dameron:

> Babs and Tad are the backbone of this surprising group, the former a thin, eager little guy who fronts the Bips and takes most of the solos, the latter a quiet, scholarly disciple of The Bop who serves importantly at the piano. . . . The arrangements, all carefully scored and rehearsed by pianist Tad Dameron, . . . are the most interesting yet written down for a vocal group, the closest approach voices have yet made to a band style.[17]

The first session, recorded Monday, February 24, featured three of Gonzales's compositions and Edgar Sampson's "Stompin' at the Savoy." For this date Blue Note added two ringers to the group, alto saxophonist Rudy Williams and drummer Charles Simon. They also printed a promotional poster. It seems that the sales of at least one of the 78s were good. Gonzales recalled sales of forty-five thousand for "Oop-Pop-A-Da" b/w "Stompin' at the Savoy" (BN 534),[18] and Blue Note had the group back in the studio on May 7. It is in this second set of tunes that we find the apparently unused "Wildroot Cream Oil Charlie," as a scat vocal now titled "Do-Bla-Bli."

Dameron's presence as an arranger is clearly audible in the eight Blue Note sides, especially in the first session, where the voices, guitar, piano, and bass of the Gonzales band are augmented by alto sax and drums. By carefully contrasting the sounds of the different instruments, Dameron creates arrangements that could be easily reorchestrated for a big band, especially "Stompin' at the Savoy." The tunes recorded in the second session, without the sax and drums, are given a simpler combo-type treatment but are still quite recognizably Dameron's work.

Dameron's one contribution, as a composer, to the Blue Note recordings is "Do-Bla-Bli." There are deposits for both "Do-Bla-Bli" and "Cream Oil Charlie," and the melody, as recorded, is somewhat different from each of the copyrighted versions, most significantly in that the bridge is open.[19] In AABA form, the song is a contrafact of Juan Tizol's "Perdido." In addition to using its harmonic structure, the song similarly duplicates the focus of the opening phrase on the dominant note ($E\flat$ in the key of $A\flat$). This is not to say that "Do-Bla-Bli" lacks its own distinct character—Dameron takes his melody in a different direction from Tizol's—but the reference is easy to hear. With only a couple of exceptions, even Dameron's less popular melodies are distinct and attractive, and "Do-Bla-Bli" deserves to be played more often.

Tadd probably left the group soon after the second recording session. After a year working with Gonzales, he apparently grew tired of being a piano-playing back-up singer. Later, he told Ira Gitler, "All of a sudden it dawned on me, 'I can't go through life doing this. This is not my story.'"[20] Gonzales later recalled, "Tad had to cut out and travel with Basie, so I replaced him with Bobby Tucker who was idle because Lady Day had gotten busted."[21] Billie Holiday's trial for heroin possession took place on May 27, and she was incarcerated almost immediately,[22] so Tucker was available—possibly even from the middle of May—and he is the pianist on Babs's next recording session in August. If Dameron did leave to work for Basie for a while, as Gonzales recounts, he probably would have been rehearsing the band in some new material for the band's summer-long stay at the Paradise in Atlantic City.

Tadd was working with other musicians by this time, as well. He joined Dizzy Gillespie and others in a broadcast of the "Saturday Night Swing Session" in April or May,[23] and earlier, in February and March, he took part in publicized jam sessions at Club Sudan and Smalls' Paradise in Harlem. Among the musicians taking part in these sessions was trumpeter Fats Navarro, with whom he recorded his first complete session as a pianist. Fats, who was second only to Gillespie among bebop trumpeters, had quit the Billy Eckstine band—and indeed big bands in general—in June of 1946, just before the filming of *Rhythm in a Riff*. After that he concentrated on small-group work with only an occasional studio session in larger bands. Fats's January 29, 1947, session for Savoy documents the beginning of a fruitful musical friendship between Dameron and Navarro, and Tadd's presence here suggests he may have been on some of Fats's combo gigs around New York prior to the recording, in addition to his work with Babs Gonzales. Gil Fuller claimed to have produced these sessions,[24] and Dameron's connections with Fuller may also have been a factor in his participation.

Dameron is credited as cocomposer with Navarro on one of the tunes recorded on January 29, "Ice Freezes Red," a contrafact of "(Back Home in) Indiana." This memorable ABAC melody (which quotes the opening phrase of Jimmie McHugh and Frank Loesser's "I Get the Neck of the Chicken") has "holes" for Navarro and Dameron to fill—an extension of the "open bridge" idea.[25] As a pianist, Tadd acquits himself well on the session, but in his solos one can hear the traces of his experience working without a bass player. Here he cannot stop himself from playing a bass line for his right-hand single-note melody, even though he has ample support from Gene Ramey. Although this kind of left-hand playing was part of the pre-bop piano style, Dameron's lines do not mesh well with Ramey's. In time he would work out a way to play bass lines that would not get in the bass player's way. Tadd himself said he developed his style in the 1930s while playing in Cleveland with his brother, Caesar, who did not have a bass in his band at the time.[26]

The summer of 1947 would see Tadd's emergence as an important bandleader. It was also on an evening that summer that a young William Gottlieb took a set of photographs at a party hosted by Mary Lou Williams, which documented some of Tadd's otherwise private social life. It seems that Mary Lou wanted to show what a party at her place was like. With two exceptions, the guests were professional musicians: Tadd, Dizzy, pianist Hank Jones, composer and orchestrator Milt Orent (with whom Mary was romantically involved at the time), trombonist Jack Teagarden, his girlfriend Dixie Bailey, and of course Bill Gottlieb. Gottlieb recalled that "at that Mary Lou party, I was the 'guest of honor,' so to speak. I had a solid relationship with Mary and Diz, and even with Jack T. But the others were somewhat incidental."[27] Even though the photographer could not recall much else about the party, his photographs preserve moments from the evening. Of course, we find that each of the pianists takes a turn at the piano. In one, while Dizzy plays the piano, Jack and Milt appear to be repairing the phonograph, to which the group listens intently in a couple of the other pictures. In one of these Tadd seems to be commenting on some detail in the music. There is also a scene of Mary, Dizzy, and Tadd playing cards. It is not known if an article was planned to accompany these photos, but they give us a rare glimpse into the life of these musicians off the bandstand.[28]

It was probably in the spring or summer of 1947 that Monte Kay, Sid Torin, and quite possibly others urged Tadd to form his own band. Dameron recalled that Kay and Torin told him, "Look, you ought to get your own group. With your style of writing and your playing, get six pieces."[29] Disc jockey Sid Torin and the promoter Monte Kay were two of the strongest backers of the bebop movement. Kay had been very active on the midtown jazz scene since 1942, when he became involved in producing Sunday-afternoon jam sessions at Kelly's Stable along with his friend Pete Kameron and a third man, Jerry White. Kay and Kameron had some experience with this, having run Sunday jam sessions at Nick's in Greenwich Village. At the Kelly's Stable sessions they started to mix older players with younger players. Dizzy Gillespie would come up from Philadelphia for these sessions, even though the travel cost him almost as much as he earned.

In 1945 Kay, a publicist by profession, formed a loose alliance with Mal Braveman and Sid Torin. With Braveman he also founded the New Jazz Foundation and started promoting jazz concerts at Town Hall featuring Charlie Parker and Dizzy Gillespie, among others. Sid Torin, better known as Symphony Sid, had a program featuring swing and jump music on radio station WHOM at the time. Monte introduced Sid to the new music of Parker and Gillespie, and Sid took to it readily. Kay made him a 50 percent partner in his concert operations, provided he play the records of the newer artists. Later, in the 1950s, this sort of thing might have been the subject of criminal action. However, it is quite clear that these men were acting out of love for the music, and the sums of money involved, even with the success they had, were rather small.

Monte Kay became Tadd's manager, and he was likely instrumental in getting the shy composer and pianist into the clubs on Fifty-second Street. Not that Tadd was a stranger to "The Street" and its club owners: he had been a regular there for some time. Saxophonist and composer Yusef Lateef tells a story about his first meeting with Tadd. Lateef had come to New York from Detroit to join Lucky Millinder's band, but for some reason he could not start when he had planned to. In the meantime, he was without work and could not afford to sit at a table when he went to hear Charlie Parker at one of the clubs, possibly the Three Deuces. Lateef had his saxophone with him but had not come to jam. However, with Tadd's gentle encouragement he ended up playing with Bird that night. As he recalled it, Tadd did have a table and was very well dressed.[30] Of course, Dameron had played some of these clubs with Babs Gonzales and possibly others. Still, by all accounts he was a reticent, soft-spoken man and possibly not entirely comfortable with hustling gigs. His alliance with the more assertive young publicist would get him on the bandstand. After that, the quality of the music he organized ensured that he would be booked again.

Dameron's sextet-plus-vocalist was supposed to open at the Famous Door on Monday, July 28, but the engagement was canceled because the club wanted Dameron to cut back to a quartet. Instead, the band opened down the street at the Nocturne the following Friday, August 1. Listed in the band were Doug Mettome, trumpet; Allen Eager and Eddie Shu, saxophones; Gene Ramey, bass; Kenny Clarke, drums; and vocalist Kay Penton. This is the band—with Shu and Ramey replaced by Ernie Henry and Nelson Boyd, respectively—that recorded sometime later in August for V-Disc, as "Kay Penton, accompanied by Tad Dameron and his group." Penton was working around New York at the time and had recorded with Teddy Wilson for Musicraft, so it is likely that V-Disc had engaged her for this session, and she in turn called upon Dameron to back her up.

Added to the band for this session was vibraphonist Terry Gibbs. However, there seem to be no parts for Gibbs in the arrangements, so he plays just the cadenzas in the codas. Although Gibbs was reported in *Down Beat* to be leaving Chicago to join Dameron's band, Gibbs said that he was called up only for this date and was never sure just why or how.[31] The two songs that were recorded, Fields and Levant's "Don't Take Your Love from Me" and Dameron's own "I Think I'll Go Away," with words by Albert Carlo, show that Dameron's approach to writing for a sextet with three horns was well developed at this point.

The band on the V-Disc record, without Gibbs, opened at Fifty-second Street's Onyx Club on Friday, September 12. In mid-September, "Tadd Dameron and His Orchestra" opened at the Famous Door, but the band seems to have become a quintet, although Kay Penton was probably still singing with the group. Later that month, on September 26, Dameron made his first recordings as a leader.[32] For this Blue Note session, Ernie Henry and Nelson Boyd are still in the band, but Fats Navarro is on trumpet, Charlie Rouse is on tenor sax, and the drummer is Shadow Wilson. All four of the tunes are Dameron originals: "Our Delight," "Dameronia," "The Squirrel," and "The Chase" (not to be confused with the Dexter Gordon tune). These would prove to be among the most remembered and influential recordings of the bop era.

"Our Delight" gets a well-developed arrangement, as does "Dameronia," making the ensemble something of a "little big band." Although there is no introduction for "Our Delight," the three horns are harmonized, and there is some of the internal line movement from the big-band arrangement, as well as a two-bar "send off" at the beginning of the first solo. After the round of solos, there is a sixteen-bar ensemble, followed by a variation on the bridge and the closing A melody from the big-band arrangement. For "Dameronia," the composer wrote an eight-bar introduction that gets a very full sound from the three horns. The tune, AABA with an open bridge, is played in unison. However, the second A has a different melody from the first. The A sections use the I-bII7 harmonic movement that Dameron used first in "Mary Lou," except that the chords are one to a measure, instead of two to a measure. There is also a similarity between the harmonic scheme of "Dameronia" and "Well, You Needn't," by Thelonious Monk,[33] and we should keep in mind the close friendship enjoyed by Dameron, Monk, and their mentor Mary Lou Williams.

The remaining tunes get a simpler treatment. "The Squirrel" has no introduction, but the first two choruses hold the seeds of the larger arrangement, recorded by Gillespie. The first chorus has Dameron playing the riff melody and the horns responding with a composed set of lines that would be used in the big-band version, discussed earlier. The second chorus has the horns playing the melody and Dameron responding with block chords. Then there are two-chorus solos by each of the horn players, followed by one from the bassist and a final statement of the opening chorus.

"The Chase" is an AABA composition with an open bridge. The arrangement is very simple, akin to other small-group recordings of the time. Dameron plays an eight-bar introduction, and the band plays the tune, with Dameron soloing on the bridge. There are two-chorus solos from each of the three horn players. The outgoing statement of the melody is only a half chorus, with Dameron soloing on the bridge again and a final statement of the A section. The catchy melody in the A sections, over simple turn-around harmonies, made it a popular tune with players of the time.[34]

On the Monday following the Blue Note date, September 29, the Tadd Dameron Orchestra opened at Club 18 (previously named the Troubadour).[35] It is most likely that the personnel of the group would have been the same, including Charlie Rouse. Rouse stayed in contact with Dameron in the years after their work with Billy Eckstine. After his brief stint with Eckstine (he left after Parker but before Gillespie), the young Rouse went back to his hometown, Washington, DC. However, he was back on the scene with the 1945 Gillespie "Hep-sations" band.

Rouse would stay in New York as much as possible, but there was often not enough work, so he would go back to Washington to, in his words, "fatten up, get a little strong, and then run back up there. I was doing that off and on for four or five years." During those years the saxophonist would work with Dameron at various times. He recalled, "We played down 52nd St. in the Onyx and all those, the Downbeat." Dameron was also active in Cleveland during these years. Rouse would work with him there as well.[36]

One of the Downbeat engagements Rouse recalled probably opened on Monday, October 16, and probably lasted for three weeks, but Rouse may not have played the entire run. As we will see, the saxophone chair in Dameron's band rotated among several players. When the band recorded for Savoy on October 28, the saxophonist was Ernie Henry. For this recording Curly Russell was the bassist and Kenny Clarke the drummer. Given their frequent participation on other recordings, they were no doubt part of the working band. Two more memorable Dameron tunes were recorded on this date, "A Be Bop Carroll" and "The Tadd Walk." Kay Penton sang "There Must Be You" (by Dameron and Albert Carlo) and "Gone With the Wind" (by Magidson and Wrubel), and we should consider that she was probably still singing with the band at this point.

"A Be Bop Carroll" is one of those gems in Dameron's catalog that somehow got lost over the years. Tadd himself never recorded it again, and no one else of note has recorded it either. The very singable opening melody is likely a contrafact of "Mean to Me"—the bridge harmonies of the two tunes are especially close in their progression. The copyrighted tune is heard at the opening chorus, but the out-chorus has a different melody: the first two As are four-bar ensemble exchanges with Dameron's piano, the bridge is open, and there is a final bluesy eight-bar line that brings the piece to a close.

"The Tadd Walk," a more frenetic and "boppish" tune, is the other instrumental in this set. It may have been played frequently by Dameron's Royal Roost bands and shows up on one of the air-check recordings but has not been heard much since. The harmonies of the A sections are a variant of "Oh! Lady Be Good." The bridge, which is left open melodically, uses the bridge progression associated with "I've Got Rhythm." In the Savoy recording the ending is abbreviated: Henry's solo continues into the first sixteen bars, after which Dameron takes the bridge and the band plays the melody for the final A. However, in the live recording, the band plays the entire tune at the end.

While the two instrumentals were released soon after the recording was made, the vocals were not released until Savoy started issuing LPs in the 1950s. "Gone With the Wind" gets a straightforward but attractive treatment. A counterline to the melody starts in the four-bar introduction and continues under the song in support of the singer. The melody of the intro is developed a bit before the tag—an unusually long last eight bars of the melody—and it is brought back in the coda, tying the whole piece together neatly. Dameron's own "There Must Be You" has an intriguing formal design, with eight-bar verses and an eight-bar chorus. The overall form of the arrangement is introduction, verse 1, verse 2, chorus, two bars of interlude, verse 3, and the final chorus, which ends with a grand retard in the last two bars. However, the whole piece is oddly incomplete. The opening is strong enough, with a four-bar harmonized line played by the horns, and the verse is supported by an effective countermelody— somewhat like the one for "Gone With the Wind"—but the line does not continue into the chorus. For the first chorus, Navarro improvises an obbligato in the background, which continues into the two-bar interlude. While his improvised line is of the high quality we would expect from him, it lacks the careful construction of the written part behind the verses. As before, the third verse is accompanied by the written background, but there is nothing from the horns to support the final chorus. It is as if Tadd had not completed writing the arrangement, modest as it is, by the time of the session but recorded the tune anyway.

Dameron is also present as a sideman on other sessions late in 1947. The first of these also represents one of the likely variations of his own working group. Savoy brought "Fats Navarro and His Thin Men" back into the studio on December 5, with Charlie Rouse, Dameron, Nelson Boyd, and Art Blakey. The discographies give Dameron arranger credit on this date. His influence can definitely be heard in the music, particularly the only number that could be said to be arranged, "Nostalgia," Navarro's contrafact of "Out of Nowhere." The introduction, the opening up of the last four measures of the B and C sections for improvisation (the form is ABAC), and the treatment of the outgoing half chorus are typical of Dameron's work. The remaining tunes are all in the more common "head-solos-head" format typical of small group jazz performances. While some have speculated that "Nostalgia" is a joint composition, it seems fairly certain that the melody is Navarro's. One could say that Dameron influenced Navarro, but it also clear that the two men had a profound aesthetic sympathy. As in the case of Dameron's collaborations with Dizzy Gillespie, it is probably more to the point to speak of the development of a common concept than it is to try to make a case for the influence of one musician over another.

The next week found Dameron present on another important bebop date for Savoy and represented as arranger on yet another significant date for Victor. On Thursday, December 11, the "Thin Men" rhythm section backed up a front line of Dexter Gordon and his former Eckstine bandmate Leo Parker. Dameron contributed one tune to this session, a blues titled "So Easy," which he would score later for Ted Heath and Artie Shaw. On the same day as the first Dexter Gordon date—and a year after voting for him as "New Star Arranger" in *Esquire*'s poll—Coleman Hawkins recorded four Dameron arrangements. The titles included a Dameron original. "Half-Step Down, Please,"[37] as well as three ballads, Harburg and Duke's "April In Paris"; Prozorovsky, Brant, Kahn, and Stothart's "How Strange"; and Hank Jones's "Angel Face." The ballads are treated in much the same manner as the two recorded by Kay Penton: the soloist is highlighted by discrete *obligati*, generally played by the horns in block chords.

Dameron finished the year with a second Dexter Gordon session (again for Savoy), with Fats Navarro on trumpet. For this date he contributed "Dextrose" and "Dextivity," as well as collaborating with Gordon on "Dexter's Mood," which is more like an improvisation on an original chord progression, having only the suggestion of a melody. There has been some confusion about "Dextrose" and "Dextivity." It was long assumed that these were written by Dexter Gordon, but research for a CD reissue of Gordon's Savoy recordings from the 1940s has turned up evidence that Dameron was the composer.[38] These two melodies do sound very much like Dameron's compositions from the time. "Dextrose" is a rather simple yet memorable ABAC tune with a riff melody for the A and open in the B and C sections. "Dextivity" has an urgent, attention-getting six-bar introduction that leads to another riff-based melody with a more relaxed affect. It is an AABA tune, with the A sections built on the harmonic progression of the As of Fields and McHugh's "Exactly Like You" and the bridge built on Dameron's favorite common bridge formula. In the alternate take there is a half-chorus "shout" in the final chorus, before Dameron solos over the bridge and the horns play the A theme one final time, by now something of a "trademark" Dameron device that he liked to use as an alternative to the more obvious repetition of the opening chorus.

Two Ds

Late in 1947, Tadley Dameron changed the spelling of his nickname from Tad to Tadd. On the copyright deposits for "The Chase," "Dameronia," and "The Squirrel," filed on December 5, 1947, and written in his own hand, his name is spelled with two *d*s, the earliest known instance of this spelling. In the articles and captions regarding Tadd that were printed in *Metronome* up through the November 1947 issue, his name is still spelled with one *d*. By January of 1948, when Orrin Keepnews interviewed Dameron for "The Case for Modern Music," Tadd was making sure that the new spelling was observed. One possible reason for this is that Tadd liked to play with his name. He had already used the name "Tadlow Lamar Dameron" on some of his copyright registrations. In light of this, the spelling of his first name as "Tadleau" in the 1940 Cleveland City Directory was undoubtedly his idea as well.

Another possible reason for the change in spelling may have had something to do with numerology, as suggested by Ian MacDonald in his book *Tadd*. While MacDonald does not cite his sources, and Dameron was never known to be superstitious, Gerun Moore, who had some connections with Billy Shaw (Eckstine and Gillespie's manager), had written an article in *Down Beat* promoting the idea of adjusting the spelling of one's name to conform to some numerological formula in order to improve one's luck.[39] While Moore's article reads like a lecture by the comedian and master of "double-talk" Professor Irwin Corey, and the article was written in 1939, the idea may have come from him since his association with Shaw seems to have been long-running. If it did, it was probably seen as a good publicity move. The change in spelling would give people another reason to talk about Dameron. Indeed, "Tadd" has become something of a brand for his work.

With this name change, Dameron was about to emerge as an influential leader of the sort of small jazz bands that would dominate the idiom as the big-band era ended.

6

1948—The Royal Roost

After his busy late summer and fall as a leader and recording sideman, Dameron went out on the road with Dexter Gordon. For this trip Gordon formed a band with Dameron, trumpeter Kenny Dorham, bassist Curly Russell, vocalist Earl Coleman, and drummer Roy Porter. Porter, a friend of Gordon's from the West Coast, took the gig in part to get out of Los Angeles, but he was also happy to be playing with Dameron. He recalled later, "[Tadd Dameron] was a big influence on my career as a composer and arranger and was such a fine piano player." In January 1948, they played at the Pershing Lounge and the Hotel Du Sable Lounge, in Chicago, as well as the Sunset Terrace Ballroom in Indianapolis. After returning to New York, they played at one of Fred Robbins's ongoing series of concerts at Town Hall (Jan. 24), along with Machito and his Afro-Cuban Orchestra. The next day they took part in a marathon show at Club 845, in the Bronx.[1] Finally, the group played at the Three Deuces, probably from February 19 through March 3. After that they disbanded, apparently because Dexter's heroin addiction was interfering with his ability to take care of business.[2] By several accounts, Tadd's involvement with this drug had started by this time as well, but he was still able to function very effectively, as the events of the next year and a half show.

The Chicken Shack

Tadd probably took part in a show at the Apollo Theater in February or March of 1948, produced or at least promoted by Monte Kay and Sid Torin. Kay was frustrated with what he called "a clip-joint attitude" developing in the venues on Fifty-second Street, an attitude that was not friendly to the younger audiences that he felt were important for the evolving modern jazz. Accordingly, he started to look for venues off "the street," and that was when he found the Royal Roost. Ralph Watkins and Morris Levy had opened the Royal Roost Chicken Shack, opposite the Strand Theater, in the basement of a building at Broadway and Forty-seventh Street, sometime in December 1947. By the beginning of 1948 they were presenting music. Initially, the performers were swing/mainstream musicians of the day who were working the New York night clubs, such as Cozy Cole, the Three Flames,[3] and Sylvia Simms.

One evening, Kay heard the Lunceford Orchestra playing there (after the death of its leader). The band was playing well, but the audience was small, and Kay thought that this would be a good place to present the new music to new audiences. Kay recalled later, "Watkins was skeptical about the modern stuff. But I managed to talk him into letting me and Symphony Sid produce a concert on an off-night. He picked Tuesday."[4] The Tuesday-night series, known as "Symphony Sid's Bop Concert," began on April 6, with a lineup including Dameron, Denzil Best, Allen Eager, Dexter Gordon, Chubby Jackson, Fats Navarro, Lucky Thompson, and George Wallington. The venue had a long bar as one entered, and in front of it an area with chairs, called the "bleechers," where those who were too young to drink alcohol could sit and listen for the admission price of ninety cents. Beyond the bar, packed with tables, was the main room, which separated the lounge and the "bleechers" from the bandstand.

"Symphony Sid's Bop Concert" was an immediate success, with an overflow crowd on the very first night—requiring police presence to assist in its management[5]—and another overfull house the next week. On the strength of this, bop performers were added on the weekends starting Friday, April 30. Dameron seems to have been a fixture in these bands from the beginning, although he was not in fact there for a continuous thirty-nine weeks, as has been reported in various places. He was, however, the pianist in the shows billed as "Symphony Sid's Bop Concerts" from April 6 through June 3, as well as in Charlie Parker's group during the next two weeks. After two weeks off, Dameron returned on Wednesday, June 30, leading a band under his own name, and he remained on the bill at the Roost through September 4.[6]

The group playing under Symphony Sid's name was probably just a jam session, for the critical response was not positive. The *New Yorker* liked Thelonious Monk, who played there frequently in the spring, but was not impressed with the Symphony Sid group.[7] However, reviews of the band playing under Dameron's name were more favorable, and the broadcast and studio recordings from the end of Dameron's summer-long stand give us an idea of the generally high quality of their performances. In light of this, Tadd was probably not calling the tunes on the Symphony Sid shows.

Long-time chronicler of the jazz scene Dan Morgenstern later recalled:

> I first met Tadd Dameron in 1948 at the Royal Roost. We went to there with two really good looking girls, so naturally, they got some attention from the musicians, and nobody paid any attention to me except Tadd. Tadd was a gentleman. Tadd was genuinely interested when he heard that I had recently come over from Europe. I told him that one of the things performed by the Don Redman band was "For Europeans Only." So he was very interested in that because at that time he never got to hear that particular arrangement.[8]

Dameron was not at the Royal Roost for most of September. It was during this break that he recorded for Blue Note with a band that was essentially the lineup he had been using most recently at the Roost: Fats Navarro, Wardell Gray, Allen Eager, Curly Russell, Kenny Clarke, and vocalist Kenny Hagood. Because of the second AFM recording strike, which had started at the beginning of 1948, this would be his first commercial recording since the second date with Dexter Gordon and his first as a leader since October of 1947. On this set of recordings, made on September 13, 1948, he introduced two more new compositions, "Jahbero" and "Symphonette." He also recorded the small-group version of "Lady Bird" and a second arrangement of "I Think I'll Go Away."

In the fall of 1947, Dizzy Gillespie formally introduced the fusion of Afro-Cuban rhythms with the swing of bebop, with pieces such as "Algo Bueno" and "Manteca." "Jahbero," a contrafact of Kern and Hammerstein's "All The Things You Are," is Tadd Dameron's take on this development and the first of several pieces in which he would incorporate Caribbean rhythms into his work. Its arrangement is a masterpiece of formal construction. "All The Things You Are" has an unusual form itself, a modification of the AABA form in which the second A repeats the first, but in a key a fifth higher. The final A is extended to twelve measures, and the tune's form is better described as AA1BA2. As in some earlier works for larger ensembles, Dameron makes this arrangement a composition of its own, one that both contains and transcends the piece being arranged. There is a twenty-bar introduction that begins with the bongos of Chino Pozo and builds up through the rhythm section in four-bar segments, followed by the horns playing the melody up to A2, which becomes a twelve-bar solo for Wardell Gray's tenor saxophone. There is an eight-bar drum interlude led by the bongos, followed by a solo from Navarro. Navarro's solo stops at the end of the bridge, and another tenor saxophonist, Allen Eager, takes the last twelve bars of the form, recalling the structure of the opening chorus. Then the piece concludes with the horns playing the final section of the melody. It is as if "Jahbero" were a dollhouse that could be opened up to reveal its contents. The first three segments of the tune are presented at the beginning, but the final segment is saved for the end, with the solos and interlude revealing otherwise "hidden" aspects of the tune:

1. Introduction: twenty measures, tension increasing every four measures
2. Opening chorus:
    Ensemble: A, A1, B
    Sax solo: A2
3. Drum interlude: eight measures, developing opening rhythm figures from introduction
4. Solo chorus:
    Trumpet solo: A, A1, B
    Sax solo: A2
5. A closing ensemble plays the composed melody for A2, which has not yet been heard.

"Symphonette" (named for Symphony Sid's daughter) is a melodically sophisticated take on the A section of "Rhythm Changes," with a unique set of changes for the bridge. With its relatively simple harmonic scheme treated dissonantly in the melodic line, often using the intervals of ♭5 and ♭9 over the perceived root, it is similar to "Hot House." However, unlike "Hot House," the overall tone of "Symphonette" is buoyant, even jolly, and the rhythmic interaction between the melody and accompaniment gives the tune a playful quality, somewhat like "The Squirrel." The arrangement is rather straightforward, with just an eight-bar introduction line for the horns to "dress it up."

"Lady Bird," while not as intricately arranged, has much of the same concise elegance of form as "Jahbero." As mentioned in the previous chapter, both the copyright deposit and the first known recording of "Lady Bird" are ambiguous in regard to the length of the form, either sixteen or thirty-two measures. This recording, which at the time was the definitive statement, makes it quite clear that this is a sixteen-bar composition. There is an eight-bar introduction, followed by the melody, played by the three horns in block-chord harmony. Navarro takes a two-chorus solo, followed by a one-chorus solo by Eager. Then the eight-bar shout, as much a part of "Lady Bird" as the copyrighted melody, is followed by a short, eight-bar piano solo, setting up Wardell Gray's chorus. In conclusion, there is one more statement of the melody that finally ends on an extra measure outside of the form.

The shout, which is the essence of the closing chorus of the big-band chart written for Gillespie, shows up in the work of others who have made contrafacts of "Lady Bird." Notable in this regard are Miles Davis and J. J. Johnson, both of whom played with Dameron. In his 1956 Prestige recording of "Half Nelson,"[9] Miles Davis uses the shout as an eight-bar exchange with drummer Philly Joe Jones. In "Kev,"[10] actually an improvisation on the chords to "Lady Bird," recorded by Johnson in 1957 for Columbia, the trombonist uses the shout twice, once to set up Paul Chambers's bass solo, the second time to set up Max Roach's drum solo.

The influence of this tune is not only formal. Lewis Porter, in *John Coltrane: His Life and Music,* makes a strong case for a connection between "Lady Bird" and Coltrane's "Lazy Bird," as well as the saxophonist's development of root progressions based on major thirds.[11] We have seen the beginnings of Dameron's interest in root and key relationships a third apart in various pieces: for instance, the codas of his arrangements of "Good Bait" (minor third) and "Zakat" (major third) for Lunceford, as well as the surprise ending for "You're Not the Kind" (major third) for Sarah Vaughan. In "Lady Bird," there is the relationship between the home key of C and the key of Eb (a minor third away) followed by a relationship between the keys of C and Ab (a major third away). In addition, the turn-around progression in the last two measures of "Lady Bird," C-EbMa7-AbMa7-Db7(#11),[12] commonly called the "Dameron turn-around," has long since entered into the common practice of modern jazz. In Dameron's own work, this progression first appears as early as 1945, in "Moo-See-Ka" (see chap. 5), where he uses this turn-around at the end of the first A: Bb DbMa7 | GbMa7 F7 B+7|| Bb ... There is also a suggestion of this in his reharmonization of "Bewildered" (see chap. 3).

"I Think I'll Go Away," sung here by Kenny Hagood, gets an improved arrangement this time around—the Kay Penton version of 1947 was not as well developed.[13] Tadd seems to have had some fondness for this melody. Not only did he record it twice in a little over a year, but he put two other lyrics to it. One of these, "Love Took the 7:10," written by Irving Reid from 1962 or 1963, survives. The other is mentioned only as a title in the reassignment document of several titles from Monogram to Robbins Music. The tune is identified as "I Think I'll Go Away/I Found a New Romance." The second lyric implied here has yet to be discovered.

Another of Dameron's songs appearing in 1948 is "Kitchenette across the Hall," with lyrics by Shirley Jones. A novelty song that was never commercially recorded, it was sung by Kenny Hagood in a broadcast from the Royal Roost on August 29, 1948. At some point Mary Lou Williams took an interest in the song and wrote a transcription of it.[14] Presumably she was interested in performing the song, but just when or where is unknown. The melody is straightforward but attractive, just the same. However, the lyric is dated in both setting and attitude, and to date, no one, with the possible exception of Williams, has chosen to add it to their repertoire.

Tadd Dameron returned to the Royal Roost on September 26, in the first of a new Sunday-afternoon matinee series organized by Monte Kay, again called "Symphony Sid's Bop Concert." Presumably, this was another jam session like the "Bop Concerts" presented in the spring. The next evening Dameron and his band returned to the regular billing and remained there until the middle of November. The Dizzy Gillespie Orchestra shared the bill with Tadd when he returned, playing several of his charts in the broadcasts,[15] including "Soulphony in Three Hearts," which they had premiered in Los Angeles at the end of August.

Dameron went to Cleveland around Thanksgiving of 1948 to work up the material for his next set of recordings. These would feature the Big Ten, which had five horns and an expanded rhythm section, including guitar and bongo or conga drums. Back in New York sometime after New Year's to record the band for Capitol, on January 18, 1949, he returned to the Roost with the Big Ten for a broadcast on Saturday, February 12, 1949. The band continued playing the club from February 16 through Tuesday, March 9, or possibly March 15. After this, in spite of a lingering listing of his name in *Variety*, Dameron did not play at the Roost again. The Royal Roost closed by the end of May, after Watkins and company opened Bop City across the street in the middle of April.

The Big Ten

It is more than a coincidence that Miles Davis was involved with both his own Tuba Band and Dameron's expanded combo. The Tuba Band, which recorded the so-called Birth of the Cool sessions for Capitol, played at the Roost and took part in the September 4 broadcast. Miles also had a history with Tadd. They had first met in East St. Louis in August of 1944, when Miles sat in with the Billy Eckstine Orchestra at the Riviera for the ailing Buddy Anderson. A little later Charlie Parker reintroduced them in New York, and Dameron became one of Davis's mentors, sharing his knowledge of harmony with the young trumpeter and encouraging his study of piano. Both men were part of the scene in Harlem and on Fifty-second Street, and both were quiet and intensely dedicated to music. By 1948, Tadd's relationship with Miles was evolving from that of mentor to colleague, and it does not stretch the imagination to consider that Miles's nonet and Tadd's Big Ten are related in several ways. Although Miles, Gil Evans, and Gerry Mulligan are clearly the guiding lights of the Davis band, Bill Cole, in his biography of Miles's early years, asserts that "Dameron assisted in the formulation of many of the ideas that Miles brought to his experimental band."[16] We also know that Dameron and Gil Evans were friends in the 1960s, after Tadd's release from prison. There is evidence of a friendship between Dameron and Mulligan as well. It seems unlikely that these like-minded musicians would not have been in communication in the close-knit modern jazz community of the late 1940s.

It would appear from the dates of these two bands that Miles's daring in presenting a larger and more formally arranged ensemble may well have inspired Dameron to take such a chance himself. There seems little doubt that Dameron would have liked more instruments to work with; despite his protestations that he hated to arrange, orchestrating was definitely part of the compositional process for him. Even a casual look at his total body of work makes this very clear. Although Dameron's use of the larger band is not as radical as Davis's, the two bands are aesthetically similar in their refined and generally mellow sound, a sound that resonates not only in the cooler "West Coast" sound of the early 1950s but in the writing of arrangers on the East Coast, as well. There is also the impact these sessions had on their producer, Pete Rugolo, who would go on to have a successful career scoring for film and television. Since the title "Birth of the Cool" was applied to the Davis nonet sessions only after the fact, we should, perhaps, consider the entire Capitol output of both leaders under this rubric.[17]

Capitol was also recording another band at this time that featured some of Dameron's writing: the short-lived "Bebop" band of Benny Goodman. This band made its first recording in a live broadcast from the Hotel Syracuse in New York on December 12, 1948, and its final recordings for Capitol on April 14, 1949. The writers for this band included Chico O'Farrill (chief arranger), Gerry Mulligan, and Billy Byers,[18] but the band did not last very long because Goodman was ambivalent about moving in a modernist direction.

With the first Big Ten recordings for Capitol (Jan. 18, 1949), Tadd Dameron introduced what we will call his "octet style"[19] and a series of works extending into the 1960s built around a five-part horn arrangement. Sometimes the groups are larger than eight pieces, as in the case of the "Big Ten," where he has added either conga and bongos or guitar and conga to the ensemble. However, the pieces are all distinguished by the sound of five, sometimes six horns, often in block voicing. It is a sound that comes to the minds of many listeners when they think of Tadd Dameron, for these Capitol recordings, and those for Prestige made in the 1950s, are his best-known works. The first of Dameron's tunes recorded for Capitol is "Sid's Delight," also titled "Webb's Delight" in the broadcasts from the Royal Roost on February 12 and 19. Miles Davis recorded the tune in the mid-1950s as "Tadd's Delight," and it has become best known by this title.[20]

"Sid's (Webb's/Tadd's) Delight" is in thirty-two-bar ABAC form with a straightforward harmonic scheme and derives its strong character from the dynamism of its melodic rhythm. In the Capitol recording there is no introduction. The opening chorus is arranged in block-chord fashion with the trumpet leading the ensemble. Fats Navarro takes a half-chorus solo with a background played by the rest of the ensemble, followed by half-chorus solos by Kai Winding and Dexter Gordon, with accompaniment by just the rhythm section. An ensemble passage, without trumpet, finishes the chorus started by Gordon. The full ensemble reprises the beginning chorus from its middle to end the piece. In the two live performances recorded at the Royal Roost, on February 12 and 19, 1949, Dameron gives himself a half-chorus solo before the last half-chorus ensemble. In the second performance he also extends the solo space for the other players, but the basic elements of the arrangement remain the same.

The other piece recorded on January 18 was "Casbah," a contrafact of Green and Heyman's "Out of Nowhere." Here the ensemble is joined by the soprano voice of Rea Pearl, a combination that calls to mind Ellington's "Creole Love Call." However, Dameron's inspiration for this may have come from necessity. Jeannie Cheatham recalled running through "Casbah" and other tunes from this time with Dameron at a roadhouse on the Ohio/Pennsylvania border. "Ohio had blue laws," she recalled,

> which meant no night clubs on Sunday, so Tadd hung out at a club in Sharon, Pennsylvania. He rehearsed all his new arrangements there. We all gathered there to watch his magic; arrangers and players. It was like a workshop. I often sang the trumpet parts when there was no trumpet player at the sessions, including the lead vocal on "Casbah," one of my favorites.[21]

Although we cannot know what exactly inspired Dameron to use this instrumentation, the result is very effective. "Casbah" is one of those Dameron pieces that is more a complete composition than an arrangement of a tune. The main theme is played only once at the beginning, and the later ensemble sections are new material based on its chord progression, much as in "A Be Bop Carroll" or "Dameronia," only with more complexity. There is an introduction that starts with four measures of just bongos and conga establishing an Afro-Cuban time-feel, followed by six more measures of the full ensemble. The lead of the melody is divided between voice and piano in the opening chorus, followed by a six-bar interlude modulating from the key of D♭ to G, leading to Fats Navarro's half-chorus trumpet solo over an ensemble background. A sax solo finishes the second half of the chorus. The next chorus is divided between an alto sax soli, with just the rhythm section, and a final ensemble led by the trumpet.

In the one live recording of "Casbah," from February 26, 1949, John Collins's guitar takes the part of the voice in the opening chorus, and the arrangement is changed a bit. Collins takes the first half chorus, but without background. The chorus is completed with the ensemble, as before, followed with Miles Davis's half-chorus solo with background. This chorus ends with a half chorus from Dameron. The sax soli is omitted, and the last chorus is played as on the Capitol recording.

The next session (May 8, 1949) would be Dameron's last until the spring of 1953, and it documents the beginning of a few months of collaboration with Miles Davis, who took over the trumpet chair from Fats Navarro in the "Big Ten" in the middle of February. Dameron also dropped bongos from the band and added guitarist John Collins around that time. For these recordings, Kay Penton returned as vocalist on two of the four titles and may have been singing with the band at the Royal Roost, as well. Two more new Dameron compositions, "Heaven's Doors Are Open Wide" and "Focus," as well as a tune cowritten with John Collins, "John's Delight," were introduced at this session. "John's Delight" is essentially an ABAC-form tune, with an eight-bar introduction, led by the guitar, followed by the melody, arranged for the ensemble in block chords. In the opening chorus, the guitar doubles the trumpet's lead an octave lower and is brought forward in the mix so that it really becomes the lead instrument. There is a half-chorus solo from Collins's guitar, with the other half taken by trombonist Kai Winding. The next chorus is split between a sax soli and a piano solo. The recorded arrangement concludes with the trumpet leading a reprise of the second half of the opening chorus, instead of the guitar. One can imagine that in live performance the elements of this chart could easily accommodate longer solos.

Kay Penton sang two songs on this date. The first, Burke and Haggart's "What's New," is taken at a very slow tempo, about 63 beats per minute, so the performance is just one chorus, along with a four-bar introduction and a very effective six-bar coda ending an appropriately tragic-sounding minor-ninth chord. Since there is no such extension of the song in the sheet music versions, one would assume that Dameron himself wrote the words for this coda, and they work very well. Unfortunately, the lyric for the second song, Dameron's

"Heaven's Doors Are Open Wide," is not so successful. It is awkwardly erotic, with lines such as "We'll go sailing into space. Won't that please you?" Dameron never submitted a copyright deposit for "Heaven's Doors," and the only official mention of it is in an assignment document from 1963. The melody is another graceful Dameron creation, and one regrets that he did not see fit to put another lyric to it later, as he did with "I Think I'll Go Away."[22] The arrangement is slightly more complex than that of "What's New." Taken only a little faster than the other ballad—presenting a chorus and a half of the song—it has a compositionally interesting five-bar introduction and a tag ending.

The last piece to be recorded at this session was "Focus," a sophisticated composition in which, for the first time in his smaller-group work, Dameron stretches beyond common practice in a manner akin to some of the pieces we have seen for larger ensembles. The copyrighted tune is twenty-eight bars long in ABAC form, perhaps more accurately described as AA₁B, since the second section is only four bars long and grows directly out of the second four bars of the A. The tune almost defies this sort of conventional form description. The solo sections use a different but not unrelated harmonic progression, with an AABA form. The connection is in the A of the tune and the A of the chord changes for improvising, which can be expressed generally as:

F G-7 | A-7 G-7 | F G-7 | A-7 D7 |

G-7 | C7 |F (D-7)| G-7 C7 ||

The progression for the first segment of the melody of "Focus" can be seen as this progression with a four-bar tag. In figure 6.1, the harmonies for the tune are taken from the copyright deposit, a grand-staff score that corresponds very closely to the recorded arrangement, and are written directly above the staff. The progression for the solos is written above, and the omitted "tag" is under a bracket. It is this connection that gives the whole piece cohesion, while allowing the soloists to work with a form that is more familiar and comfortable. We have seen Dameron use different chord sequences for melody and solo sections in "Frolic at Five" and "Moo-See-Ka," and we will see him explore this strategy more frequently in the coming years.

A broadcast transcription of the "Big Ten" documents two other arrangements. "April in Paris" is the same arrangement that Dameron wrote for Coleman Hawkins a little over a year earlier, with John Collins taking Hawkins's feature part. The other is titled "Miles" (not to be confused with Tadd's own tune by this name from 1962) on the few commercial issues of it. The tune is actually

ex. 6.1

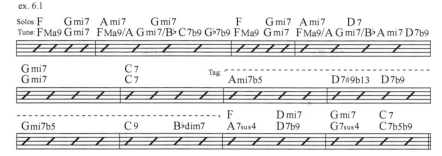

Fig. 6.1. Chord sequence from Dameron's "Focus."

John Lewis's "Milano," and the arrangement is stylistically different from Dameron's other work of this period. The baritone sax part sounds unlike anything Dameron ever wrote for that instrument, and there is more detail in the various parts than he uses for a group of this size, at least until 1956 and "Fontainebleau." It is possible that Dameron had arranged this John Lewis tune and was now experimenting with some arranging techniques that would only appear later in his work, but it is more likely that this is completely Lewis's work and that Lewis contributed it to the band's book.

The music Dameron's groups recorded and broadcast during the Royal Roost period is among the most influential of the late 1940s. The September 1948 sextet session for Blue Note and the earlier quintet sessions helped lay the foundations for much of the small-group jazz of the 1950s and '60s. With their introductions and ensemble interludes they incorporate the overall compositional structure of big-band arrangements with the more solo-oriented bebop aesthetic, and their influence is heard clearly in the work of such admitted Dameronians as Gigi Gryce, Benny Golson, Frank Foster, Quincy Jones, and Horace Silver. The 1950s work of West Coast–based musicians, such as Shorty Rogers, resonates with the Dameron aesthetic as well. In addition, the octet/nonet/dectet sound of Dameron's early 1949 recordings finds resonance in the similar recordings made by musicians on both coasts and Europe—and, of course, in the writing for these midsized groups by Gryce, Golson, and Jones. Dameron certainly did not invent this sort of "little big band," but his writing for it set a standard and tone that most of his successors would find hard to avoid, even if they wanted to.

On Saturday, April 9, 1949, the *Pittsburgh Courier*, one of the foremost African

American newspapers of the time, held its Third Annual Midnight Concert at Carnegie Hall in New York. The event was held to honor those musicians who had had an impact on mainstream American culture and thereby brought honor to the African American community in general. In an item in the English music journal *Melody Maker* a month later, Dameron is reported to have been awarded a statuette by the *Courier* "as being the most advanced Negro musician of the day."[23] By the spring of 1949, Tadd Dameron was clearly gaining recognition as a leading voice in modern American music and was about to embark on a journey that would mark the high point of his career.

Club 11, London, June 1949. Behind Tadd are two African-British jazz enthusiasts, one of whom, playing bongos or a small drum, is probably Chico Eyo, a Nigerian. Val Wilmer. © Val Wilmer Collection. Courtesy of David Chilver.

Courtesy of the Institute of Jazz Studies.

At home, 490 West End Ave., New York, May 1962. Photo by Val Wilmer, © Val Wilmer.

Paris Jazz Festival, May 1949. Left to Right: Al Haig, Dameron, Bernard Peiffer, and British pianist Steve Race who attended the event to review it for the *Musical Express*. Val Wilmer. Photographer unknown. © Val Wilmer Collection.

Dameron, age 23, as he went to work for Harlan Leonard. Courtesy of *DownBeat*.

MONTE KAY
— Presents —
SYMPHONY SID'S
'BOP' CONCERT
Sunday Afternoon, October 10, 1948 4-8 p.m.

CHANO POZO
(MONTECA)

Tadd Dameron   **Fats Navarro**
(The SQUIRREL)

Dexter Gordon   **Allen Eagers**
TENOR SAX

Max Roach   **Art Blakey**
The Gonest on DRUMS

Al Haig   **Milt Jackson**
PIANO   VIBES

James Moody   **Cecil Payne**
Dizzy's TENOR & BARITONE SAX STARS

Nelson Boyd   **Tommy Potter**
Two Great BASSISTS

ADMISSION $1.50   No minimum or cabaret tax

THE HOUSE THAT BOP BUILT

Royal Roost
1580 Broadway, Cor. 47th St., Opp. Strand Theatre

Courtesy of Frank Driggs.

Tadd with one of Mia's cats, Hotel Almac, New York, ca. December 1963. Courtesy of Mia Dameron.

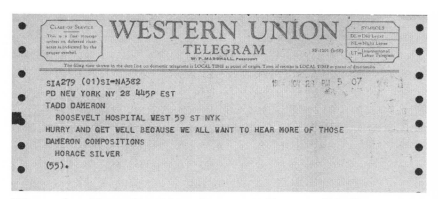

Telegram from Horace Silver, November 28, 1964. Courtesy of Mia Dameron.

Melody Maker editor Ray Sonin with Margo and Tadd, London, June 1949. © Max Jones Collection. Courtesy of Val Wilmer and Max Jones.

7

1949—International Fame

Paris

In the summer of 1948 Nicole Barclay, Charles Delaunay, and others were already involved in planning the 1949 Paris Jazz Festival. Nicole Barclay and Kenny Clarke had become good friends by this time, no doubt because of her interest in promoting jazz in Paris and because her husband, Eddie, a pianist and bandleader and owner of Barclay Records, was interested in recording the music for distribution in Europe. Nicole promised Kenny, who had stayed on in Paris after the 1948 Gillespie tour, that he would have an important role in the festival. She made good on that promise when she came to New York in the spring of 1949 to book the artists for the festival. According to Clarke, Nicole gave him the final word on those musicians to be engaged.[1]

The festival ran for eight days starting Sunday, May 8, 1949, with a series of concerts presenting American as well as European musicians, playing in both the new and the older styles. The Americans included the older musicians Sidney Bechet, Bill Coleman, Jimmy McPartland, "Big Chief" Russell Moore, and Hot Lips Page. The modern school was represented by Don Byas and two bands: Charlie Parker's working quintet, with Kenny Dorham, Al Haig, Tommy Potter, and Max Roach; and the Miles Davis/Tadd Dameron Quintet, which included Kenny Clarke, as well as James Moody and bassist Barney Spieler, who were already in Europe. The Europeans were represented by the Kentonesque band of Vic Lewis;[2] Carlo Krammer's Chicagoans; the Swedish All-Stars; Pierre Braslavsky's band, which backed up Sidney Bechet; and some freelancers such as pianist Bernard Peiffer and guitarist Toots Thielemans.

It seems there had also been some earlier contacts between Delaunay (and possibly the Barclays) and Tadd Dameron about a visit the year before the Paris Jazz Festival. In the December 17, 1947, issue of *Down Beat* the following item appeared:

TADD TO FRANCE

New York—Tadd Dameron, pianist and arranger, has signed as musical director for Charles Delaunay's Blue Star record company in Paris, France, starting March 3. He will also be staff arranger for Tony Proteau's orchestra. Tadd will leave for Paris about mid-February.[3]

Despite the article's claim, Tadd Dameron did not go to France in March of 1948. We do not know why these plans were abandoned, assuming the initial claim was correct. Still, it seems clear that there had been communications between the festival organizers and Dameron as early as the fall of 1947 and, indeed, Dameron wrote for Proteau, probably later on, while in Paris.[4]

Even though Dameron did not get to go to Europe in 1948, Europeans did hear some of his music during the Dizzy Gillespie Orchestra's tour that year. Performances of "Our Delight" and "Good Bait" are documented in recordings made at the Vinterpalastset in Stockholm and at Salle Pleyel in Paris. No doubt the band played others of their Dameron charts, as well.

On Friday, May 6, the American contingent—those not already on the continent—flew into Paris. This was a day earlier than had been planned by the festival organizers, but that did not seem to bother Tadd and his friends. English musician and commentator Steve Race reported that "Dameron, Kenny Clarke and Co. have been sitting in various night clubs to kill the time. You can't keep a good musician away from his instrument."[5] Unfortunately, despite their extracurricular playing, it seems that they were not able to rehearse adequately before the first night's performance. Race goes on to report the inconsistent quality of the Davis/Dameron quintet's playing, some of it good but much of it tentative and sloppy. However, the band would have five more sets in the coming days of the festival, and, as André Hodier reported, they improved night by night.[6] The recordings from the festival seem to bear witness to this, although the tracks are not identified by dates. The ones with better sound present uncharacteristically poor performances by Miles Davis and presumably come from the first night. The ones with poor sound have better performances from Davis, but it is very hard to hear the rhythm section. The band introduces no new tunes, and the arrangements are the same as they would have been at the Royal Roost. Still, these are historically significant recordings and should be listened to, if only to understand the impact these American musicians had on a European audience, even when not able to play at the top of their form.[7]

The festival and the following weeks Dameron spent in England give us a rare chance to witness part of his life with an extraordinary degree of detail. Certain British musicians were particularly fascinated with Tadd's music, and they have left us with clear accounts of meeting him. One of them was Ivor Mairants, who played guitar in the Geraldo Orchestra. He would go on to a very successful career as a studio musician, educator, and retailer of musical instruments. Geraldo's band was a rather commercial dance band that played swing music as part of its overall repertoire. Just the same, there were a number of jazz musicians in the band. Ivor, as well as some of his bandmates, was quite taken with the new jazz coming out of America after World War II, and of course Dameron's music caught his ear. "I first heard his music around 1945," recalled Mairants, "when I used to get some records from America, before they were on sale here. There was a record of Dizzy Gillespie playing 'Our Delight.' This 'Our Delight' was so advanced. Can you imagine in 1945, these close brass harmonies and Dizzy Gillespie's solo in the middle of it?"[8] Mairants went on to explain that "the Geraldo Orchestra used to spotlight an American jazz orchestra every week in one of our broadcasts. We used to do nine a week and needed a lot of material. They would get one of their orchestrators to transcribe the arrangements from the records, 'Our Delight' among them."

The Geraldo Orchestra continued to transcribe the new music coming out of America for the next few years, and Mairants developed a great interest in the various arrangers, including Bill Finegan, who was also in Paris at the time of the festival. Mairants explained: "I heard that in the 1949 Paris Jazz Festival there'd be a lot of these [American musicians] around. One was this same Tadd Dameron who had written and arranged 'Our Delight.' So I asked Gerry, if I took a holiday in Paris to see this, would he give me carte blanche to get [Dameron] to arrange for him."

When Mairants arrived in Paris, bassist Barney Spieler, with whom he had been in correspondence, took him to Salle Playel, where Spieler was to rehearse with Dameron and the others. As Ivor recalled,

> They were rehearsing for the following concerts, and I was introduced to Tadd Dameron and Miles Davis. Tadd Dameron was obviously feeding Miles Davis the notes that he should be playing, and Miles Davis, sitting on a high stool, said, "Man, can I play those notes here?" Dameron said, "Sure you can," and he played them. So I could see that this wasn't just an ordinary rehearsal. Although

it looked just very cool, it was an intensive practice, and I saw the capabilities of Tadd Dameron as well as the others.

English music journalist Denis Preston was also present at a Dameron rehearsal, perhaps the same one. He shared his recollections a couple of months after the fact in the August 27 *Melody Maker*. Here he is comparing the rehearsal styles of Sidney Bechet, who would run his tunes straight through as if in performance, with those of Dameron and company:

> We found an atmosphere so casual that it was hard to believe a serious rehearsal was, in fact, in progress. Davis in his overcoat, mooching disconsolately around the vast Salle Pleyel stage, occasionally playing some fragmentary phrase in a husky overtone. Kenny Clarke (and drums) in a far corner working out intricate rhythmic patterns. James Moody holding a sax and looking thoughtful, and Tadd Dameron (also in overcoat!) trying over "Good Bait" harmonies with an untried bassist. Every now and then, as if by telepathy, the horn men would gather 'round the piano and, for a few bars, something like coordinated music-making would take place. But as much seemed to be achieved vocally as instrumentally, the musicians making their various contributions to the proceedings with little snatches of bop scat.[9]

As is often the case, there was no doubt something in the live performance of Tadd and Miles's opening concert that cannot be recorded. Our noting of the recorded inconsistences in the Davis/Dameron performance aside, Ivor Mairants observed that it was "a most marvelous concert." The next day Mairants went to visit Dameron at his hotel, "a very, very nice hotel, right in the middle of Paris." When he arrived,

> a beautiful girl opened the door, an Italian looking girl. She introduced herself as Margo, and I said I wanted to see Tadd Dameron. "Oh," she said, "he's in his bath." So she took me to the bathroom and there's Tadd Dameron in his bath, he was nude. He was a very languid, sort of upper class person, but very pleasant. I said, "I play in Geraldo's band," and he's never heard of Geraldo's band. I said, "I've got permission to commission you to write some arrangements for him, including 'Our Delight.'" "Oh," so he can hear that I knew something about him. And from then on we became quite friendly.

Margo and Tadd had been lovers for a couple of years by this point. Both Ray Brown and James Moody recalled her accompanying Dameron to rehearsals of the Gillespie band,[10] and since both men were in the band at the same time, from November of 1946 through sometime in September of 1947, we have a general time for the beginning of the relationship. Margo would be Tadd's companion until some time in 1950, and then she seems to disappear into thin air. Those who remember her from the trip to Europe recall that she had a strong presence, and she may have been something of Dameron's advisor as well as his companion.

Ivor Mairants also remembered having some after-hours fun with Dameron:

> We, that is, Tadd Dameron, Barney Spieler, Bill Finegan, and I, did the rounds of the Paris cafés and so on, and wherever there was a piano and a bit of a guitar we used to set up. Bill Finegan was a trumpet player, and we did a little jam session and so on. [We] finally made it home about three or four in the morning ready for the following day.

As the week passed, Mairants and Dameron made arrangements for a meeting with the Geraldo band in London. There must have been talk already of his writing for Ted Heath, and Vic Lewis as well, for Steve Race mentions this at the end of his review of the opening concert. The British music press was very excited about Dameron's arrival. On the front page of the May 14 edition of *Melody Maker*, there was an item with the headline "Dameron to score for British bands." A photo of Tadd at the piano was at the head of the text.[11]

London

The May 28 issue of *Melody Maker* announced the arrival of Tadd and Margo in London on Monday, May 23. Dameron had probably used the week in between to write some of the arrangements he brought to London. There would have been "Our Delight," as Ivor Mairants had requested, and likely other other arrangement for Geraldo. Some of the pieces Dameron would do with Ted Heath may have been written at this time, and he may also have been planning other work for his return visit to Paris a month later.

Ivor Mairants described Dameron's first meeting with the Geraldo Orchestra:

> We arranged that he would come to the [BBC] Maida Vale studio at rehearsal. Tadd Dameron came into the studio in an immaculate double-breasted, powder

blue suit, and he looked the great impresario. We'd never seen a suit like that. I put the parts out, Geraldo went into the control room, and Tadd Dameron stood with his hands up ready to conduct the band. I could see the brass—brass is always the most reactionary section—looking at him as if to say, "Who the hell is this black!" The saxes were eager to go, the rhythm was eager to go, but the brass took an instant dislike to him.[12]

After a rough start, the band did master "Our Delight" and broadcast it. However, it did not suit the taste of either Geraldo or the BBC, and there was great disagreement between the saxes and the rhythm section, whose members liked the chart, and the brass section, whose members did not. Dameron brought a second chart, but it was not recorded. As Mairants recalled later, "What [was] I going to do? I asked him to come over. I said he'll get paid for these arrangements but I've got to find him some work. So I found Ted Heath."

Dameron's less detailed account supports Mairants's observations. He said to a reporter for *Melody Maker* that

there was some talk of my tying up in some way with Geraldo and he broadcast my original "Our Delight." I might say that I have heard this number played by Dizzy Gillespie, Boyd Raeburn, and Billy Eckstine, but from the musicianly point of view, I have never heard it played better than by Geraldo's excellent musicians. However, several of the boys in his orchestra seemed to be quite out of sympathy with that type of music—so that was that.[13]

Perhaps Ivor Mairants's memory, forty-two years after the fact, was a little fuzzy with regard to the Heath band, for several sources suggest that Ted Heath had been expecting Dameron to write for him, as well, from the start. Ted Heath subsequently recorded four of Tadd's arrangements: Hoagy Carmichael's "The Nearness of You," Charlie Ventura's "Euphoria," and Dameron's own "So Easy" and "Lyonia." Earlier in 1949, George Shearing had written an arrangement of "Lady Bird" for Ted Heath, which the band had recorded in March of that year, but it is possible that Tadd wrote another for him, one that included a singer. Lyricist Moira Heath (Ted's wife) later recalled, "I wrote a lyric to 'Lady Bird.' Ted rang me up from his office and said Tadd was with him. He said, 'We want a lyric. Will you do it and ring me back?' So he hummed it and I wrote it down, just in dots, to get the rhythm, and I did it."[14]

Moira Heath continued: "They [Heath and Dameron] liked each other immensely, but Ted never brought him home—Ted was so very private—but he thought the world of Tadd. He thought he was a brilliant musician."

As much as Heath may have admired Dameron as a man and a musician, he may have been ambivalent about the style of his music. Trombonist Maurice Pratt, who as a young musician was definitely excited about the new music, recalled that Heath "never wanted a bebop band, he just got swept along by the tide and bebop was the thing at the time. Ted's wasn't a bebop band, it was more Glenn Miller."[15]

Tadd socialized with several musicians while in London, either at their homes or at the flat he and Margo rented in the classy Shepherd Market district of Mayfair. Tadd and Margo, of course, spent time with Ivor and his wife, talking about music and politics; when asked about Tadd's political views, Ivor responded that his were "the same as mine . . . that is, left." On at least one occasion, Ivor's daughter played the piano for Dameron:

> My daughter was about sixteen, and she was a very good pianist. She played a brilliant little sonata by Kabalevski without any qualms or mistakes, and Tadd looked on, amazed. He says, "Have you got the music of that?" So she showed him the music, and he went through this music at a snail's pace, and he couldn't get on with it. How could a man who could write at such speed not be able to play the notes that he saw on the paper? It was because one came from his mind and he knew that this note represented a C or whatever, but he didn't know what it looked like to refer back to his mind from the paper.

Tadd and Margo also socialized with Max Jones and his wife, Betty. Jones, who was a full-time staff writer for *Melody Maker*, wrote a profile, quoted elsewhere in this book, that stands as one of the handful of significant articles on Dameron. Unfortunately, in addition to shedding light on Dameron's aesthetic, it also perpetuates some of the misinformation about his early years, particularly the business of his studying medicine before going into music. Like others who met the couple, Max and Betty Jones doubted that Tadd and Margo were really married, even though they presented themselves as such.[16] The couple also visited Maurice Burman, Geraldo's drummer, who had responded favorably to his music. Aubrey Frank, saxophonist and a former member of Heath's band, was there as well.

Not surprisingly, Tadd spent some time at Lyon's Corner House,[17] an all-night restaurant on several floors that was frequented by many of London's musicians. That was where he met journalist Roy Carr, son of swing violinist and band leader Tony Carr. Carr was only a boy at the time, but the well-dressed Dameron made an impression on him that he remembered more than forty years later: "People would ask Tadd about stuff he'd recorded with Allen Eager and Fats and he was amused! Like so many American artists, his jaw would drop open when you could give him the date of the record and the name of the bass player and all that."[18]

On the front page of the June 3 *Musical Express* was a moderately large photograph of Tadd with accordionist Tito Burns, one of England's foremost exponents of bebop at the time—Dameron called him "the Charlie Ventura of England."[19] The picture appears to have been taken in a house or apartment, presumably Burns's, with Tadd at the piano, playing and conversing with Tito. On the cover of the following week's *Melody Maker* appeared another photo of Dameron and Burns. This time the caption describes Tadd's visit to Decca's studios for the recording session of the Tito Burns Septet's first commercial release. The photo shows the members of the band and a couple of Decca's people gathered around Dameron, who is seated at a grand piano.[20]

Dameron also began a friendship with the saxophonist Ronnie Scott, the same Ronnie Scott who, in later years, would operate the London nightclub that bore his name. If the two had not been introduced already during the Paris Festival,[21] they began their friendship at Club Eleven, a cooperative venture run by several of London's young, progressive musicians—Scott among them—and the only bop-oriented venue in England at the time. The May 28 *Melody Maker* item announcing Dameron's arrival in London concludes, "He has already received big welcomes when he made surprise visits to the London Jazz Club and Club Eleven." The June 4 issue ran a photograph on page 1 captioned "Tadd looks in at 'Club Eleven.'" Included in the photo are Scott, drummer Tony Crombie, and five other British musicians. Many years later, drummer Lennie Breslaw recalled, "I saw Tadd Dameron at Club Eleven and it was wonderful. He looked like some kind of Black god. His hair—it was just like a film star, something we'd only seen in magazines—all slicked back, black and shiny. He came down with a white suit on, and just sat down and played—oh, *chords!* I was carried away."[22] Another visitor to the club recalled "an evening at Club Eleven when Tad Dameron took over the piano and Ronnie [Scott] played like a man inspired."[23]

It seems that there may have been a larger purpose to Tadd's sojourn in England than just arranging for Geraldo and Heath. Roy Carr recalled that "he was thinking of living here." However, Carr envisioned some problems for Tadd: "I don't know how many arrangements he wrote for Ted Heath, but with only five or six big bands at the most, there was a limit to how many bands could ever pay him. The Union would have made it difficult, too." Still, Carr could imagine an interesting possibility: "I'm sure that if he'd come to someone like Ronnie Scott, they'd have made it by putting a band together."[24]

It is not unrealistic to consider that Tadd Dameron, having become a celebrated musician over the previous two years, was considering using his reputation and skills to make a new life for himself in Europe. His good friend Kenny Clarke would certainly have been looking seriously at this possibility after his peacetime return to France. Tadd would have heard about the warm receptions greeting musicians who went to Europe with Don Redman and Dizzy Gillespie, as well. Many years later, Aubrey Frank reflected on Dameron's likely intentions: "I think he was interested in keeping away from America, that was the impression I got."[25]

Ivor Mairants was directly involved in Tadd's efforts to stay in England. Some years later, he wrote in a profile of Dameron that "Tadd was very anxious to settle in London so I put his name forward to the BBC with the suggestion that he be employed in a freelance capacity, but there were obstacles. The big hurdle to overcome was a work permit which could only be applied for from abroad." On Monday, June 20, Tadd and Margo returned to Paris. Publicly, Dameron did not express any hopes. He told the *Melody Maker*, "My wife and I made some very good friends during my short stay in London, and I did hope to be able to settle down and work here ultimately. But, there do not seem to be the same opportunities for my kind of music as exist on the Continent, so I have no option but to go back to France."[26]

Tadd and Ivor exchanged a couple of cards and letters on this matter. This one, from Dameron, was postmarked July 18, 1949:

Hello Ivor,

I hope this letter finds you and your family well. Please give my best regards to "Lil," "Val," and Stewart. Margo and I are hoping to see all of you soon.

I've been very busy since I've come back to France, but can't get the good sounds of English bands out of my ears.

I wrote the Ministry, as you can see, so—now it's left in the hands of Jim Davidson, or Ted Heath. Could you see about this matter for me? Thanks a million!

I haven't forgotten your guitar leads, I'll send them to you next week.

Your friendship was very precious to us during our stay in London; I don't know how we can ever repay you.

Please write and tell me all the news. Regards to all.

Progressively yours,
Tadd Dameron[27]

During his month in Paris, Dameron probably wrote some more arrangements for Tony Proteau and Aime Barelli,[28] and there is a title, but no music, for a tune honoring the French saxophonist Hubert Fol, "And Now Hubert Fol." Tadd also scored several pieces for the short-lived all-star octet that Kenny Clarke and French bassist Pierre Michelot led at the club Frisco's International Atomic Bopera House.[29] The band included Don Byas, Bill Coleman, James Moody (identified as leader of this group in some sources), trombonist Nat Peck, baritone saxophonist Henri Aspar, and pianist Jean-Paul Mengeon.[30] The young Annie Ross was one of its singers. Clarke had fond memories of the band, including Tadd's arrangements. Moody, however, recalled being disappointed with the charts, even though he was generally a fan of Dameron's music.[31]

There is one recorded Dameron tune that he may well have written during his stay in France, "Bah-U-Bah,"[32] recorded in Paris by Coleman Hawkins on December 21, 1949. The other musicians on the date included trombonist Nat Peck, Hubert Fol, Pierre Michelot, and Kenny Clarke, all members of the Frisco's band—James Moody was also playing around Europe with Hawkins's band, but he was not present for this particular recording. One has to at least consider that "Bah-U-Bah" may have been in the Frisco's band book and that the arrangement, while not necessarily the same, was probably influenced by it. "Bah-U-Bah" is a contrafact of "Sweet Georgia Brown" with alternating rhumba and swing sections. The voicings certainly sound like Dameron's, but then again so do some of the arrangements on the recordings James Moody made in Sweden around this time.

Back in the USA

On Tuesday, July 19, Tadd and Margo flew out of Paris for New York. For close to three months Dameron had been treated with a kind of dignity and respect he had never experienced in America. As Ivor Mairants put it, "He found England marvelous. He found it living like a normal human being. He wasn't short [of money] or anything, and he had a beautiful girl."

Whatever disappointment and frustration he may have felt—and in the long term it must have been profound—he still had other options to fall back on. He and Miles Davis had a plan for a large jazz ensemble, and there were arranging commissions, perhaps more than he could handle alone. Still, when he got back to the United States, there seemed to be a drop in the energy level of the New York scene. Miles Davis, who had returned to New York sometime at the end of May or beginning of June, had trouble finding work and was depressed for other personal reasons. Davis soon turned to drugs, which he had avoided up until this time, and headed into a four-year-long nightmare. Dameron, as we shall see, would have an even longer nightmare, one that probably hastened his death.

In August and perhaps early September, Tadd and Miles rehearsed a sixteen-, seventeen-, or eighteen-piece orchestra—depending on which notice one reads. Max Jones had already mentioned this "Capitol recording orchestra" in his article on Tadd's departure from Paris.[33] Such a project certainly would have made sense, given both men's efforts earlier in the year and their musical friendship. In another article in *Melody Maker*, this one written by Leonard Feather and dated September 10, we get a better idea of the band's makeup, as well as the challenges it faced. "If the band can just find a suitable place—or indeed, any place—to work," Feather wrote, "it may well prove a sensation. Sax section at rehearsal included Charlie Kennedy, Jimmy Ford (altos), Allen Eager, Zoot Sims (tenors), Cecil Payne (bari), Red Rodney, Lamar Wright, Jr. (tpts), 3 trombones and French-horn, Shadow Wilson (d), Nelson Boyd (b), Pancho Hagood (vcls)." Yet another notice in *Down Beat*, dated September 23, gave a similar partial list of personnel, indicating there would be five trombones. Kai Winding and Matthew Gee were named, and the article said there would be two more, plus Johnny Mandel on bass trombone. It did not say anything about French horns, but guitarist John Collins was included in the rhythm section. The *Down Beat* article mentioned that "[the band] will have a book entirely written by Tadd. He has been working on it since his return from Paris in mid-summer."[34]

Despite all the press, however, the project was abandoned fairly quickly, and there are no reports of the band ever recording or performing publicly. It was hard to find work for such a large band, and Pete Rugulo's progressive policy at Capitol—which yielded not only Tadd's and Miles's midsized band session but also recordings by Lennie Tristano—was beginning to run into resistance from the management.

On the back of one of the scores Dameron wrote for Artie Shaw around this time there is an interesting but ultimately mysterious notation written in Dameron's hand:

```
Trumpets—Bernie Glow
        —Red Rodney
        —Johnny Mandel
        —Lamar Wright
Bones   —Kai Winding
        —Mathew [sic] Gee
```

	—Milt Gold
	—Rip
Saxes	—Jimmy Ford
	—Charlie Kennedy
	—Allen Eager
	—Cecil Payne
	—Sonny Rollins
Rhy	—John Collins
	—Art Blakey
	—Nelson Boyd
	—Tadd Dameron[35]

There are check marks next to the names of Glow, Rodney, Mandel, Winding, Gee, and Rip, but not the others, probably noting that they had been contacted or had confirmed their availability. Next to this list are the words "Premier Hotel, Fallsburg, N.Y." Although we cannot know for sure, the list might suggest that Tadd tried to keep the band going after Miles gave up on it. If so, his efforts appear to have been unsuccessful. The engagement seems never to have taken place. For his part Sonny Rollins said, "I never made this job—or performed as part of Tadd's band."[36] However, the overlap of personnel among those musicians reported by Leonard Feather, mentioned in *Down Beat,* and found on this list, which dates from late in 1949, indicates that Dameron was at least trying to organize a big band after his return from Europe.

Ted Heath and Artie Shaw

The Artie Shaw band, for which Tadd wrote in 1949, represented the clarinetist's try at a modern-jazz-style band. It had several well-known, young, progressive musicians on board: trumpeter Don Fagerquist; saxophonists Frank Socolow, Herbie Steward, Al Cohn, Zoot Sims, and Danny Bank; guitarist Jimmy Raney; and drummer Irv Kluger. Tadd wrote three scores for the band, all of his own compositions. Two were rewrites of arrangements made for Ted Heath, "Lyonia" and "So Easy." The third was a new piece, "Fred's Delight."[37] "Lyonia" was never recorded by Shaw, but the other two were recorded in December 1949 and January 1950, respectively.

"Lyonia" could be thought of as a piece of "Soulphony." While not through-composed, it does have a unique structure and is completely written out, with no improvised solos. The form is similar to the usual AABA or ABAC song-form structures, only more complex.[38] Using the letter system, it would be best described as ABCDA1ABC. It starts with a somewhat rumbalike rhythm in the drums and the bass, over which a five-measure vamplike melody is repeated three times, with increasing intensity: first by the saxes alone, then with the trombones added a fourth higher, and finally with the trumpets an octave above the trombones. When the opening theme is introduced, Dameron creates a subtle rhythmic tension by having the drums switch to a 4/4 swing time-feel while the melody and the rest of the accompaniment stay with the Latin time-feel. With the next strain the entire band switches to the swing feel, returning to Latin at times. While the switch between swing and Latin is not at all unusual, the superimposition of one over the other in this manner is, especially in 1949.

Comparisons between the Heath recording and the Shaw score show a few small differences, but the overall structure of the piece is the same. This might be unusual for Dameron were this not a complete composition within itself. Nevertheless, in the Shaw score we find some alterations, probably made by Shaw. Most of these are just redistributions of parts, made as he reduced the number of musicians in his band before breaking it up completely. There is a fourth trombone part, found with the score. that shows an open drum solo inserted before the return of letter A. Whether this was Dameron's idea or Shaw's is unknown. This solo would change the proportions of the piece, but it would not necessarily alter it in an unfavorable way. The trombone part also shows some dynamics penciled in. There are no dynamics indicated in the score, yet the Heath performance reveals how important dynamic detail is to the beauty and effectiveness of this work. Most likely, Dameron's intention was to rehearse Shaw's band, as we know he rehearsed Heath's.

The other arrangement written for both Heath and Shaw, "So Easy," is the twelve-bar blues that Dameron recorded with Dexter Gordon on Gordon's December 11, 1947, session for Savoy. The small-group treatment is very straightforward, but it contains the suggestion of some elements of a larger arrangement, as do most Dameron small-group arrangements. There are significant differences between the two charts, which strengthens the case for "Lyonia" being a complete composition rather than an arrangement open to tailoring by the bandleader. The Shaw arrangement is, of course, built around the leader's clarinet, while the Heath version presents the whole band. There is an eight-bar introduction in the Shaw, but the Heath has no introduction and starts with two choruses of the tune. The backgrounds are different, too, and while the Heath performance is taken at about 160 beats per minute, the Shaw is more relaxed at 110, giving it a different feeling. There are some things that both versions share, the call-and-response from the small-group version and an ensemble chorus following the opening statement of the tune. Both end with two tags of the last phrase of the tune, but these are orchestrated differently.

There are also important differences between Dameron's score for Artie Shaw and the recorded performance. The score has the trumpets present the tune in the opening choruses and indicates a repeat of the tune before going to the ensemble. Instead, Shaw himself plays the tune, and there is no repeat. There are also cuts of some of the background passages behind Shaw's solo, and the clarinetist plays fills before each of the tags at the end. Whether these changes were made collaboratively or were Shaw's alone is not known.

The arrangement of "The Nearness of You" written for Heath is simple but elegant. Taken slowly, in cut time, it recalls Dameron's arrangement of "Bewildered" for Lunceford, with its interesting harmonic substitutions and its orchestration full of finely detailed little solo passages in the background. Dameron also brings out the variety of sonorities that the big band has, making the listener appreciate the fact that it really is an *orchestra*.

For Charlie Ventura's "Euphoria," a contrafact of George and Ira Gershwin's "S' Wonderful," Dameron wrote Heath a simple chart designed to give solo space to the remarkable trombonist Jackie Armstrong and one of the tenor saxophonists, most likely Tommy Whittle. There is a somewhat mysterious-sounding eight-bar introduction, played by the saxes. The saxes, led by the baritone, continue with a unison statement of the A section. The full ensemble comes in for the bridge, with the trumpets carrying the melody, and then the saxes return, alone, for the last A. Armstrong takes a chorus with a background, the tenor saxophonist takes another chorus with a different background, and the band reenters from the bridge as played at the beginning. The saxes finish the piece with the full band in for the last chord.

Dameron's third chart for Artie Shaw is an AABA original titled "Fred's Delight." The tune is pleasant, but not one of Dameron's strongest. The A sections are a harmonic variant of the "rhythm changes," and there is too much arpeggiation of the harmonies in the melody. Dameron is usually very effective in his use of arpeggios, as in "If You Could See Me Now." Here the effect is more perfunctory, at least to the author's ears. The bridge, which moves from the key of C to A♭, is more interesting, and one wishes that Dameron had worked with "Fred's Delight" a bit longer. In the bridge he cleverly reworks the harmonic scheme of the A section so that the sequence that normally occurs in the fifth and sixth measures comes back to the tonic of the section (A♭) rather than going to the subdominant (D♭). By doing this he sets up the last two bars for a return to the key of C (fig. 7.1). The arrangement seems to be best suited for dancing, and perhaps this has something to do with the blandness of the melody. Still, it

Fig. 7.1. First A section, eight bars, and bridge of Dameron's "Fred's Delight." © 1978, Twenty-Eighth Street Music

is a typically well-crafted chart, mostly focused on the ensemble. There are only two solos, each eight measures long, one for guitar and the other—the bridge in the out-going half chorus—for Shaw.

The scores for Artie Shaw are written on "Stan Kenton Orchestra" score paper. While it has been suggested that various arrangers were given the unused pads of paper when Kenton disbanded his big band in 1948, it is also possible that Dameron had done some writing for Kenton prior to that. Dameron was submitting scores for Kenton's 1950 Innovations In Modern Music Orchestra at this time; however, the score paper he used for the Shaw arrangements would not have sufficed for these charts. The Innovations Orchestra had forty instruments, including a sixteen-piece string section. Writing for this unique precursor to the Third Stream movement would have been of great interest to Dameron, given his "Soulphony" pieces and his taste for classical music at the time, and it is unfortunate that his contributions were not performed publicly. Even though Tadd's music was not used on the tour, he had been invited to submit the music. Kenton said later, "I chose guys whom I respect, and who know what I can do."[39] Trombonist Milt Bernhart played in the orchestra and later recalled that

> at the first rehearsal it became evident that Stan had commissioned more music than the program could accommodate. . . . Some of the pieces were just plain more accessible than the others, . . . but I don't even recall what Tadd Dameron's

piece sounded like. George Russell also wrote a twelve-tone exercise, and I think that both Russell's and Dameron's works got played down only once or twice and that was the last of them.[40]

There is also the distinct probability that Tadd Dameron arranged two numbers for an Illinois Jacquet session for Victor on December 14, 1949, and the date of the recording would suggest that these were written after his return from Europe. The treatment of "Blue Satin," a blues credited to Cedric Haywood, Maurice Simon, and Jacquet, sounds like a scaled-down version of some of the charts written for Gillespie's big band. The Dameron touch is even more evident on the ballad "Stay Away," by Isaac Royal and Jacquet, especially in the coda and in the lines behind the singer when he returns after Jacquet's solo.[41] Near the end of his life, Jacquet told Don Sickler that Dameron had contributed many arrangements to his book.[42]

In addition to all this writing, Dameron was still playing in small bands when he got back to New York. Drummer and radio producer Don Manning was in New York in 1949 and 1950. He remembers a jazz scene that was still pretty lively, and certainly the playing on the 1950 air-checks by Miles Davis and others shows no sign of depression. Even though the clubs on Fifty-second Street were in decline, there was still music on "The Street," and Manning recalls hearing a Dameron-led group there that included John Collins and Cecil Payne. He also recalls Dameron playing with others.[43]

We know for certain that Tadd played in Wardell Gray's quintet at the Orchid Club on Fifty-second Street for a week, starting on Friday, October 7, 1949.[44] The engagement at the Orchid came to an end suddenly when the club decided to abandon its modern jazz policy. The next week Dameron and Miles Davis co-led a quartet at Soldier Meyer's in Brooklyn—referred to in *Down Beat* as "Brooklyn's new Bop haven."[45]

It seems most likely that Dameron went back to Cleveland for a visit in the fall. His hometown friends Buddy Crewe and Myron Styles recalled a trip to New York with Tadd and Buster Harding, as well as some other people, in the fall of 1949. The party was formed to go see a Giants football game and hear Tadd play at a club "down around 48th St." Harding, another successful arranger, had grown up in Cleveland, and his father managed one of the nightclubs there at the time. Certainly he and Tadd were friends from the New York scene, and their friendship may well have gone back many years, to the 1930s in Cleveland. Crewe and Styles's recollection of going to hear Tadd play suggests that Dameron put a band together for a week or so at either Birdland or Bop City, sometime during the football season.

In December, Dameron was reported to be playing at Café Society with a quartet. Although the specific dates are not known, he may have stayed there into January 1950. It was also in December, while working on the cruise ship *Caronia*, that Ronnie Scott and bassist Pete Blannin visited Tadd and Margo in New York. "I remember Tadd invited us up to his place for dinner, Pete and I," recalled Scott. "He was there with his wife, a white lady as I remember, and . . . I remember that he was playing some records and Pete asked him if he had such-and-such a record and Tadd said 'No, no, I have only *beautiful* music.'"[46]

At the conclusion of one of Leonard Feather's "Blindfold Tests," published later in the year, Feather quotes Dameron as saying, "Personally, when I'm at home just listening to music, d'you know what I play? Ravel, Delius, Stravinsky, Villa-Lobos—just to mention a few!" Dameron was not the first to voice a preference for music outside of jazz; Coleman Hawkins said he favored listening to opera at home.

Throughout his "Blindfold Test," Tadd shows himself to be open to a wide range of musical styles and very particular about good musicianship. He responds favorably to Jimmy Dorsey's Columbia recording of "Johnson Rag": "I don't know who it is, but for Dixieland I'd say it's one of the best I've heard. I can see why people like Dixieland; it has a beat and is easy for anyone to understand. Three stars." An obscure—at least to the modern listener—Basie recording of "Solid as a Rock," recorded for Victor, gets a firm rejection: "This sounds like Basie. It's very poor. In spots it has a good beat, but that's about all . . . sounds like the old Basie era; group and unison vocal poor. The composition? Horrible! One star." In response to the Parker-with-strings version of "Just Friends," Dameron responds, "Charlie Parker—the world's greatest instrumentalist! . . . That must be Mitch Miller on oboe. . . . This is a very nice arrangement and the piano solo is good. I like the tune too—'Just Friends,' isn't it? This is one of the best things out of the album. Four Stars." He also appreciates Tex Beneke's band for the quality of its ensemble work, even though, he remarks, "I can't say I care too much for the style." An Erskine Hawkins recording of "St. Louis Blues" is firmly criticized for poor intonation and weak solos. Dameron also made a general assessment of some of his contemporaries: "Arrangers? I like Gerry Mulligan's writing very much. Miles is the farthest advanced musician of his day, and 'Boplicity' is one of the best small-group sounds I've heard. Tristano is so far advanced that it's hard to get with it and understand what he's playing. I don't know what bop is—but of course that remark has been made a thousand times."[47]

Dameron and Jimmy Mundy had been writing arrangements for Pearl Bailey's stage show late in 1949,[48] and in February of 1950, Bailey recorded a

Dameron arrangement of "Nothin' for Nothin'," by Dorothy Fields and Morton Gould, for Columbia. The ensemble consists of string orchestra, flute, guitar, piano, bass, and drums. The rhythm section is generally subdued, but there are a few solo lines for the guitar, and the bass is bowed along with the higher strings in the coda. The flute is heard clearly only at the very end of the arrangement, and at times, it sounds as if it might be playing along with the first violins, as one might expect. Simple as it is, this arrangement further documents Dameron's skill in writing for an ensemble made up primarily of strings.

February also finds Tadd and Miles working together again. In the fall Davis had been employing Bud Powell on his few New York gigs (other than the week at Soldier Meyer's). By February, Powell had his own trio, and Dameron was playing piano for the Miles Davis Sextet in an engagement at Birdland that opened on February 9 and continued into March. The lineup included Stan Getz—sometimes listed as co-leader, J. J. Johnson, Dameron, Gene Ramey, and either Art Blakey or Max Roach. The band was recorded in broadcasts on three consecutive nights in February. The sextet was back at Birdland again in May, with Brew Moore replacing Getz and Curly Russell in place of Ramey. Once again, they broadcast for several nights, with Tadd's fellow Clevelander Jimmy Scott joining them on Memorial Day. As much as Tadd is a part of this band, it is only as a pianist, and "Hot House" is the only one of his compositions represented in the transcriptions of these broadcasts. The previous year's hero had made no new recordings of his own and was now just the pianist in the band of his former protégé

The Miles Davis Sextet was booked into Birdland for one more week, from June 30 to July 6. According to some sources, Dameron played with the band on the broadcast on June 30, but he gave up his chair to Walter Bishop Jr. before the week was out. Others have questioned the dating of this broadcast, for various reasons. If it is correct, it seems he went to Cleveland for a visit and returned to make the opening of the stand at Birdland. An article in the July 1 edition of the *Cleveland Call and Post* has Tadd trying to put a good face on matters. It opens by saying that he has "returned home from Europe this week to spend a few days with his family." The article goes on to give a reasonable, if somewhat boastful, summary of his place in the bop movement. However, in three and a half paragraphs near the end, the article starts to move from reality into fantasy:

> After several years, Dameron left New York for Europe, where he has been arranger for the British Broadcasting Company and a number of Continental broadcast stations.
> In addition to his work for the BBC the young composer—he is now 34—

also composes and arranges for virtually every "name" band in the United States, and frequently publishes music of his own.

Dameron will be in Cleveland for about a week, after which he will return to England, with his wife. He appeared here twice last week on radio programs, once with the Bill Hawkins show and the other time Thursday night, when he took over the Symphony Sid program over WDOK.

The former Clevelander is not definite as to his future plans. He will catch up on his work with the BBC in London, then will set out for Rio de Janeiro. He plans, he says, to travel "all around the world at least once" before taking up permanent residence anywhere.[49]

The article concludes by saying that Tadd would play for a week with his brother Caesar's band. By the end of September he had a regular gig at Amvets Post number 29, on Cedar Avenue.[50] In January 1951, Tadd was running the jam session at the Sky Bar, one of Cleveland's longest-running jazz venues. By the fall of 1951, he was writing arrangements for Benjamin "Bull Moose" Jackson, his childhood friend from the neighborhood, now a star on the R&B circuit. So much for returning to Europe with his beautiful and charming wife before moving on to Brazil: instead of building on his transnational successes, he retreated to Cleveland, without Margo. Something had gone terribly wrong in Tadley Dameron's life, and whether the cause or a symptom, drugs had something to do with it.

8

1950–55—Into The Shadows

In the *Call and Post* article of July 1, 1950, Tadd Dameron presents his dream of what might have been, had he stayed in England or France. Perhaps the article would not be quite so disturbing if Dameron's comments, which have so little connection with reality, had been addressed to a community where he was not very well known. One has to wonder what he was thinking when he was telling the *Call and Post* interviewer about his travels, his career with the BBC and other European radio stations, his planned return to England with Margo, and their intention to go to Brazil. It is not clear why he did not stay in France as an alternative to England—his intention as told to an interviewer from the English magazine *Music Fare*. It may have been too complicated to get an extension on his French visa, or it may have been because French law was not particularly tolerant of heroin users. Various observers have suggested that Dameron was drawn to England because of a more lenient policy toward drug addicts.

So far, Tadd Dameron's use of drugs had been discreet, making little discernible impact on his activities. However, he does seem to have been playing around with drugs for a few years. Gene Ramey recalled that "when Bird got to New York and was hanging out with Tadd Dameron, they were experimenting with everything."[1] Ramey seems to be referring to the fall of 1942, after Parker left Andy Kirk and before he joined Earl Hines, but it could have been later in 1943 or 1944. Orrin Keepnews recalled that at the time of their meeting in late 1947, Tadd was part of a group of "well-dressed junkies."[2] Still, the general sense of Dameron's heroin use is that he was not, at first, an intravenous user, and it is not entirely clear if one can really say that he was an addict until the late 1940s. Stan Levy, who would know an addict if he saw one, said, "When I knew him in

1945 he wasn't using any drugs—maybe smoking a little marijuana."[3] As noted before, Levy's contact with Dameron at that time was not just limited to the Diz and Bird rehearsals: they socialized after work and were on the road together with Georgie Auld.

Dameron's affliction seems to have been part of a more general compulsion to intoxicate himself. One friend, who could speak with authority on the matter, felt that Tadd had a bigger problem with cocaine than with heroin.[4] Considering this, it is interesting to note that the British musician Denis Rose once said that he and Tadd "did coke together" during Dameron's London sojourn.[5] Several people also reported witnessing Tadd drink to great excess on various occasions, although he was not thought to be an alcoholic. Still, it is clear that by 1950, heroin had taken a firm hold on him.

By the time Dameron returned to Cleveland in the summer of 1950, it also appears that his relationship with Margo was about to end, if it had not ended already. We do not know if she was a drug user herself or if Tadd's indulgences were just something she tolerated. If the latter is the case, it is worth considering Tadd's addiction as a factor in the collapse of this relationship. John Collins, guitarist with the "Big Ten" band, recalled,

> I don't know when Tadd would have started taking drugs but it was before the Paris trip. I never saw him "take off," Tadd wasn't like that, but it was fairly obvious to anyone who knew him. I kept well clear of it. I remember once I was at his home when there was a knock at the door. Tadd went to the door and came back with [someone Collins knew to be an addict]. Well, I was straight out of there. I knew what they were going to do.[6]

Not surprisingly, Miles Davis was also a visitor to Tadd and Margo's apartment.[7] Davis said that after his return from Paris, "Some of the younger guys like Dexter Gordon, Tadd Dameron, Art Blakey, J. J. Johnson, Sonny Rollins, Jackie McLean and myself—all of us—started to get heavily into heroin."[8] Dexter Gordon, with whom Tadd had worked in various situations, was already having difficulties keeping a band together because of his addiction, and Art Blakey was an associate of Dameron's since the early days of the Eckstine band; both of these men probably came to the apartment as well. It would seem likely that after the return from Europe, several of the visitors to Margo's home were addicts with heroin taking over their lives. This, along with Tadd's increasing dependency, may very well have become intolerable.

Even in Cleveland there were suspicions about Dameron's drug use as early as the late 1940s. Venus Irving-Prescott was a young woman living in Cleveland at the time. She knew the Damerons from the neighborhood, especially Ruth and Caesar, and had a bit of a crush on Tadd. She remembered going out with him to Val's-in-the-Alley or one of the other clubs and hearing Art Tatum and Erroll Garner (with none other than Dinah Washington playing bass). However, she was aware that Tadd was already into heroin and decided to keep her distance from him, in spite of his charm.[9]

Some have wondered why Dameron did not take the tragic death of his childhood friend Freddie Webster, from a heroin overdose in 1947, as a wake-up call. One could ask the same question in regard to the then-recent death of another of Tadd's trumpet-playing associates, Fats Navarro, in the summer of 1950—but then addiction is not a particularly logical phenomenon.

Charlie Rouse also had memories of this period, particularly how the combination of professional frustration and concerted effort on the part of drug dealers to sell to musicians—as well as other performing artists—made heroin use hard to avoid:

> Man, the market was flooded, they had it all out in the streets. I mean around the musicians; the average person didn't know anything about it. The drug pushers went to the clubs, to the musicians, and the musicians got hung up in it, I imagine, through a lot of different aspects of their lives. Some of your hours was unusual, you figured you could play better. I would do that. I would figure I could play better because I realized Bird and all of them, they was on it, you know— 'till you find out. Then there was the fact that they knew they was being exploited, and there was nothing they could do. During that time, Tadd and all of them when they were recording, couldn't record unless they gave the company the rights to their tunes.[10]

As several members of Dameron's generation recall this time, a sort of terrible gloom had fallen over the community of younger jazz musicians by the end of 1950. Fifty-second Street had gone to strip joints, Bop City had closed or was about to close, and there were not even big bands to play in anymore. Tadd and Miles had been treated with respect and admiration in Europe just a year before, only to return home and have the feeling that few people cared about their skills and accomplishments. We have no way of knowing, but it is easy to imagine that Margo must have felt this disappointment as well, and it is easy to see the young couple drifting apart emotionally, especially if Tadd was turning more and more to intoxication. The fact that Tadd was still referring to Margo as his wife as late as the summer of 1950 leads us to suspect the separation was not something that he wanted or welcomed. The couple had been together for something like three or four years. From what little we know of this part of his life, this was the most successful relationship of its kind he would enjoy, save his marriage to Mabel Sopper near the end of his life.

So, in this gloomy time, Dameron shifted his base of operations to Cleveland, where he was a hometown hero and could always find work, musical or otherwise. Sometime in late 1949 or the beginning of 1950, Caesar Dameron opened a restaurant, Dameron's Hut. According to Buddy Crewe and Myron Styles, Tadd and Caesar's longtime friends, Caesar bought the restaurant for their mother, Ruth. Crewe recalled that "Tadd and his mother was workin' in it, and he was helpin' her open up and close the place. He was workin' there for a while, then he would go out and play, then he'd come back, then sometimes he'd disappear and be gone for four or five days." To this Myron Styles added, "And then his brother, Caesar, was with the Musicians Union. He didn't have to go to the hiring hall, the hiring hall came to him."[11]

Donald Meade, a jazz historian from Chicago and a long-time observer of the modern jazz scene, recalled seeing Tadd working in the kitchen of Dameron's Hut on occasion in the early 1950s.[12] Willie Smith, an arranger and saxophonist from Cleveland, confirmed the general pattern of Tadd's working for a while at Dameron's Hut, and then either going out on the road for a bit or going to New York for a visit.[13] Even though he was spending more time in Cleveland, he apparently kept a place in New York and was playing piano for Charlie Parker on occasion.[14] There is also anecdotal evidence that he still was in demand as an arranger during the period of 1949–53. Jimmy Boyd, a pianist and arranger based in Cleveland, orchestrated arrangements for Dameron on a regular basis; apparently Tadd had too many assignments to be able to finish them all by himself. According to bassist Ron Javorsky, who worked with Boyd in the 1980s, Dameron would give Boyd a grand staff score, like the one deposited with the copyright office for "Focus." After a bit of discussion regarding which lines would go with which instruments, Boyd would produce the conductor's score, from which the copyist would write the parts.[15]

Dameron may have had other commitments in Cleveland. There are various stories about a child or children that Tadd had by a woman or women who lived in Cleveland. The stories are secondhand, and since we have no names for any of the possible mothers or children, we cannot say anything conclusive. However, since these stories come from various unrelated sources, they cannot be dismissed out of hand. Donald Kennedy, who knew the Dameron family as a neighbor, heard of a writer who had tracked down a woman who was supposed to be Tadd's daughter.[16] The writer came to her door, and when she heard that he had come to talk to her about her father, she slammed it in his face. The trumpeter Bill Hardman, who worked in Cleveland with Dameron in the 1950s, told fellow trumpeter Don Sickler that he encountered a man who looked very familiar to him in a bar one night. Hardman could not place the man and found himself staring at him. Not wanting to appear rude, he went over to the man, introduced himself, and explained why he was looking at him. The man said that people often mistook him for his father. When Hardman asked him who his father was, the man said, "Tadd Dameron."[17]

Willie Smith, who became a truly close friend to Dameron in the 1950s, remembered that there was a Cleveland woman with whom Tadd lived on and off, who filed child-support complaints against Tadd with the authorities. Dameron clearly had more than a casual relationship with this woman, for when he died, she had possession of a significant number of his manuscripts, which have since been lost. It has not been documented whether the child or children in question were really Tadd's, but this stormy relationship left Dameron depressed on several occasions.[18] Tadd would sometimes leave town just to get away from it.

Whatever the actual details of Dameron's difficulties with women, children, and drugs, one can easily understand how it would have been very difficult for him to focus on his own creative efforts in the 1950s. Looked at in this light, the small and intermittent output of work under his own name from this time could be considered rather remarkable, even heroic. While he was writing arrangements for others and playing piano for Charlie Parker and Bull Moose Jackson at various times, he was not continuing to present his own music much, if at all, after his return from Europe—certainly not to the extent that it was being recorded or promoted.

Bull Moose Jackson

In October of 1951, Bull Moose Jackson recorded three Dameron arrangements, among other things, for the King label. By now Dameron was working with some regularity with Jackson, whose 1947 recording of "I Love You, Yes I Do" is reputed to be the first rhythm-and-blues record to sell a million copies.[19] Along with Dameron, the band included Johnny Coles on trumpet, Benny Golson on tenor sax, and Jymie Merritt on bass. From this edition of Jackson's band came Dameron's next notable project, the nonet that recorded for Prestige in June of 1953 and then worked briefly, but legendarily, in Atlantic City.

In the early 1950s, there was not a lot of work for jazz musicians, except for well-established stars, but there was work for musicians willing to play for floor shows and rhythm-and-blues dances. Jackson was well established and very popular in the early 1950s. From an employment standpoint, it was a "good gig"—the work was steady, and the leader was both competent and kind. Benny Golson recalled that Tadd was already in the band when he joined in 1951. As other players were needed, Benny recruited some of his friends from Philadelphia, first Coles and Merritt and later drummer Philly Joe Jones, who was to become one of Tadd's closest friends.

The three Dameron arrangements recorded on October 17, 1951, were "I'll Be Home for Christmas," "I've Had a Hard Way to Go," and "I Never Loved Anyone but You."[20] Dameron himself was also in the band, and the rest of the personnel suggests that this was the band that Jackson worked with off and on for several months in 1951 and 1952. "I'll Be Home" is simply a vocal arrangement with rhythm section (organ, celeste, guitar, bass), with some subtle touches: the opening phrase of "Silent Night" paraphrased in the guitar introduction and the harmonies Dameron uses in the few places where the voices are harmonized. "Hard Way" is a medium-slow blues shuffle with some very effective ensemble kicks. Here, Dameron's voice is heard most clearly in the voicings for the horn section. "I Never Loved" is a classic Dameron small-band ballad arrangement with a four-bar introduction that teasingly suggests the first phrase of the melody of the song without giving it away. The accompanying lines in the horns weave in and around the melody, reminiscent of the arrangement of "What's New" from 1949, tying all the phrases of the song together into a beautiful flowing movement from beginning to end. Along with this there is a very soft obligato played by celeste running throughout the performance, which works here in a manner similar to the obligato played by Bud Powell in Sarah Vaughan's recording of "I Can Make You Love Me."

We also need to consider seriously that these were not the first arrangements Dameron had written for his old neighborhood friend. In spite of the lack of documentation, it is hard to imagine that anyone other than Tadd Dameron could have written the arrangement of "I Love You, Yes I Do," Jackson's big 1947 hit, with its voicings and lines that are so very much like those in Dameron's other arrangements of vocals from the same time. The same can be said about "All My Love Belongs to You," also from 1947, and "Don't Ask Me Why,"[21] from 1949.

Since Jackson's recorded up-tempo numbers do not sound like Dameron's work, it seems likely that Bull Moose called upon Tadd primarily for arranging ballads. However, when Dameron was with the band, Jackson also let him present his own instrumentals in the opening "warm-up" numbers of their sets. It was, and in many cases still is, customary for the band accompanying a singer to play two or three instrumental numbers before the singer makes his or her entrance. Golson recalled that often two audiences would show up for Bull Moose's performances, one of blues and R&B fans and the other a more "sophisticated" group that came to hear Dameron's instrumentals. Golson also recalled that this was "just fine" as far as the leader was concerned.[22] Not only was this good for business, but Jackson was himself one of these sophisticated listeners.

Benny Golson considered his time in the Jackson band to be his "postgraduate" work. In an interview with Harry Frost for a profile in *Down Beat* in 1958 he said, "After hearing things like [Dameron's] 'Our Delight' and 'Lady Bird,' I had more of a definite goal. I wanted to do more than play tenor sax. I wanted to write." Golson was referring to his early years at Howard University, where he wrote his first arrangements. Imagine his surprise and delight to find Dameron playing piano in the first band he worked with full-time after leaving Howard. When traveling, Benny would often ride with Tadd so he could discuss the art of writing music with his hero. Golson said that "he was very open with me and taught me so many things. He didn't have any trade secrets, he was a completely open book, and I still have fond memories of him for that."[23] Of course Benny, too, would write for the band and he later recalled,

> Tadd has been a big influence on my life. The very first thing I wrote was called "Shades of Dameron." We played it, and people would come up to Tadd and say, "Man, I like that arrangement of your tune 'Shades of Dameron.'" He'd say, "What a drag!," but he'd only be kidding. . . . He'd come up and give me the whole act. "Man, what a drag. They come and thank me for something that you wrote." But he was really commending me, you know. He was very proud of it since it *did* sound like his composition.[24]

The Harry Frost Interview

When the Bull Moose Jackson Band played St. Louis in the spring of 1952, Tadd and Benny were interviewed by local jazz disc jockey Harry Frost. It is the only recording of Dameron's voice known to the author[25] and an important source of information about him. At the time, he and Golson were excited about a studio date for Atlantic Records, scheduled for August. Although never realized, their plans were well set: they were going to be in Atlantic City with Bull Moose and intended to use his band,[26] with the addition of J. J. Johnson, Cecil Payne, and Clifford Brown, the latter of whom was still unrecorded at that time. The album was to feature compositions and arrangements by both men. It is, to say the least, a pity that it never came about. Dameron expressed his regard for Golson in terms so prescient that ten years later Frost was able to use that portion of the interview in a radio program about Golson's rise as an important musician.

Between Dameron's lies about his life in the press and his general reticence, it is hard, at times, to know if he was telling the truth. Frost asked about the title of the tune "Jahbero," and Dameron replied, "It's an African bird. It's very beautiful. . . . You'll be walking down the street and he sweeps down on you; almost touches your head, but he won't bother you." "So there was a *bird* influence in that composition," interjected Frost, humorously. Tadd's reply was, "Yeah, when I was in North Africa." Maybe there is such a bird, but even if Tadd took a side trip to North Africa before returning to New York from Paris, it would have been after he wrote and recorded "Jahbero."[27] Dameron also says that he wrote the arrangement of Gerald Wilson's "Yard Dog Mazurka" for the Jimmie Lunceford Orchestra, but the notes on an MCA LP reissue of this recording say it was arranged by Wilson and Roger Segure,[28] a fact pointed out to him in the interview. Neither man says anything more about it, but it feels like an awkward moment. When asked about this by the author, Gerald Wilson himself was adamant that it was his arrangement and that Tadd did not join the band until he was just about to leave, a couple of months after the recording of "Yard Dog Mazurka," which was made in August of 1941.[29]

Although Tadd was working a lot with Bull Moose Jackson during this time, he was not working with him exclusively. Sometime in 1952 he played on the debut recording of Philadelphia-based singer Billy Paul, released on the Jubilee label. Jerry Blaine, president of Jubilee Records, requested Dameron for the recording session, but Paul and Dameron had already met. Billy Paul recalled that he first met Tadd sometime in 1951 at Club Harlem, in Philadelphia, when he was introduced to Charlie Parker by his manager, Jules Malamut. Dameron was playing piano for Parker on this engagement. Paul sang a few songs with the band, and Dameron offered to coach him. They would meet for coaching sessions at odd intervals, in either New York or Philadelphia, from the time of their first meeting until sometime in 1955.[30]

Dr. Willis Kirk, former president of San Francisco City College, was a working drummer in 1952, with a steady gig in Columbus, Ohio. He remembered Dameron playing at another club in the same neighborhood with his own small group a few times that year.[31] A little later, on January 17, 1953, Tadd and his orchestra played for the "Mayor of Harlem" ball at the Pla-Mor Ball Room in Cleveland. Whether this orchestra was drawn from the ranks of the Bull Moose Jackson band or put together from Cleveland regulars like Curtis Shepherd, Bobby Smith, and Willie Smith was not reported. The Mayor of

Harlem was an honor bestowed on an outstanding businessman from the black community not only in Cleveland but in other cities as well, for there was an Association of U.S. Mayors of Harlem.[32]

Duke Ellington's Opening Theme

Around this time, Dameron submitted a score and parts to Duke Ellington. Titled "Duke Ellington's Opening Theme," it was intended as a feature for Clark Terry. There is no date on the score, but Terry joined Ellington toward the end of 1951,[33] and in the 1952 interview with Harry Frost, Frost mentions that Dameron had written for Ellington. To our knowledge, no other Dameron scores have been found in the Ellington collections,[34] nor have any others been recorded or mentioned in print.

One of the score's outstanding features also provides evidence for dating it during this period: the tune is essentially the same as one recorded by Miles Davis in 1954, titled "Spring Swing." While it might be interesting to speculate about this, given Dameron and Davis's professional and personal relationship, we can say nothing more without further documentation.

The instrumentation of the arrangement is odd in that it calls for four trombones; Ellington used only three. While it is subtitled "featuring Clark Terry," there is no indication in the score identifying Terry's part. Was Terry to be a fifth, solo trumpet? The bridge in the opening chorus sounds like a background, but there is music scored for all four of the trumpets. Ellington did record with five trumpets in December of 1952, and there are earlier and later instances of a five-trumpet section, but these are only for recordings. And why four trombones? It is not likely that Dameron was unaware of the instrumentation of Ellington's band. Was this written for a special performance that was planned but never took place, or did Dameron just decide to send his hero a score? Although it is unclear whether the piece was ever even given a reading,[35] someone else wrote in a drum part, which Dameron had not provided. Dameron did not often write drum parts in his scores, but then, neither did Ellington.

Whatever its provenance, "Duke Ellington's Opening Theme" is a fascinating piece of music with strong elements of bitonality, or even polytonality. The tune at the heart of the piece is a very sophisticated variant of the "rhythm changes" design. An examination of the presentation of the first eight bars of the melody itself shows some of the harmonic complexity. After the introduction, the A melody is played by the alto and tenor saxes, over an F drone bass, played by baritone sax, fourth trombone, bass, and piano. Against this there

ex. 8.1

Fig. 8.1. Reduction of voicings used at the beginning of the third phrase of the A section of Dameron's "Duke Ellington's Opening Theme."

is essentially an E7 in the three other trombones (E, A♭ [G♯], and D) and a quartal chord in the trumpets (C, E♭, F, and B♭). The beginning of the third phrase of the A melody, while brief, is powerful and exemplifies Dameron's harmonic daring in this piece. Here he has the saxes and fourth trombone moving in contrary motion to the trumpets and the rest of the trombones. On their first note they combine to make Gmi7 chord, on the next an Ami7 over D. As the lines continue to diverge, the next two harmonies (marked * and ** in fig. 8.1) defy conventional notation but could be described as a B♭ major triad over an A♭Ma7, and an E♭Ma7/F, except that the C of the A♭Ma7 is in the descending line and is heard as leading to the F of the next harmony. This F is heard in both the lowest and the highest voices, while inside of these outer voices there is an E♭Ma7 chord. The C in the third trombone, given its distance from the B♭ in the second trombone, is heard as reinforcing the F. The effect is that of colossal flower opening up.[36]

In "Duke Ellington's Opening Theme" Dameron is working again with his concept of harmonic evolution as a developmental element. Later in the piece he presents two different chord progressions for the tune. These, along with the polytonal/modal treatment described above and a probable standard "rhythm changes" progression for a solo, make four different harmonic variations.[37] Dameron is also probably incorporating some of the harmonic concepts that he was hearing in the work of European composers such as Debussy, Ravel, and Delius, all of whom he mentioned listening to with great interest in the late 1940s and early 1950s. As with others of his lost and unrecorded works, it is a pity that, for whatever reasons, this one was never heard.

A Study in Dameronia

Even though Dameron and Golson never got to make their record for Atlantic, something would eventually come of this project. Sometime in the spring of 1953, while playing with the Jackson band at the Apollo Theater,[38] Golson recalled, someone came from Prestige Records to talk with Dameron about making an LP that would be titled *A Study in Dameronia*.[39] While the Atlantic project was supposed to be a twelve-inch record, allowing for eight selections, the one for Prestige would be a ten-inch record and would have room for only four. Benny's writing debut would have to wait for a while. On June 11, 1953, Tadd took a band of young, strong players into a studio in New York and recorded four new compositions: "Philly J. J.," "Choose Now," "Dial 'B' for Beauty," and "Theme of No Repeat." The musicians, Idrees Sulieman and Clifford Brown on trumpet, Gigi Gryce on alto sax, Benny Golson on tenor, Cecil Payne on baritone, Percy Heath on bass and Philly Joe Jones on drums, would all distinguish themselves in the coming years. Jones, Sulieman, and Payne were the oldest, thirty or thirty-one years old, with respectable resumés. Sulieman may well have been one of the musicians selected for the Atlantic album, for he claims to have been the first to mention Clifford Brown to Dameron.

Idrees first encountered Clifford at a club in Philadelphia, where someone told him that this hot young trumpet player was in the audience. Sulieman invited Brown to sit in, but Brown demurred, preferring to listen. Brown came back the next night, again only to listen, but on the third night he brought his horn and played, to Sulieman's amazement and delight. According to Sulieman, "when I got back to New York, I called Tadd up and I said, 'Hey Tadd, you got to hear this little trumpet player named Clifford Brown.' So Tadd said, 'Yeah, but I want to [use] you.' I said, 'No, because you got to hear him first.'" Dameron finally heard Brown and decided to use both trumpeters on this date.[40]

Gigi Gryce had arrived in New York only a few months before, but he was already establishing himself. Prior to the date with Dameron he had recorded with Howard McGhee and Max Roach. Gryce and Golson met in New York in the summer of 1951, before Benny joined the Jackson band, and it was probably on Golson's recommendation that Tadd chose him for this session. His selection must have delighted Gryce, for he was already an admirer of Dameron's work. Gigi felt that Tadd was "one of the greatest, most creative and exploring arrangers of our time."[41] Percy Heath, who had worked for two years with Dizzy Gillespie in his post-big-band groups, would soon be a founding member of the Modern Jazz Quartet. He is generally regarded as one of the foremost bassists of his generation. Philly Joe Jones,[42] the melodic and masterful drummer who was already working intermittently with Miles Davis, would later be a member of one of the trumpeter's most memorable bands. As noted, Philly Joe would remain a close friend of Dameron's; he had already made enough of an impression on the composer to warrant a tune dedicated to him on this session.

"Philly J. J.," the feature for Jones, starts with an introduction—three two-bar exchanges between the ensemble and Jones, after which he takes another sixteen or so measures of solo—and a statement of the tune. The bass and drums play in double time. With the tune taken at around 180 beats per minute, this puts the rhythm section at a ferocious tempo of 360. The melody, as played by the band, has an AABAC form, but the solos by Brown and Golson are taken over an AABA form that uses the same harmonic progression as Dizzy Gillespie's "Woody'n You," which is related in its A sections to those supporting the opening melody.[43]

Clifford Brown solos first, taking two choruses. The background of the first chorus is essentially a simplification of the melodic material of the A section, rhythmically augmented, of course, to match the slower-moving harmonies. The second chorus is accompanied only by the rhythm section. In the first chorus of Golson's solo, the As of the first chorus have a four-bar exchange between ensemble and saxophonist, yet another paraphrase of the melody. As in Brown's solo, the second chorus does not get a background. A brief fanfare introduces an open solo by Jones, which he keeps to roughly the proportions of the AABA chorus—the first half lasts around twenty measures, instead of sixteen. There is a "bridge" of new material, a simple repeated-note motif of eight measures (or ten, if one includes the two bars of setup by Jones). Jones resumes his solo for another eleven bars, the final two of which reestablish the ferocious double tempo, setting up a reprise of the opening melody from the B section. There is a coda comprised of a solo cadenza by the drummer and a double-forte four-note final cadence from the ensemble.

"Dial 'B' for Beauty" is actually a two-part medley of the title tune and another piece, "Kayepyn," which was copyrighted in 1949, at the same time as "Focus" and "Woody's Workshop." Compositionally, the two melodies have little in common, outside of the shared ABAC form. However, there is a continuity of mood between them, and this seems to be enough to make the entire recorded piece work. It is interesting to note that Dameron subtitled "Kayepyn" with the word "Idyll" on the deposit lead sheet[44] filed with the Copyright Office. Indeed, there is something idyllic and dreamlike about the entire "Dial 'B' for Beauty." A four-measure introduction from the ensemble is followed by a meandering passage of twenty-four measures played by Dameron, with just the accompaniment of Jones's brushes. In spite of its meandering character, this section has clearly been well thought out beforehand, and it concludes with two phrases that are motivically related to the melody of "Dial 'B' for Beauty." Structurally this section acts like a verse to the following song-form chorus. Dameron plays "Dial 'B'" completely solo and outside of a strict tempo, concluding with a brief transitional interlude that leads to "Kayepyn."

The deposit for "Kayepyn" is written in the five-voice "octet style" that evolved in Dameron's writing in the late 1940s, and the orchestration for this ensemble is very close to what he wrote four years before. Although the form is the same as in "Dial 'B' for Beauty," it works very differently. The A section, when first heard, sounds like an introduction to the B section, whereas in the other tune the B section is more of a first ending to the A, the latter being the more usual sense of the ABAC form. Only when the A repeats in "Kayepin" does the form start to become clear. The C section of "Kayepyn" begins with four measures of Dameron's piano, accompanied only by bowed bass. This helps to tie the entire work together by recalling the texture of the first part of the piece.

If one were to think of "Dial 'B' for Beauty" in visual art terms, it could be considered a triptych. The introduction and verselike segment would be one panel, the tune itself—along with the transitional material—the second panel, and "Kayepyn" the third. To continue this analogy, we might consider "Theme of No Repeat" to be a diptych. The opening melody is unrelated to the solos and the out-going melody except in key and tempo. A strange and perhaps not completely successful construction, it works well enough in that the melodies and the solos are strong, but careful listening reveals the lack of connection between the opening melody and the solos.

The first panel of this diptych is an interesting thirty-two-bar AABA tune in which Dameron blurs the line between the second A and the bridge by making the last phrase of the second A sound as if it were the first phrase of the bridge. He does this by moving momentarily from the key of B♭ to the key of C. The first A concludes with a turn-around—Dmin7 G7♭9 | Cmin7 F7♭9 ||—bringing the progression back to the tonic, B♭. In the second (and the third) A the progression is Dmin7 G7♭9 | Cmaj7 ||. There is an eight-bar introduction that is skillfully developed from the opening motif of the tune. An unconventional fourteen-bar interlude that is tagged onto the last bar wanders around but holds the listeners attention anyway, like a child leading an adult to a secret place in the woods.

The second panel consists of solos by Clifford Brown and Tadd Dameron, followed by a concluding tune with an unconventional relationship to the solos. The solos are taken over a chord progression made up of rhythm changes A sections and Dameron's favorite common bridge: in this case Fmin7 | B♭7 | E♭ | E♭ | G-7 | C7 | Cmin7 | F7||. The out-going tune is derived from a figure that Dameron plays at the end of the bridge of his first solo chorus. The A sections have their own progression, but the bridge is open, and Dameron solos on it.

One can only speculate on the rationale for the overall composition of "Theme of No Repeat," but it is worth considering Dameron's piano solo for some clues. At medium to fast tempos, Tadd Dameron was always more effective in playing chords—either in accompanying or in his block-chord solos—than in developing single-note lines. Therefore, it is no surprise that one of the weaknesses of his earlier single-note work is his overreliance on arpeggios. However, his soloing on the tracks on this album shows a great improvement in single-note melodic improvisation. He had obviously been working on this area of his playing, but he may not have gotten to the point where he was confident playing over any progressions except the more common ones: blues and rhythm changes. He may also have wanted to push himself to step out and take longer solos and perhaps cooked up this arrangement so that he could do both. It is also possible that he was working out ideas about building pieces of music out of marginally related elements, as he did in "Dial 'B' for Beauty."

"Choose Now" is reminiscent of the music Dameron wrote for the "Big Ten." Built on the same progression that is used for the solos in "Theme of No Repeat," it opens with an eight-bar introduction that is developed from the opening motif of the tune. In the opening chorus Dameron solos over the bridge changes, but there is a melody for the bridge, which is heard later. After an eight-bar interlude—the sixth or seventh bar of which is 2/4 instead of 4/4—Clifford Brown solos. In his first chorus he plays over the first two As, and then the saxes play a soli in the bridge, before receding into the background as Brown returns for the last eight measures of the chorus, after which the trumpeter takes another chorus with only the rhythm section. Next, Dameron takes a single chorus solo,[45] followed by a chorus and a half from Benny Golson. The ensemble returns with the bridge melody and the final A, and the interlude returns as the coda.

Atlantic City

Dameron had been engaged for a summerlong stand at the Paradise, one of Atlantic City's two major black nightclubs, where he would write the backgrounds for a floor show and provide dance music. Atlantic City was strictly segregated in the early 1950s, but it was a popular vacation spot with African Americans nonetheless. Many of the foremost black entertainers performed in these clubs during the summer months, so even though this was in no way a jazz gig, it was potentially a very good place for Dameron to set up shop. He used the same instrumentation at the Paradise that he had used on the Prestige recording—two trumpets; trombone; alto, tenor, and baritone saxes; and piano, bass, and drums, with the addition of congas—and most of the same musicians. The exceptions were Steve Pullum on trombone and Jymie Merritt on bass. The identity of the conga player is unknown. The band members and the audience were in agreement that Tadd had created something exceptional. Art Blakey went to the show one night and felt that it was some of the most beautiful music he had ever heard.[46] Johnny Coles called it "a poppin' little band."[47] Saxophonist Andy McGee and tap dancer Jimmie Slyde were both in Atlantic City that summer and concurred that this band was exceptionally good.[48]

Kellice Swagerty, who would substitute for Cecil Payne from time to time, described the general form of the show, which was built around a cruise to the Carribean. The MC would describe the tour and introduce the acts, then tap dancer Bobby Ephram opened the show, followed by comedienne Anita Nichols. There followed a string of singers and dancers. Interspersed among the singers and dancers would be little scenes featuring actors Princess De-Paure, Joel Noble, and possibly others. Finally the headlining comedy team of Stump and Stumpy would close the show, sometimes with one or two of the other performers, sometimes alone. The band also played for dancing between the shows and, on the weekends, for a breakfast dance as well.[49] On Saturdays they would start at 9:00 P.M. and would not finish until 5:00 the next morning. They made something like $100 or $125 a week, which was not bad for the early 1950s, unless you consider the hours and the fact that the shows ran seven nights a week.

Kellice Swagerty also taped the show one evening. Although the sound quality is poor, it gives us a little more information about the music. While there are some songs by Dameron, like one most likely titled "Haiti," which he would revisit in the 1960s as "Weekend," most of his original work is limited to transitional passages. The bulk of the arrangements were of standard popular songs, such as "I've Got You under My Skin," "Orange Colored Sky," and a medley of "Love for Sale/Temptation/Old Black Magic." This last was for an extended feature for the dancers. In addition to the regular cast, there were guests in the review at the Paradise, and the young Betty Carter is heard on this tape singing "Moonlight in Vermont"[50]

From the standpoint of Tadd Dameron, who was trying to get back into the action after a couple of years of working out of Cleveland, this engagement could have been very important. He had already established himself as a superior arranger for big bands and an important leader of and composer for small jazz bands, and he even had one really great ballad to his credit. Now he showed that he could write for a complicated floor show as well, with the same high quality of composition that distinguished his other work. In the coming years, black entertainers would continue to work their way past the racial discrimination and segregation that permeated American society and become nationally recognized mainstream stars in ever greater numbers. Then there were the established stars who would drop by for the breakfast dance. Kellice Swagerty remembered the time that Sammy Davis Jr., who was working at another Atlantic City club, sat in with the band. "Yeah, early Sunday morning," said Swagerty. "Sammy played the drums about a half-hour. Played everything!"[51] According to Swagerty, other stars, such as Frank Sinatra and Dean Martin, attended as well. This could have been the beginning of a lucrative phase of Dameron's career.

All this came to a grinding halt one Sunday morning when there was a raid on the Paradise.[52] It seems there were a lot of drugs around, especially among the dancers. Someone got word to both Tadd and Cecil Payne, with just enough time for them to find subs for the night. Not surprisingly, recollections of the day's event are murky. One assumes that both Dameron and Payne were worried that it would not be enough just to be clean when the raid happened. Or they may have figured it would be wiser not to be around on general principle. Cecil Payne called Kellice Swagerty to sub for him, and since Swagerty was a cab driver, Payne got a ride to the train station as well. We do not know who sat in for Dameron.

Years later, Swagerty, still angry about being left in the lurch, confronted Payne verbally on a New York subway.[53] Dameron, too, never forgot his anger, but his was directed at Swagerty, whom he thought had tipped off the police. It is not likely that the police were looking for Dameron specifically, since they could have picked him up at his hotel. Still, Tadd's paranoia around this incident suggests he was more than a semi-innocent bystander. Cecil Payne recalled that he and Tadd returned to New York, although not together.

On Quincy Jones's recommendation, Gigi Gryce and Clifford Brown left to join Lionel Hampton, who was about to tour Europe. Benny Golson stayed on to rehearse the new members of the band at the Paradise Club.

The possibility of work with major American stars was not all that was lost in the raid. Dameron was in communication with Ronnie Scott at this time as well. An item in the *New Musical Express*, which appeared, ironically, about the same time as the raid, presented some extraordinary news:

Tadd Dameron, the famous American arranger/composer/pianist who, amongst others [other compositions], wrote "Ladybyrd" [*sic*], a standard bop number all over the world, is due in Europe shortly with a 37-piece all-coloured show, and has been cabled an invitation by Ronnie Scott to score for the Scott band.[54]

This news suggests that Dameron was looking for a way to take the Paradise show, or something like it, to England. How far he had gone with these plans and who was involved we do not know. However, the band that Tadd was being invited to write for was Ronnie Scott's new nine-piece group, similar in instrumentation to the Paradise band. Scott's idea was to try to do something that was both commercially acceptable and still based in the modern jazz idiom, an elusive mix that was part of Dameron's own aesthetic. Neither the tour nor the arrangements for Scott materialized. Thus, a potentially significant opportunity for Tadd to build on his various successes of the previous five years was lost. This, along with the loss of the opportunity to network with established stars provided by the residency at the Paradise, was a most unfortunate turn of events, especially since there also seemed to be little work for arrangers at the end of 1953. Quincy Jones recalled that all of the best arrangers, Dameron among them, were struggling when he came back from the European tour with Lionel Hampton.[55] Still, when things turned around for the arranging community in the next couple of years, Dameron continued to go missing.

Retreat

After his departure from Atlantic City, and the few unproductive months in New York, Tadd retreated to Cleveland. We will never know why Dameron walked away from the momentum he had been building over the previous two years, but the raid and his continuing addiction almost certainly have a connection with his retreat of 1954 and 1955. Still it seems difficult to blame the drugs entirely, for other entertainers and musicians ran afoul of the law over narcotics from time to time but kept going in spite of it. It is ironic that after the summer in Atlantic City, Clifford Brown and Gigi Gryce would go to Paris and lay the foundation of their legendary status (much as Tadd had done only four years earlier), while Dameron, who had helped bring them together, just disappeared. It is also ironic that the younger men built on their European experience upon their return, while Dameron was never to return to the glory of the spring of 1949.

Tadd seems to have lain low for quite a while after the Atlantic City catastrophe, for there appears to be no mention of him anywhere until an ad in the April 2, 1955, issue of the *Call and Post* announced that he would be playing with drummer Jacktown Jackson's Town Criers at the Club Congo, in Cleveland. The other members of the band listed are bassist Bill Brown and tenor saxophonist Tony "Big T" Lovano (father of saxophonist Joe Lovano). What did he do during the two years in between? According to Dameron himself, "I did nothing."[56]

The recollections of Willie Smith shed some light on this period of time. Willie first got to know Tadd in the late 1940s, when Dameron made periodic returns to Cleveland, and the two remained friends until Dameron died. When recalling the times he spent with Tadd Dameron, Smith often had difficulty pinpointing the exact year. Still, some things he recalled are associated with events for which we have dates. For instance, Willie remembered the times that he hung out with Tadd and Thelonious Monk. Dameron and Monk had a friendship that went back to the early 1940s at Minton's and the time they spent with their mutual friend Mary Lou Williams. At one point, perhaps when Tadd was working with Bull Moose Jackson, Tadd introduced Smith to Monk. Later, when Monk came through Cleveland as a traveling "single," he sought Smith's help in putting a band together for his stay there. Willie recalls this as having something to do with the beginning of a modern jazz policy started at the Loop Lounge around 1954. The Loop had been presenting music as early as 1949, but the musicians were locals, such as Tadd's brother, Caesar,[57] who were playing either mainstream swing or rhythm and blues. According to Smith, "The people I was tight with, the people that owned the joint, they wasn't hip to the musicians. All the dudes that come through, I'd get 'em to come to the Loop. So this is how the Loop got real important." Indeed, the Loop Lounge became one of Cleveland's major modern jazz clubs. Charlie Parker, Miles Davis, Chet Baker, Lockjaw Davis, James Moody, and the Max Roach/Clifford Brown Quintet were among the attractions presented at the Loop in 1954 and '55.

The three men, Tadd, Monk, and Willie, would find a piano somewhere and spend all day playing for each other and discussing music. As Smith recalled,

> Tadd happened to be here when Monk came through, and him and Monk was good friends, too. All we'd do during the day is go somewhere and sit down and come up with tunes. Tadd liked to play all the time, anywhere we go, and there's a piano he's gonna sit down and play. Monk, he was in that same type of groove, too. He wasn't ever shy about gettin' with the musicians and doin' stuff. That's why I started workin' with Monk.

Tadd and Willie would run small rehearsal bands as well. Willie was yet another Dameronian, a younger writer who, in the late 1940s, fell under the spell of Demeron's special way with a five-to-ten-piece group. Smith started to do some arranging when he and Benny Bailey were working in California with Scatman Crothers in the mid-1940s. With Dameron in Cleveland for such an extended period of time, and Smith somewhat bored with playing the dances and floor shows that were the staple of his work, the two men found it comforting to try out their own music informally. Smith recalled,

> Tadd had a lot of his music, and he always wanted to play his stuff. He was writing, I was writing, so we were trying to form a little old band. There was a lot of musicians around town that wanted get in on anything that Tadd was doing. And I was on the scene, too, so we were able to get some of the better musicians around town and play some of his things. We'd call rehearsals and have eight, ten guys show up—too many guys to play some of the octet things we had! We started rehearsing just to keep active. Tadd wanted to rehearse, you see.[58]

We do have two other fragments of information regarding the years 1954 and 1955. First is the copyright registration of "Hot House" in 1954 by Bregman, Vocco and Conn. Even though the piece was recorded by Dizzy Gillespie and Charlie Parker in 1945—and BVC copyrighted three other Dameron compositions that year—there is no record of copyright protection for this important and famous melody until December 6, 1954. The written music itself is not in Dameron's hand, but it includes a piano accompaniment with a four-bar introduction that probably came from the composer. Most likely, someone at BVC noticed that the tune was not protected. There are no other copyright registrations of work by Dameron between August 8, 1951, when "John's Delight" (recorded at the 1949 Capitol session) was finally covered, and April 11, 1956, after he had resumed activities in New York.

The second reveals the extent of Dameron's retreat from the world of professional music. By the summer of 1955, Dameron was working in some sort of heavy industry. Trumpeter Sam Noto and saxophonist Charlie Mariano were touring the Midwest with the Stan Kenton band that summer. While on a walk one afternoon, they stopped to have a drink at a bar in an industrial neighborhood. As they were drinking, a group of workers in overalls and hard hats entered the bar, most likely after finishing their shift. One of the men caught Mariano's eye because he looked so much like Tadd Dameron. When the saxophonist pointed him out to his companion, Noto agreed. When the two musicians asked the man who he was, he said that he was indeed Tadd. The three went on to discuss music for a while before going their separate ways.[59]

As much as he had exiled himself, Dameron would still keep in touch with his old friends. Supposedly, sometime in late 1955 or early 1956, Dizzy Gillespie came through Cleveland. While catching up with Tadd, he urged him to come back to New York. Then, on February 6, 1956,[60] Clifford Brown and Max Roach came to Cleveland to play at the Loop for a week. After closing on Sunday, February 12, Brown and Roach had to get back to New York for a recording session on the following Thursday. According to Dameron, "Max said he was so tired he couldn't drive, and he said 'Tadd, why don't you come back to New York?'" So, in return for taking a turn at the wheel, Dameron got a lift back to the center of the jazz universe and another brief period of visibility.

9

1956—Back in Action

After over two years of near-total obscurity, Tadd Dameron returned to the jazz world again in 1956. The first project Dameron was connected with was finishing the Clifford Brown/Max Roach album *At Basin Street*,[1] one of the seminal recordings of the style that would become known as "hard bop." Three of the selections, "Step Lightly (a.k.a. Junior's Arrival)," by Benny Golson, "Gertrude's Bounce," and "Powell's Prances," by Richie Powell, had already been recorded at a session on January 4. The remaining six tunes were recorded at another session on February 17.[2] Dameron was in attendance at this second session and took part in arranging the tunes, two of which he had composed: "Flossie Lou" and "The Scene Is Clean." These two would also be recorded at his own octet session a few weeks later, the session that first introduced "Fontainebleau." All of the musicians present at the Brown/Roach session were capable small-group arrangers, and the results, for the most part, were probably a collaborative effort. Nevertheless, Tadd's presence is clearly heard in his own compositions, and he is credited with arranging his own tunes, as well as Cole Porter's "What Is This Thing Called Love."[3] One of the distinguishing features of the hard-bop style is the attention to arranging details, and the performances on *At Basin Street* include well-thought-out introductions and codas, as well as ensemble interludes. All of these devices were frequently present in Dameron's small-group work of the late 1940s, and his involvement in this recording is significant.

Just three weeks later, on Friday, March 9, Dameron was in Rudy Van Gelder's studio with a band of his own to make a record for Prestige, using material he may have developed while leading rehearsal bands in Cleveland in 1954 and '55. On hand were Kenny Dorham on trumpet, Henry Coker on trombone,

Sahib Shihab on alto sax, Joe Alexander on tenor sax, Cecil Payne on baritone sax, John Simmons on bass, and Shadow Wilson on drums. The title track on the LP released from this session is "Fontainebleau," a through-composed piece with no solos—the next work in his "Soulphony" series.[4] The rest of the album has suggestions of a band concept that is never quite realized.

Some of the weaknesses of this album may be the result of Prestige's approach to production: while Prestige released many important records, it was not known for providing much, if any, support for rehearsals. On his 1953 album, which features more consistent performances, Dameron had the advantage of having worked with several of the musicians just prior to the recording. The *Fontainebleau* LP is a mixture of the introduction of a very important Dameron composition, "Fontainebleau," one other really strong performance, "Delirium," and three not-too-well-focused takes, "Flossie Lou," "The Scene Is Clean," and "Bule-Beige." It gives the impression that Tadd was not really ready to make a complete album. Nevertheless, the record was well received and earned four stars (out of five) in a *Down Beat* review.

"Flossie Lou" is a contrafact of Johnny Mercer and Harry Warren's "Jeepers Creepers," and both the quintet and octet arrangements are rather simple. The Brown/Roach version has a four-bar introduction in the piano, followed by the trumpet carrying the melody throughout and the tenor sax cycling among counterlines, harmony, and octave doubling. There are no ensembles, and the tune ends suddenly with no coda. The octet version, a feature for trombonist Henry Coker, has an eight-bar introduction that returns at the end of the arrangement. The A section of the tune consists of two short phrases and one long phrase, the former played by the ensemble in unison and the latter harmonized with some little contrapuntal details as well. Dameron paraphrases the bridge melody at the piano, and the last A is the same as the first two. Coker takes three choruses with only the rhythm section, and the piece concludes—without returning to the tune—with the introduction, a short cadenza from Coker, and a "stinger" from the ensemble. The Brown/Roach version is taken at a moderately brisk 180 beats per minute. The octet version is more sedate at 120.

"The Scene Is Clean" is one of Dameron's most striking tunes. In ABAC form, with a unique chord sequence, it is both harmonically sophisticated and memorably lyrical. The two versions are fairly simple in their arrangement, both sharing the same rhumba-based, vamp introduction, except that Brown, Roach, and company extend the introduction considerably, from eight measures to twenty-eight. In the quintet version the tune is played in octaves, and it has a little tag phrase in the last bar. The octet version is fully harmonized, but there are no interludes or backgrounds. On the quintet recording Brown, Rollins,

Powell, and Roach all solo. Interestingly, Powell "comps" for Roach's solo, an unusual but probably appropriate gesture, for the tune is complex in its harmonies,
and Roach was a particularly melodic drummer. On the octet recording only
Dameron solos, shying away from his own complex harmonic creation by soloing over "rhythm" As with his favorite bridge—the same sequence he used for
the solos in "Theme of No Repeat." This time he does not manage to make a
good case for this incongruity (see chap. 8). The quintet version ends by returning to the vamp after restating the opening melody. The octet version has no
coda and simply ends with the last note of the tune.

"Delirium," a feature for Dameron's fellow Clevelander, tenor saxophonist
Joe Alexander, is the liveliest of the five tracks on the *Fontainebleau* LP. Next
to the title piece, it is also the most fully developed. The melody is written as a
call-and-response between the ensemble and the tenor saxophonist. Beginning
with an eight-bar introduction (notated in the copyright deposit), it has two
two-bar figures, each with two bars open for Alexander's improvised response.
The tune itself continues with this call-and-response format, but here the
segments are four measures instead of two. The harmonic sequence is, again,
rhythm changes in the As and the common bridge. One of the indications of
Tadd Dameron's powers of invention is the way he can return so often to this
particular harmonic "well" and continue to come up with distinct and memorable compositions.

The whole piece is structured as an arch. After the opening chorus, there is
a two-chorus solo by Alexander, the second chorus accompanied by a riff background in the ensemble, followed by a two-chorus solo by trumpeter Kenny
Dorham, which could be thought of as the keystone of the arch. Alexander returns for another two choruses, the second of which is again accompanied by a
riff in the other horns. Finally the tune is played as at the beginning, and there
is a cadenza-type coda.

"The Bula-Beige" actually dates from 1953 and can be heard on an obscure
Italian release of informal recordings of Clifford Brown made during the Dameron Band's stand at the Paradise Club in Atlantic City.[5] It is a twelve-bar blues,
which is used in a loose, jam-session sort of way on the *Fontainebleau* LP but
gets considerable development in an arrangement for the Dorsey brothers, for
whom Dameron was writing at the time. In the Dameron performance, the pianist plays a chorus of blues in which he suggests the riff, which makes up the
tune. Then the ensemble plays the tune in unison for two more choruses. There
is a series of long solos from Dameron, Coker, Alexander, Shihab, and Payne; a
two-chorus waking solo from bassist John Simmons; and a final two choruses
from Dameron again. The piece concludes with a two-chorus ensemble, playing

new melodic material that is structured in a through-composed manner, much the same as an improvisation.

The big-band arrangement, which was written around the same time, is in an arch form—very much like the design of "Delirium"—opening with muted trumpets stating the riff theme in unison, first soli, then accompanied by background figures in the trombones and saxes. Next, alto saxophonist Jimmy Dorsey solos over an ensemble background that develops some of the ideas in the previous chorus's background. This is followed by a trumpet soli, with saxophone-section background, and a trombone soli without background. Dorsey returns for another chorus, with yet another background. This one with open trumpets foreshadows their lead in the last two choruses, which are a re-orchestration of the final two heard in the octet recording. The Dorsey brothers seem to have liked this chart, since they are reported to have recorded it as part of live broadcasts on three occasions in 1956.

"Fontainebleau"

"Fontainebleau" is the most outstanding of the pieces in the vein of "Nearness," "Soulphony," and—as has been suggested—"Lyonia." That is, it is a composition without improvised solos,[6] written for jazz ensemble and requiring a jazz sensibility on the part of the players. The work, inspired by a visit to the famous French palace, is in four parts: an introduction, "Le Forêt," "Les Cygnes," and "L'Adieu." "Le Forêt" refers to the vast game refuge that surrounds the palace, "Les Cygnes" to the swans swimming in the decorative ponds and canals that are part of the grounds, and "L'Adieu" to Napoleon Bonaparte's departure from the palace to begin his exile on the island of Elba. The whole piece is held together by subtle manipulations of various motifs, similar to the technique used in "Nearness" and "Soulphony in Three Hearts." There are three distinct versions of the piece, Dameron 1956, Dameron 1962, and Goodman 1962,[7] as well as a copyright deposit lead sheet. The existence of these four somewhat different expressions of one of these extended compositions is exceptional in the body of Dameron's work.

The first of the motifs is a descending triplet of eighth notes, followed by a note of longer value. This returns in many guises, the most readily recognizable its repetition in different voices at the end of the piece, as Napoleon bids farewell to the place that stood for his greatest accomplishments. While the intervals are not exactly the same, the relationship is quite clear enough to refer back to the beginning of the piece and its ominous tone, which is now to be understood as a foreshadowing of the somber ending. This motif is heard at other points during the course of the piece as well. At the end of the fourth phrase of "Le Forêt" the motif is heard with the triplets[8] ascending in the upper voices, answered by a chromatic descending line of three eighth notes and a half note, a clearly audible variation on the opening motif. As he has done elsewhere, Dameron plays with what we can call the "poetic rhythm" of this motif. Where in the opening the stress is on the triplets, in "Le Forêt" it is on the longer note. The opening motif also shows up in the fourth, fifth, and sixth phrases of "Les Cygnes."

Two other unifying elements in "Fontainebleau" are the rhythmic figure of a quarter note and two eighth notes and manipulations of the *clave* rhythm. The first rhythm is gently suggested by the baritone saxophone in a solo passage at the end of the introduction. It then generates most of the melodic rhythm of the entire "Le Forêt" section. The figure also generates the last four bars before the beginning of the transition to the last section, "L'Adieu." The final appearance of this rhythmic figure is in the ostinato at the beginning of "L'Adieu."

The clave, in which pulses are grouped $3+3+2$,[9] shows up clearly for the first time in the first six measures of "Les Cygnes." The high obligato figure uses this clave rhythm, and the melody in the lower instruments is organized around the same rhythm but augmented so that it covers two measures. This rhythm is found again in the low voices, at the beginning of the transition from "Les Cygnes" to "L'Adieu," this time diminished rhythmically, so that it creates a doubling of tempo. The clave is also found at the end of the piece, augmented rhythmically, where it creates the illusion of an allargando.

Near the end of the piece we hear another unifying element, the reappearance of the beginning of the first phrase of "Les Cygnes" at the beginning of "L'Adieu." In addition, this phrase is followed by a phrase incorporating the opening motif in its final form, which will be heard by itself in the following measures. There are more subtle motivic connections between the sections of this work, but these should make the point regarding the thematic coherence of "Fontainebleau."[10]

Carmen McRae

A few weeks after recording "Fontainebleau," on March 28, Dameron conducted an orchestra in four of his arrangements for Carmen McRae's *Blue Moon* LP.[11] The songs were "Blue Moon," by Rodgers and Hart; "I Was Doing All Right," by George and Ira Gershwin; Irving Berlin's "I'm Putting All My Eggs in One Basket"; and Joe Mooney's somewhat obscure "Nowhere." With the exception of his work for Pearl Bailey, this was the first time since working with Sarah Vaughan ten years before that Dameron had a chance to write for a truly great singer.[12] Accordingly, he gives Carmen the kind of strong, swinging backgrounds that she can really dig into, which serve as an aesthetic foil for the more pop-oriented string arrangements that Jimmy Mundy was commissioned to write for the balance of the LP.

Tadd's arrangements are compact, fitting the requirements of jukebox singles, and all follow the same general design. Nonetheless, they all fit the singer so well that it seems quite likely that Dameron worked out some details with McRae before writing the arrangements. The two had a mutual connection in McRae's former husband, Kenny Clarke, and no doubt shared many other friends and associates. In addition, Dameron continued to freelance as a pianist on the East Coast in the 1950–53 period and may have previously accompanied the singer in live performance. When listening to these arrangements, it is tempting to picture the two of them sitting at a piano, exchanging ideas on how they should go.

The band's exact instrumentation is not documented, but it sounds as if there are three trumpets, three (perhaps only two) trombones, five saxes, piano, guitar, bass, and drums. While Dameron, in the manner of his generation of arrangers, does not use cross-sectional combinations of instruments, he does manage to exploit the varied colors of the ensemble to wonderful effect. For instance, in "I Was Doin' Alright" he uses frequent variation of the instrumental colors to create depth to the background for the song, as well as a sense of giddy joy that reflects the lyric. Careful attention to dynamics, in addition to the shift in instrumental colors, helps to bring out the full effect of this arrangement. We should remember that Dameron was directing the band on this session.

Except for the "Big Ten" and the arrangement of "Nothin' for Nothin'" for Pearl Bailey, Dameron did not include guitar in his bands. However, he makes good use of it here. Again, dynamics are key to his good results. Sometimes the instrument is just strummed subtly as part of the rhythm section. Other times, as in "Blue Moon," the guitar comes forward as another melodic voice in the ensemble. With the increased prominence of the guitar since the late 1960s, this sort of use of the instrument in large-ensemble jazz writing has by now become quite common. In 1956, although not unheard of, it was still somewhat unusual.

As Billy Vera comments in his notes to a reissue of this album, "By 1956, when the album *Blue Moon* was recorded, McRae was on the verge of a major breakthrough, as America[ns were] becoming familiar with her via the small screens in their living rooms."[13] Television was changing the entertainment business, and many of the fine musicians who had come up through the big bands and the small club scenes in New York, Los Angeles, Chicago, and other cities were beginning to have an influence on American music again. In addition, Dizzy Gillespie was about to start a world tour as a cultural ambassador for the United States—he already had "Cool Breeze" in the book, and Dameron was writing for Tommy Dorsey. In spite of the unevenness of the *Fontainebleau* album, Tadd was once again in a good position to make a comeback.

First Arrest

Despite his renewed musical activity, it was not his recordings that made Dameron the subject of this item in the New York *Daily News* on Tuesday, April 10:

JAZZ MAN'S BAIL 10G IN DOPE RAP

[Wednesday, April 11, 1956] Jazz pianist Tadd Damerson [*sic*], 39, of 122 W. 47th St., was held in $10,000 bail yesterday in Felony Court for action by the grand jury on a charge of possessing narcotics with intent to sell. A similar charge against harmonica player Florence Key, 32, who lives with him, was dismissed for lack of evidence. They were arrested in their home Monday night after a half-ounce packet of heroin was found on a window sill.[14]

Although a half ounce may sound like an insignificant amount, this was a serious offense. The average heroin addict uses about a gram, or maybe a little more, of the drug per day. Given that there are approximately thirty-one grams in an ounce, Dameron was in possession of at least fifteen doses. According to law-enforcement personnel familiar with drug offenses, this was probably a case of one person picking up doses for several people and then redistributing them. It is most likely that Dameron would have received something of a wholesale discount and would have earned his own fix this way.

As for the dismissal of Florence Key, this may have been part of the method of making the arrest. According to a fellow inmate of Dameron's at the Federal Prison Hospital (where he would be incarcerated in 1958), most of the people at the hospital had been arrested under the Boggs-Daniels Act (the Narcotics Control Act of 1956). Under this federal law, anyone caught selling narcotics would be put away for five years for the first offense, ten for the second, and life for the third.[15] This fellow inmate, who requested anonymity and will be referred to as "A", went on to say that many of those arrested under Boggs-Daniels were victims of entrapment by U.S. Treasury agents. The agents would get a captured user to make an introduction to another user, and then the agent would get the second user to obtain drugs for him. The first, and supposedly less significant, addict would not be prosecuted. This was how Tadd was caught the second time, in 1958.[16] The relatively small but still significant amount of the drug and the obscure girlfriend, whose charges were dropped, point to the likelihood that the city or state police had fashioned their strategies along federal lines.

In May, Dameron was indicted, and the entire charge was expanded to three offenses: possessing narcotics, possessing narcotics with intent to sell, and possessing a hypodermic needle. We do not know when his sentence was handed down, but the information we have comes from the October 3 issue of *Down Beat*.[17] Typically, sentencing takes place some time after a conviction, at the convenience of the court, and it is possible that this did not take place until August or September. When sentenced, Dameron was given three to five years in a workhouse. However, the sentence was suspended, and Tadd was put on probation. No further information seems to be available regarding the trial. Records of the arrest have gone missing, and there was no mention of this sentence when Dameron was later brought before federal court in 1958 (see chap. 10). We will probably never have the answers to the questions these facts raise.

With so high a bail, we are left to wonder who would have had this much money to post. The first person to come to mind would be Tadd's brother, Caesar. Between his various business interests and real estate, he may have been able to come up with this much cash. Willie Smith, who knew both brothers, opined later that posting bail for Tadd was one of the issues of contention between the two brothers. He also implied that there may have been other arrests, but we know of only this and the second one, in 1958.[18]

Two other people who may have come to Dameron's aid entered his life around this time. One is Maely Dufty, who, as will be discussed later, most likely became friendly with Tadd before his 1958 incarceration. It is not known if she would have had the resources to contribute more than a portion of the total needed. The other is Richard Carpenter, a shadowy figure in the jazz world. Until 1956, Dameron's main publisher had been Bregman, Vocco and Conn, which held the rights to various titles, including some of Dameron's best-known work.[19] All five of the compositions released on the *Fontainebleau* LP are held by BVC and were registered, ironically, on April 11, 1956, the day of his first arrest. The compositions recorded on the *Mating Call* LP, which would be recorded in November, were instead published by companies owned by Carpenter.

Richard Carpenter is reputed to have taken advantage of addicted musicians by signing publishing agreements with them and advancing them money against their royalties. This in itself is not a crime. If we understand the situation correctly, the only offense committed by Carpenter was withholding royalty payments and accounting statements without justification. Richard Carpenter certainly had some company in the commitment of this offense. What is particularly troubling about his business practices, however, is that he dealt almost exclusively with addicts, who were, by their very nature, ill equipped to defend their intellectual property rights. Dameron's change of publishers between the prearrest *Fontainebleau* and his next album, recorded in November, makes us wonder if this was repayment for a loan or for some other favor. Tadd must have known Carpenter's reputation, and by all accounts, he had always enjoyed a good relationship with the more prestigious Bregman, Vocco and Conn.

There can be little doubt that Dameron was under considerable stress in the spring and summer of 1956. Either he had to raise $10,000, or he had to spend at least some time in jail. There also would have been strain on his family relationships. One can imagine the grief his arrest must have brought to his mother. They had been working together on and off for five or six years at Dameron's Hut, and she probably at least sensed that he was in some sort of trouble. Willie Smith, Buddy Crewe, and Myron Styles, who knew both Tadd and Caesar, indicated that the bothers were often at odds. It would not have been easy for Tadd to ask Caesar for bail money or be in debt to him. Further, the arrest itself would not have helped their relationship. Whether an individual is habituated or addicted—and by now there is little doubt of Dameron's addiction—the struggle with drugs causes a complex kind of anguish, posing extreme challenges for even the heartiest of souls, not to mention one with the stresses in his life that Dameron was subject to. There is even some indication that the legibility of his manuscripts was suffering. In all the examples available, Dameron's handwriting, whether of music or text, is always neat and clear. However, George Vedegis, one of Dorsey's copyists, is known to have complained about the sloppiness of the charts Dameron wrote for his employer around this time and how difficult they were to work with.[20]

The October announcement of Tadd's arrest and trial in *Down Beat* ended with a positive note: "Dameron is now lining up a new Prestige LP in which all his best known instrumental hits of the 1940s will be revived, among them 'The Squirrel,' 'Our Delight,' and 'Hot House.'" It goes on to mention his writing for Tommy Dorsey. Sadly, less than two months after the publication of this item, Dorsey would die in a freak choking accident.

Instead of releasing a reprise of his earlier successes, as *Down Beat* had suggested, Dameron now recorded an album of six new compositions, *Mating Call*, featuring John Coltrane. It has been said that this recording was to feature a quintet but that the trumpet player did not make it to the session. However, Bob Weinstock, the session's producer, confirmed that this was always planned as a quartet date.[21]

The choice of Coltrane for this project was probably not a casual decision. 'Trane had a relationship with Willie Smith that went back to the time when he was with Dizzy Gillespie, in 1951. Smith recalled that "[Coltrane] used to come down on my gig and sit in."[22] Smith went on to say, "He worked with Bull Moose, yes he did. He went out on the road with him for a minute. But he came right on back, he didn't stay all that long."[23] If Coltrane gigged a bit with Jackson, it would have been around the same time that Dameron was working with that band. Perhaps of greater significance, Coltrane was a member of the Cleveland-based Gay Crosse band for two stints in 1952: one from sometime in January to late March, the other during the last two months of that year.[24] Clearly, Coltrane and Dameron were in Cleveland at the same time and shared friends and associates, including Benny Golson. Dameron, with his keen ear for talent, had most likely been watching Coltrane's progress and may have had this collaboration in mind for some time.

Although less ambitious than *Fontainebleau*, *Mating Call* yielded two of Dameron's most popular compositions, "Soultrane" and "On a Misty Night," as well as four other titles. In addition to John Coltrane, for whom "Soultrane" is named, the band included Philly Joe Jones and bassist John Simmons. "Soultrane" is a thirty-two-bar, AABA ballad with a subtle and graceful melody in which Dameron avoids using any of his personal clichés, such as his favorite harmonic formulas. It is eloquent enough as a composition that a straightforward instrumental ballad presentation of it is all that is needed.

"On a Misty Night" is most likely a contrafact of Dubin and Warren's "September in the Rain" (again thirty-two bars in AABA form), but Dameron has taken the model as just a starting point. For instance, the bridge of "September" follows a commonly used harmonic pattern closely related to the one that Dameron often uses, but he modifies it just enough it to make it something unique to this particular composition:

Key of Eb:

"September in the Rain" bridge changes: .

Bbmi7 Eb7 | Bbmi7 Eb7 | AbMa7 | AbMa7 |

Cmi7 F7 | Cmi7 F7 | Fmi7 | Bb7 ||

"On a Misty Night" bridge changes:

Bmi7 E7 | B♭mi7 E♭7 | A♭Ma7 | A♭Ma7 |

D♭mi7 G♭7 | Cmi7 F7 | Fmi7 | B♭7 ||

As played on the *Mating Call* LP, "On a Misty Night" has an open bridge. Dameron solos on the opening statement, and Simmons solos on the closing one. There is a bridge melody written in the copyright deposit that was filed in March of 1962. The music appears to be written by Dameron, but with the exception of a posthumous version with a lyric written by Georgie Fame, this melody is never used. It is not the bridge that Dameron used in his 1962 recording, *The Magic Touch*; the arrangement for Benny Goodman; or the arrangement for Sonny Stitt. In all three of these instances the bridge melody is one that comes from the first chorus of Dameron's piano solo on the *Mating Call* LP.

The other four tunes from this set are the title track, "Mating Call," "Super Jet," "Gnid," and "Romas." "Mating Call" is in AABA form, but the As are eight measures long, and the bridge is sixteen measures in length, giving it more weight than is usual. The harmonic structure is unique to the tune, with the A section starting as if it might be heading for the key of B♭, the subdominant of the actual key, F. In a general way, this is similar to the A of "What Is This Thing Called Love." The bridge takes a long meandering journey from A♭ back to the opening Cmi7 through two sequential eight-bar segments. The first four bars of the melody, with their vamplike Cmi7 | D♭9 | oscillation, are used as an introduction and as a coda. In the bridge of the out-going chorus, Dameron improvises two-bar exchanges with Jones.

"Gnid," also known as "Handy Andy," is a more conventional AABA composition. In the recording, it has a lyrical eight-bar introduction, with an eight-bar interlude tagged at the last bar of the form, which also serves as a coda. As with "Mating Call," the harmonic sequence in the bridge begins in the key of the bIII, A♭ in the key of F. "Super Jet," which might be a contrafact of "Sometimes I'm Happy'" is an up-tempo tune in ABAC form in which the A are built around a descending sequence of dominant 7 chords, B♭9 | A♭9 | G♭9 | F9|. The tension created by this is released by the more diatonic B and C sections. "Romas" is a slow blues that does not seem to have a clear theme, in spite of Chet Baker's 1965 recording of a blues with this title. It is just a good old-fashioned slow blues "jam."

Throughout this set of performances, one is impressed by the evolution of Tadd Dameron's piano playing. Where in the previous recordings he seems to have shied away from more challenging chord progressions, as in "The Scene Is Clean," here he takes everything in stride. He also continues to break free of his own personal clichés. For John Coltrane this was another in a series of important albums he played on in 1956. These include the best of the Prestige recordings of Miles Davis's first great quintet, as well as his collaboration with Sonny Rollins, titled *Tenor Maddness,* and his recordings with the revered but obscure composer and pianist Elmo Hope.

When one considers the state of Dameron's personal life at this time, it is striking that his music maintains a kind of serenity, in spite of the chaos and strife that surrounded him. In this, he is like Wolfgang Mozart, whose music never reveals the emotions in his life but seems to exist in a world of its own—most notably the pieces written at the time of his mother's death. Some artists use their art as a cathartic outlet for the emotional elements of their lives; others, such as Dameron, use it as a sanctuary. As he stated so clearly to Barry Ulanov in the 1947 *Metronome* profile, Tadd felt that his mission was to create beauty and harmony in the world as a balm for the ugliness and conflict so often present in human existence. Whatever one may think of the way Tadd Dameron conducted his life, one has to admit that he was steadfast in his commitment to his artistic principles. Nowhere is this more evident than in the music he created in 1956.

Throughout the 1950s, Tadd Dameron continued to develop as both a composer and a pianist, in spite of the mounting pressures in his personal life. While in comparison with the 1940s, his output is rather small in these years, the quality of this work is almost always first rate, and he is always contemporary with the leading trends in jazz. In the 1953 recording there is much in common with the work of Charles Mingus and his Jazz Workshop colleagues of the same period. It is interesting to listen to the pieces released on *A Study in Dameronia* in the context of Mingus's Savoy release from 1954, *Charlie Mingus Presents: Jazz Composers Workshop.*[25] The formal and harmonic complexity and the general tone of the music are noticeably similar, even with the distinct voices of the two composers.

Dameron's 1956 small-band work shows him to be in at the beginning of the stylistic trends generally known as "hard bop." We have the rhumba-based groove alternated with straightahead swing, a device with its roots in the late 1940s that really comes to the fore in the 1950s. There is also his move toward new formal structures, as suggested in the tune "Mating Call." Dameron would continue along this path in his writing from the 1960s, along with the composers associated with the "hard bop" movement. Additionally, if our assumption about the date is correct, "Duke Ellington's Opening Theme," with its long, essentially modal passages contrasted with sections of functional harmony, should be included in any analysis of this period. In spite of the fact that he released only three albums in the 1950s, many people know Dameron mainly, if not only, for this particular body of work. It is a body of work that is remarkably rich in its variety, and it represents the mature flowering of his musical development in the 1940s.

10

1957–1961—Incarceration

After *Mating Call*, only a couple of pieces of Dameron's music survive from the 1956–58 period. The year 1957 is another one for which we have little information, but he was probably in New York much of the time. Presumably, he would have needed to report to his probation officer on a regular basis. Jackie McLean, who worked with Art Blakey in 1956 and '57, remembered Tadd dropping by Birdland when they were playing there. McLean recalled that Dameron would join the band for a few numbers and sit in one of the booths "gossiping" with Blakey on the breaks. As a younger musician he did not get to know Dameron, and so he was not party to the conversations.[1] Also, in July of 1957, Woody Herman recorded a new composition written for him by Dameron, titled, depending on one's source, "Slightly Groovy," "Slight Groove," or "Small Crevice."[2] "Small Crevice" is a trombone feature written to spotlight Bill Harris. It may have first been documented in a live recording made in June 1957[3] and was recorded later in the year for Verve. "Small Crevice" appears to be a variation on another tune, "The Rampage," which was submitted for copyright along with "Handy Andy" (the Bregman, Vocco and Conn version of "Gnid") in the fall of 1956. Identical in ABAC form and chord changes, these two tunes also share significant portions of melodic material in the B and C sections. As heard on the Verve recording, the arrangement is brief but exciting, showing off both Harris and the band to good advantage.

There is evidence of Dameron writing for Stan Kenton in 1958. There are two items, presumably parts, labeled "Look, Stop and Listen" in the Kenton Collection at the University of North Texas. These are dated 1958, and pianist George Ziskind reported Tadd mentioning that he had written "Look, Stop and Listen" while at Rikers Island (the prison of New York City),[4] where he was held after his 1958 arrest. Unfortunately, these parts are among many that have become so dry that opening them for viewing would cause them to disintegrate. Efforts are being made to save these manuscripts, but for the time being they are off-limits. Fortunately, the score itself is in the collection of Bob Curnow, and it presents an arrangement of "Look, Stop and Listen" significantly different from the version Dameron would record on his own *Magic Touch* LP in 1962. We will consider the two versions together in the next chapter. There is a curious notation on the back of the score paper: "Look, Stop + Listen" arr. by "[Tadd's brand, with the T, A, and D incorporated into one symbol] + Jeru." Beneath this it says, "Forward to: Stan Kenton 941 La Cienaga Blvd., Hollywood, California." "Jeru," Gerry Mulligan's nickname, is crossed out and just barely visible. One does not know exactly what to make of this. The piece is so unlike anything Mulligan ever wrote that there is little question that he had no hand in composing it. Perhaps Jeru was entrusted with getting the score to Kenton.

Another piece from this time is the waltz "This Night of Stars," with a lyric by Carl Sigman. It is the only waltz in the known body of Dameron's work—although there is a reference to "two 'bop' waltzes" in the July 1949 *Music Fare* article. The tune is only thirty-two bars long, rather short for a piece in 3/4. The melody and harmonies are graceful yet deceptively difficult. It is one of those melodies that sounds simple but is actually rather sophisticated. The opening interval is a diminished fifth (E to B♭ in the key of C), and the melody is harmonized with several altered chords. To date, the tune has never been recorded, but the author has performed it. The response of both fellow musicians and audience members has been notably positive.

Second Arrest

On January 17, 1958, Tadd Dameron was indicted in federal court. The indictment reads, "The Grand Jury charges: On or about the 13th day of December 1957 in the Southern District of New York, the defendant, unlawfully, wilfully and knowingly did receive, conceal, sell and facilitate the transportation, concealment and sale of a narcotic drug . . . heroin."

Dameron was in possession of more than an ounce of the drug this time, and he was also charged with evading the taxes that would have been due on the drugs and their sale, a customary additional charge in such cases. The court records reveal that he was indicted under his professional name, Tadd, not his legal name. While perhaps this was somewhat odd for a serious legal action, it seems not to have mattered to the federal authorities. At the initial hearing Dameron waived the five-thousand-dollar bail. At the trial on February 19, represented only by a court-appointed lawyer, he pled guilty to the possession and sale charges, but not to the tax charges. Tadd's willingness to accept incarceration for his offense seems to have earned compassion from the authorities, for they accepted the not-guilty plea regarding the taxes.

Dameron was sentenced only to the five-year charge for his first federal offense, and he was not required to serve further time for the local parole violation once he was released from federal prison. It would seem that the previous arrest did not count against him. Still, this would have counted as a probation violation, but as far as we know, the city or state never brought charges against him for this. This leads us to wonder if Richard Carpenter had possibly provided more than just a loan for the earlier bail.

When Dameron's arrest records were requested, the City of New York could not find any for him being arrested in 1956.[5] It is beyond the resources of the author to solve this mystery, but it may explain the oddly powerful hold Carpenter seems to have had on Dameron later. Carpenter was known to be both crafty and unscrupulous. Given that police and court records were on paper and kept in filing cabinets, it would not have been impossible for an ally of Carpenter's inside the courts to remove the respective documents. While this is just speculation on the part of the author, we will see that after Dameron's release from the U.S. Public Health Service Hospital in Lexington, Kentucky, in 1961, Carpenter was able to get him to repeatedly go against his own best interests in signing over his royalties. Clearly, Dameron's debt to Carpenter was profound.

Dameron seemed to welcome his sentence to the Public Health Service Hospital. His sister-in-law, Dorothy, recalled Tadd expressing his willingness and even relief at going there. She said, "He wanted to get himself straightened out,"[6] and with the exception of being separated from the working jazz scene, his stay at the prison seems to have been benign. After being held for two more months in New York City, Dameron was moved, first to a facility in Virginia and then to the hospital in Kentucky. This was a minimum-security facility, where addicts were also able to go for treatment without incriminating themselves. As one inmate put it, "It was the best of all bad worlds."

Instead of cells, each inmate had a room, and it was hoped that through the provision of this hospital service, the problem of drug addiction could be dealt with in a humane way. If the Boggs-Daniels Act was meant to be the stick, then the hospital was the carrot. Still, the reality does not seem to have been so ideal. Some addicts are said to have used the place as a free vacation, since it was apparently rather porous when it came to excluding drugs. Some who were there at the time have humorous recollections of inmates being discharged in the morning only to return in the evening because they had been arrested for possession again during the day. This is probably an exaggeration, but there is likely some truth to it as well. However, by all indications, Dameron did take advantage of the hospital's services and really did kick his habit.

The accounts of Dameron's stay at Lexington are conflicting in some of their details, but all agree that he spent his time at Lexington well. When he first came to the hospital, he may have been isolated to get through the period of detoxification. At the same time, he may well have already gotten the drug out of his system during the previous four months of detention.[7] However, he was soon involved with musical activities at the hospital. In keeping with the positive philosophy of the institution, which stressed rehabilitation rather than punishment, creative activities were encouraged. With all the musicians who were there, either voluntarily or as a result of arrest, it was possible to have a very good band. Rabbi Joseph Rosenbloom, one of the chaplains at Narco, as the hospital was named by many of those associated with it, remembered the band this way:

> The big band at Narco was especially interesting because almost all the members were good soloists as well as good ensemble musicians. The band had an excellence that would have been difficult to match on "the street"; it needed to make no compromises. There were some special and unusual problems in keeping a big band going at Narco. Some of the patients were at the hospital voluntarily, and they were free to come and go. As a result, the turnover of personnel was unusually high. But even this turnover could be an advantage to the musicians, for the writers had a chance to experiment with different combinations of instruments and a variety of voicings. The players in the band also learned to be flexible in their playing, to adapt themselves to good ensemble work in spite of constantly changing section mates.[8]

Among the better-known players who are said to have been at Lexington during Tadd's stay there were trumpeters Chet Baker and Hobart Dotson, trombonists Bob Burgess and Charles Greenlee, and saxophonist Sam Rivers. Baker and Rivers would resume association with Dameron after his release in 1961. Tadd also found an old band mate in the rhythm section, bassist Curly Russell. The drummer was an interesting character named Bott Brooks, whom fellow inmate and guitarist Carl Hayse described as a "jail house drummer." Brooks did not play on the outside, only when he was in jail or at the hospital. Nevertheless, Hayse remembered him as a very good drummer who played in a style that was an amalgam of Art Blakey and Max Roach. Hayse also described one of Dameron's rehearsal strategies: he would rehearse the horns separately from the rhythm section and would have them play at a slow tempo in order to perfect their execution of the parts.[9]

Perhaps it was the instability of the band that caused Dameron to lose interest in it after a while. "A"'s recollection was that Tadd did not take part in the activities of the band except for possibly a little writing, preferring to hang out with a small group of favorites. However, both Carl Hayse and Tadd himself indicated that he was deeply involved with the band at first. Tadd claimed to have taken over conducting the band upon his arrival, and given his love for rehearsing bands, this seems quite likely. Hayse remembered that Dameron put him out of the band once he discovered that he could not read. The guitarist also remembered Tadd writing out some of Sy Oliver's Lunceford charts like "Saxology," "The Worm," and "One for the Book" from memory, and Sam Rivers has said that Tadd gave him one of these charts, which he still has.[10]

Whether working with the band or alone, Dameron was musically active, and he spent a lot of time at the piano. There was the upright in the rehearsal room and a Steinway grand at the home of Dr. Diamond, one of the staff members who had a house on the hospital grounds. Dameron was either assigned or requested the job of servant at the doctor's house, where he cooked for the family. Tadd was reputed by several people to be as creative a cook as he was a composer, able to make a delicious meal out of whatever was at hand. Later on in his time at Lexington, he was allowed to go off the hospital grounds to work as a domestic in the home of James H. Crawford. The Crawfords were apparently very supportive, providing Tadd time at their piano for practicing and writing. Dameron said to Ira Gitler that he was able to make extensive use of their piano, working "until it was time to go in, until I finished writing. They'd be so happy that I'd be writing."

Smooth as the Wind

Since he would have been working for the Crawford family toward the end of his incarceration, it is quite likely that some of the writing Tadd was doing at their piano was for a Riverside LP featuring trumpeter Blue Mitchell. Orrin Keepnews wrote in the notes to the record:

> It was Cannonball Adderley, a fellow-Floridian and old friend of Blue's, who first advanced the idea of recording him with "a few strings." In further discus-

sions with Blue and Benny Golson, the concept of full-scale brass and string backing was developed, and the pivotal suggestion of calling on Tadd Dameron was made. Dameron, long an important figure in modern jazz, is a brilliant and original writer, regarded by many of today's best young arrangers (including Golson) as their major influence and inspiration. His adventurous, richly detailed and always thoroughly sympathetic scoring of most of these selections, including his own two new compositions, is clearly the core of this album.[11]

The project was developed through the mail and possibly through phone calls. As Keepnews later recalled, "I wrote to him and broached the idea of him doing these arrangements for us from there. He did remember Blue and he was very enthusiastic about it. We picked tunes at long distance and he did those charts." Benny Golson conducted the session and contributed three of his own arrangements. Almost ten years after their time with Bull Moose Jackson, the two men were working together again.

Tadd was generally happy with the results, but he said that under different circumstances he would have done some things differently. He said later, "I like 'But Beautiful' and 'Smooth As The Wind,' but on some other things, the strings played so loud. If I'd have been there . . . because no one can direct my arrangements like I can. But it's a good record. You have to be there [to get the results you want]."[12]

The two new compositions Dameron wrote for the Blue Mitchell project were the title tune, "Smooth as the Wind," and a very interesting twelve-bar blues called simply "A Blue Time." He also arranged the American song-book tunes "But Beautiful," "The Best Things in Life Are Free," "For Heaven's Sake," "The Nearness of You," and Horace Silver's "Strollin'." The inclusion of this last tune and of the Benny Golson arrangement of Silver's "Peace" deepens the significance of this recording in expressing the importance of Dameron's work. Here we have a collaboration between a master and a former student (who had by now become a well-regarded artist in his own right), along with the compositions of an outstanding modern jazz musician who acknowledged Dameron's considerable influence on his own work. The recording of Blue Mitchell's *Smooth as the Wind* was finished on March 30, 1961, and in many ways this must have seemed an auspicious event, with Tadd's release so close at hand. It appears the record was well received. Barbara Gardner gave it four and a half stars in her *Down Beat* review.

As he had demonstrated in 1946, with the Musicraft recordings of Sarah Vaughan, Dameron could write very effectively for strings. While the lush tone of this album may have struck some listeners as "commercial," in the manner of film scores, for Dameron this was probably not an issue. He was concerned with creating beauty through melody, and his concept of modernity had to do with the freedom to follow his ear in the quest for this beauty. Dameron may also have been thinking of trying to work his way into film scoring after his release. Tadd told fellow inmate Carl Hayse, "I want to be the first black composer to crack Hollywood." True, Benny Carter, Gil Fuller, and Gerald Wilson were already in Los Angeles, but their work for the film industry was still anonymous at that time. However, that those three men knew and respected Dameron made his thinking about movie work quite reasonable.[13]

The ensemble for *Smooth as the Wind* has a brass section similar to the one he would use on his own *Magic Touch* a year later, as well as the Milt Jackson *Big Bags* and Sonny Stitt *Top Brass* LPs. There are three trumpets (not counting Mitchell), two trombones, and French horn. The reeds of the *Magic Touch* band are replaced, in a way, by a nine-piece string section. Close examination of the photos accompanying the album shows three cellos and six smaller instruments, at least one of which appears to be a viola. The rhythm section consists of piano, bass, and drums. This ensemble was almost certainly defined by Dameron and, of course, the suggestion by Cannonball Adderley at the outset of the project that Mitchell should record "with a few strings." Producer Orrin Keepnews recalled later that "this project had basically been built around the Dameron arrangements."[14]

The new compositions, "Smooth as the Wind" and "A Blue Time," exhibit a suave lyricism that, while always a part of Dameron's musical personality, has qualities unique to this period. This can be seen best by comparing Dameron's background line writing in this final period with some of his earlier work. For instance, if we compare the essentially legato background for the shout line from the 1945 Lunceford arrangement of "Good Bait" (fig. 10.1a) with the one Dameron employs in a 1962 arrangement (fig. 10.1b), we find that the later one is more singable, more memorable. That is, the uppermost part presents a melodic line of stronger character as a melody. Another good example of this strong character in a background is the line that supports a sixteen-bar trumpet solo in the 1962 "Good Bait" chart (fig. 10.1c).[15] We find these melodically strong backgrounds used throughout Dameron's arrangements for Blue Mitchell. The stronger melodies create a very rich musical texture, but they also demand a soloist of the caliber of a Blue Mitchell who will not be overwhelmed by them.[16]

"A Blue Time" is a slow twelve-bar blues with a haunting through-composed melody. Dameron achieves an expression of longing in this melody by avoiding chord roots, except as passing tones, until the final cadence in the eleventh bar of the form. Then, in the eleventh and twelfth measures he sustains the tonic ex. 10.1a.

ex. 10.1b.

ex. 10.1c.

Fig. 10.1. Comparison of various background lines used by Dameron in different arrangements of "Good Bait."

note while harmonizing it with a descending turn-around sequence (fig. 10.2). One of the hallmarks of Tadd Dameron's melodic style is his use of the upper notes of the chords that support the melody. "A Blue Time" is one of the finest examples of this, not least for its expressive power.

The arrangement of "A Blue Time" highlights an interesting feature of Dameron's approach to the whole project. While most writing for a featured instrumentalist treats the instrumentalist's role as analogous to that of a featured vocalist, Dameron treats Mitchell's trumpet as just another of the sonic elements in his compositions and arrangements. This is not to say that Mitchell's playing does not receive special attention, but his role is not the conventional one for this sort of recording. In "A Blue Time" Mitchell does not enter until the fourth twelve-bar chorus, and he does not participate in the ensembles, except to respond with his improvisation.

While "A Blue Time" is the most extreme example of Dameron's unusual use

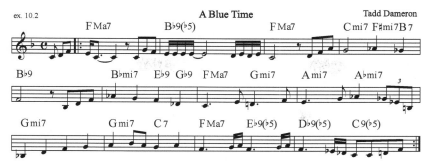

Fig. 10.2. "A Blue Time," by Tadd Dameron. © 1961, Jury Music Corp., renewed 1989 by Twenty-Eighth Street Music.

of the featured soloist, the rest of his arrangements on *Smooth as the Wind* also embody this same approach to varying degrees. In the opening chorus of the title tune, Mitchell plays only on the bridge. However, the trumpeter is the only soloist, and he gets basically two and a half choruses to tell his story, one of them with just the rhythm section. In the opening chorus of Burke and Van Heusen's "But Beautiful," Mitchell plays only four measures before becoming the focus of the listener's attention in the second and concluding chorus. The same is generally true in the opening chorus of the DeSylva, Brown, and Henderson tune "The Best Things in Life Are Free." In the ballads "For Heaven's Sake," by Meyer, Bretton, and Edwards, and "The Nearness of You," by Washington and Carmichael, Mitchell's trumpet caries the melody more often, but he has less space for improvising. Even in Horace Silver's "Strollin'," which Mitchell had played with Silver, the trumpeter does not play for any more than sixteen bars in a single passage.

Two things are worth considering here. First is one of the constants in Dameron's large ensemble writing: improvised solos are treated as a compositional element. Tadd Dameron is always striving for a balance between powerful aesthetic forces. He would say, alternately, that "the music must swing, but it has to be beautiful," and that "the music must be beautiful, but it also has to swing." Likewise he believes in the expression of an individual voice but conceives of its full meaning and significance in the context of a larger group effort. This is evident not only in *Smooth as the Wind*, but as far back as "A-La Bridges" and "Mary Lou." Even in his vocal arrangements, with a few exceptions, the singer is an integrated part of a whole composition. The second thing to remember is the extent to which Dameron put his personal stamp on this project. Even though this is a Blue Mitchell record with Mitchell's name in large type on the cover—and Dameron's in very much smaller type below—Dameron's musical personality dominates the recording. Whether this is a result of the frustration of being off the scene for five years, or just a natural expression of the power of his mature musical personality, Dameron's compositional voice would often be the strongest feature of the musical projects he would take part in during the last years of his life.

Because of his incarceration, it may have seemed that Tadd Dameron had fallen off the face of the earth to readers of the American jazz press (and in a sense he had). But jazz writers in England had not forgotten him. In the March 1960 issue of *Jazz Monthly*, there was an article by Jack Cooke titled "Tadd Dameron—An Introduction."[17] It provided a sympathetic profile and made a plea that Dameron, and by extension others, not be ignored in the face of current developments in music. Included with the article was a discography by the author's wife, Ann Cooke, which was probably the first attempt at a catalog of Dameron's recorded work. A year later, in the April 12, 1961, issue of *Jazz News*, Mike Butcher pondered the relationship between "Fontainebleau" and third-stream music (a movement concerned with merging jazz and classical idioms) in an article titled "Tadd—The Forgotten."[18]

Dameron clearly had been a good inmate, busying himself with constructive activities and carrying out his work assignments to everyone's satisfaction. Counting time served before his trial, he would not have been finished with his sentence until the middle of December 1962. Yet, on Wednesday, June 28, 1961, Tadley Ewing Dameron walked out of the U.S. Public Health Service Hospital in Lexington a relatively free man—free from his obligation to society and free from heroin addiction. But he was not free from obligations to others who had entered his life. Nor was he free from the illnesses that were probably already developing quietly inside his body.

II

1961–1962—Release

Not long after Tadd Dameron was released from prison, Groove Music, a publishing company held by Blue Note records, registered copyrights for seven of his tunes, including one titled "Bevan Beeps," named for the son of Maely Dufty. By the fall of 1961, Tadd and Maely were known to be socializing as a couple, and the following April they would take an apartment together and start a publishing company of their own. Tadd told his friends Edgar and Barbara Blakeney that Maely claimed her child Bevan was his son. The boy was around four or five years old at the time of Dameron's release, which would mean that any affair with Tadd would have started in 1957, before his federal arrest. While Tadd was not convinced the boy was his,[1] and his exact relationship to the boy remains unclear, the possibility of his being Bevan's father establishes a likely starting point for Tadd and Maely's relationship.

Following his time away from music, Tadd was anxious to restart his career. Maely, who had been on the jazz scene for some time in various professional supportive roles, had the connections and drive to help him with this. One of her former husbands, newspaperman Bill Dufty, whose name she still used at this time, had helped Billie Holiday write her autobiography, *Lady Sings the Blues*. It is the opinion of many observers who knew the Duftys that this arrangement had been brokered by Maely. Pianist George Ziskind, who got to know Tadd well enough in these last years to be a frequent dinner guest at the Dameron/Dufty home, recalled that Maely seemed to know everyone. For instance, George invited Tadd and Maely to the taping of a television program featuring Duke Ellington that a friend of his was producing. George thought he would impress his guests, but as the three of them entered the studio, Duke and Maely commenced blowing each other kisses.[2]

Dan Morgenstern, who grew friendly with Tadd shortly after his release, remembered Maely as a "Hungarian Jewish girl. I don't know what her original name was," recalled Morgenstern. "Maely had these big dark eyes, nice hair, and a pretty face, but she was fat, like Mildred Bailey size, and she was a rather dominating personality. . . . She was quick-witted and had a pretty sharp tongue. She had pretty strong likes and dislikes, nothing in between."[3]

Morgenstern, Tadd, and Maely were part of a social circle that included Danish émigrés Chris Albertson and Timme Rosenkrantz. The latter of the two had set up the Don Redman tour of Europe in 1946. Morgenstern said of his fellow Danes, "They never had any money, but they always had great parties, with lots of musicians . . . and at one of those parties Tadd played quite a lot of piano." It was also at this piano that Dameron recorded several selections in late October or early November. Albertson had hired an engineer to record a session featuring guitarist Bernard Addison at his apartment. After the Addison session, the engineer left his recorder, preferring to retrieve it a couple of weeks later, and Albertson used the machine to record Dameron one day when he came by to visit. The recording of Dameron did not take up the entire reel of tape (the only one Albertson had at the time), and Lil Hardin Armstrong, with whom Albertson was writing a book, came by later and performed some songs on the remaining unrecorded tape. Albertson let Armstrong take the tape home with her, on the condition that she send the reel back once she had the songs copied to another tape. Even though Albertson and Armstrong continued to work on the book together, the tape seems to have been forgotten and subsequently lost.[4]

The Lost Session

Dameron's return to actual studio recording came on December 14, 1961, when Blue Note recorded him leading a septet in four titles: "Lament for the Living," "Bevan Beeps," "Aloof Spoof" (all three registered by Groove in October), and Sam Rivers's "The Elder Speaks." The project was never finished, but these four titles were finally released in 1999.[5] Michael Cuscuna, in the notes to that CD, describes the recordings as "less than polished." While this criticism may be overstated, there were at least thirty-one takes—an unusually high number for a session yielding only four tunes, which suggests many false starts and aborted takes.[6] The explanation given in the notes for the less-than-satisfactory session is that there was a problem with the copyist, but the band is small and the arrangements not terribly complex, so one has to question this story. Dameron would likely have written the parts directly, without a score.

This was Tadd Dameron's last session as a pianist, and perhaps the many takes and final rejection of the project were Dameron's call. He may have been unsatisfied with his solos. Dameron told Bill Coss, in the 1962 *Down Beat* interview, "I don't think I'll play [piano] much. I'm too old for that. But I'd like to record some. I play much better now than I ever did before." While Dameron's tone is positive overall, there is an expression of ambiguity in this somewhat confusing statement, as well as criticism of his earlier piano playing. We have already noted some of the weaknesses of Tadd's technique as a soloist, and he was on record as being a harsh critic of his own work. In the same interview he said of his early recordings, "Turkeys, all of them. I've never been well represented on records." Several virtuoso modern jazz pianists had established themselves by this time, and this fact, along with Dameron's stated desire to focus on composing, were likely behind his decision to retire from playing piano publicly. Still, it is a pity that the solo tapes from November were lost and that Dameron never got the opportunity to record more. Sparse as they are, his solos on these 1961 Blue Note recordings have the same confidence and clarity found in his playing on the *Mating Call* LP, even if he does not possess the muscular virtuosity of most of the other pianists recording at the time. His ensemble work, as always, is very solid, and it is in part the way he uses the piano with the horns that makes the arrangements so satisfying, in spite of their brevity.

We will probably never know if the other tunes that had been copyrighted in October, "Doin' the Nitty Gritty," "A Pinstriped Mind," "Honey Hush," and "Cooking in Tempo," were intended for this project, but the seven Dameron tunes, along with the one by Sam Rivers, would have been enough for an LP. The copyright lead sheets for these seven titles, which present only melodies, are mysteriously unclear. The three that were recorded have little, if anything, in common with the lead sheets. Two of the others, "Doin' the Nitty Gritty" and "Cookin' in Tempo," are twelve-bar blues, but the melodies are not convincing when played. Nor do they work well with conventional or even altered blues changes. They are completely diatonic, lacking even the expected flatted sevenths characteristic of the blues, let alone the altered notes that would fit with the types of harmonies found in a modern jazz blues progression. The rest, in their deposited lead-sheet form, are thirty-two-bar AABA tunes. One, "A Pinstriped Mind," does make some semblance of harmonic sense, although it seems to be a suggestion of something that needs more work. Another, "Honey Hush!," is melodically incoherent.

It is true that copyright deposits are not always precise in their representation of the final work. They need only be close enough that there is no doubt that they represent the work in question, should they ever be contested in court. For instance, the deposit melody of the A section of "Smooth as the Wind" does not match the one that was recorded. The rhythms are the same, but the pitches are awkward and would not make for even a convincing harmony part; still, the deposit would probably hold up in court, if necessary. That said, of the three titles recorded for Blue Note, two share only the form of the copyrighted versions, and the third has absolutely nothing in common with the lead sheet. It would be impossible to connect the deposits with the recordings without their titles. Given that these seven lead sheets are clearly in Dameron's hand, we are left to wonder what his motives were for this discrepancy.

The musicians on this Blue Note session included old friends Cecil Payne and Philly Joe Jones, as well as a more recent friend, tenor saxophonist Sam Rivers. New to recording with Dameron were trumpeter Donald Byrd, trombonist Curtis Fuller, bassist Paul Chambers, and French hornist Julius Watkins. Dameron used the horn to wonderful effect in the arrangements for Blue Mitchell and would continue to use it in all of his remaining recordings, a choice that is not as surprising as it might seem at first glance. The overdue emergence of Watkins—and to a lesser degree Willie Ruff—as a well-recorded player occurred during Dameron's incarceration. By the time he was released, both players were quite active in New York. We should also remember Leonard Feather's report of a French horn in the stillborn Dameron/Davis big band of 1949 and Dameron's ongoing friendship with fellow arranger Gil Evans, who was one of the first to make extensive use of this instrument in the jazz idiom.

As mentioned earlier, Evans and Dameron were friends already by 1948, and in this final period of Dameron's life, we hear from various sources that the two men liked to spend time together. For instance, George Ziskind recalled accompanying Dameron one day on a walk to Gil Evans's apartment for an unannounced social call.[7] The use of previously neglected instruments in jazz scoring had been evolving throughout the 1950s, and whether Tadd's use of horn and flute in his later arrangements was influenced by Evans's writing or not, it would seem likely that expanding the orchestral pallet would have been a topic of discussion between the two men.

"Bevan Beeps," the first tune recorded on December 14, turns out to be a melody with an unusual twenty-bar ABA form in which the eight-bar As are twice as long as the four-bar B—completely different from the copyrighted melody. The melody evokes a child learning to walk, with a predominantly pentatonic melody punctuated with flatted thirds and augmented fifths. "Lament for the Living," as recorded, is a minor-key tune with a rhumbalike time-feel. Although the recorded melody has its own clear identity, it can also be seen as one of a long line of jazz compositions inspired by and patterned on Dizzy Gillespie's "A Night in Tunisia." "Aloof Spoof," as recorded, turns out to be the same melody as "What Ever Possessed Me," a ballad by Tadd Dameron and Bernie Hanighen that Chet Baker would record in 1964, only with a different bridge. However, as "Aloof Spoof" the melody is played at a jaunty medium-up tempo, around 148 beats per minute.

Of particular interest in these octet arrangements is the extensive use of counterpoint and the way the melodies are orchestrated. In his earlier arrangements for groups of this size Dameron generally writes trumpet-led ensembles, voiced in block chords. To provide some contrast Dameron will occasionally have the trumpet lay out, letting the alto sax lead the ensemble. Still, the other horns are almost always used as a harmonic block. The most notable exception to this practice would be "Fontainebleau," an exceptional composition in other ways as well. This is not to say that Dameron does not find ways to be creative with this approach, but the lower instruments are never brought out in the ensemble, which he uses to produce, essentially, a single voice. In these arrangements Dameron orchestrates his music in a manner that uses the instruments as individual voices. As a result the ensemble passages, while brief, are so engaging that one does not notice their brevity without repeated listening.

In Dameron's treatment of "Bevan Beeps," the trumpet and tenor sax play the melody in octaves, while the trombone and baritone sax, led by the French horn, play a harmonized counterline. In "Lament for the Living" there are essentially two melodic lines in counterpoint, divided between the tenor sax, solo, and the French horn and trombone in thirds in the first four measures. In the next two measures the trumpet caries the upper line while the others play the lower one. In the last phrase, the French horn has the upper line, and the tenor sax leads the lower one. The bridge is open, with Dameron soloing, allowing little ensemble playing by the horns. Nevertheless, what they do play makes a very strong impression because of Dameron's effective use of the various instrumental voices in orchestrating the melody. The ensemble plays only the A sections in "Aloof Spoof," as well. The trumpet plays the melody in the first, second, and fourth phrases; the French horn plays it in the third. The accompanying horns play a rich contrapuntal background. Again, while brief, these passages make a strong impression.

These arrangements lead us to wonder what the lost Atlantic Milt Jackson

LP sounded like. The band is similar in its instrumentation, and the recording session took place on January 29, 1962,[8] just a little over a month after Dameron's Blue Note session. Unfortunately, the tapes were destroyed in a fire before the project could be prepared for release, and while some have held out hope that a test pressing might exist, none has turned up. However, we do have the lead sheets for Dameron's original compositions, as well as a listing of the personnel. By now Dameron had formed, or was about to form, his own publishing company, Tadd Dameron Music Inc., and the four tunes recorded for Atlantic, "Sando Latino," "Beautifully Adorned," "Milt's Delight," and "Slightly Flighty," were registered in a folio on March 5—along with three other pieces—as belonging to that company.[9]

All of the major jazz discographies list the first session, at which these were recorded, and Claude Schlouch's discography of Kenny Dorham's work lists a second session taking place on April 16, 1962, with the same musicians and Dameron as arranger.[10] Four more tunes were recorded at this session: "Lillie," "Tahiti," "Cancel Out," and "Minor Loup." The first three were by Milt Jackson; the last, for which no records have been found, was probably Dameron's composition. In addition to Jackson's vibraphone and Dorham's trumpet, the ensemble consisted of French horn, two alto saxes (one doubling flute), and baritone sax. The players were Julius Watkins, Jerome Richardson, Leo Wright, and Cecil Payne, respectively. The rhythm section was pianist Tommy Flanagan, bassist George Duvivier, and drummer Connie Kay.

"Sando Latino" is the most unusual of the tunes recorded at the first session. Fifty measures long and in ABA form, the tune is titled in a way that suggests it should be played with a "Latin" time-feel, probably the sort of rhumba variant that Dameron frequently employs, although the melody works with the bossa-nova rhythm as well.[11] In the A section, Dameron develops the opening motif in an unusual way (fig. 11.1, under brackets). The motif lends itself naturally to a descending sequence, as in the first two measures, but when Dameron brings it back at measure 9 he gives us an ascending sequence instead that turns out to sound just as natural, but with an element of surprise. The concluding A section also has an interesting extended final cadence. The BMa7 chord in measure 15 is present in the first A, where it harmonizes an E♭ (D♯), the third of this chord. In the final A it harmonizes a B♭ (A♯), the seventh of the chord, and a D♭ (C♯), the ninth. These two notes are repeated over an E9, of which they are the #11 and the #13, respectively. The melody comes to rest on the B♭ again, where it is the fifth of the tonic E♭Maj7 chord.

"Milt's Delight" is a thirty-two-bar AABA tune, also with a very sophisticated harmonic sequence, reminiscent of the sorts of things John Coltrane was

ex. 11.1.   (last 'A' section):

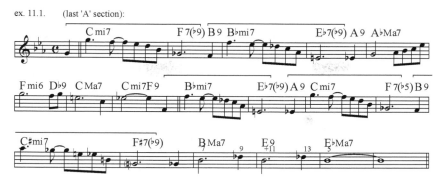

Fig. 11.1. Final A section of Dameron's "Sando Latino." © 1962, renewed 1990 Twenty-Eighth Street Music.

doing in his "Giant Steps" phase. We have already considered Lewis Porter's argument for a connection between Coltrane's "Lazy Bird" and Dameron's "Lady Bird," so this is not necessarily surprising, but compared to the relatively conventional harmonies he had employed in his previously recorded post-Lexington melodies, "Milt's Delight" and "Sando Latino" stand out in stark contrast. The remaining two tunes from this project, "Slightly Flighty" and the ballad "Beautifully Adorned," are more conventional harmonically and evoke earlier periods of Dameron's work. "Slightly Flighty" would not have been out of place in a Royal Roost broadcast, and "Beautifully Adorned" recalls the Lunceford-period ballads, although with a subtler harmonic sense.

The Magic Touch

Dameron's next projects were interconnected to a certain degree. There was a set of old and new compositions for a Riverside LP, titled *The Magic Touch*, and a set of five arrangements for Benny Goodman's upcoming tour of the USSR, which included four of the pieces on the LP. In addition, three of the arrangements on the LP were also published, with slight modifications, by Bregman, Vocco and Conn. The publication of these scores was Dameron's first venture into the educational market for big-band jazz, which was still relatively new. The recording for the LP began on February 27, with an all-star band: Joe Wilder, Clark Terry, and Ernie Royal, trumpets; Jimmy Cleveland and Britt Woodman, trombones; Julius Watkins, French horn; Leo Wright and Jerry Dodgion, alto sax/flute; Jerome Richardson, tenor sax/flute; Johnny Griffin, tenor sax; Tate

Houston, baritone sax; Bill Evans, piano; George Duvivier, bass; and Philly Joe Jones, drums. On that day they recorded three pieces, "Our Delight," "Dial 'B' for Beauty," and "Bevan's Birthday."

The "Our Delight" treatment is rather compact, perhaps in connection with the "special jazz arrangement" that would soon be published by Bregman, Vocco and Conn "for the school stage or professional dance band," as described on the arrangement's cover. Student bands often lack soloists who can develop solos of much length, if they can improvise at all. Only three choruses long, the tune is played once, followed by a half-chorus solo by Julius Watkins, and the remaining chorus and a half is a series of exchanges between the ensemble and Bill Evans. The opening chorus, in the key of A♭, is different from the original arrangement for Billy Eckstine, with a shorter introduction and a different orchestration of the melody. An eight-bar interlude modulates to the original key of D♭, with Watkins's half chorus getting a saxophone background similar to the original at this point. The ensemble passage in the bridge is new, and Evans finishes out the chorus without ensemble background. The final chorus is scored as it was originally written, first as a feature for Eckstine's valve trombone and then for Dizzy Gillespie, when he had the chart in his book. It is interesting to hear it as a feature for this, at the time, rising young piano star. Evans's own post-bop voice was well established by this time, and it is a mark of his skill as an improviser that he makes the solo feature his own, while still drawing on his roots in the bop piano tradition of musicians such as Bud Powell. The published arrangement is the same arrangement reorchestrated for four trumpets, four trombones, five saxes, piano, guitar, bass, and drums. There is also an optional part for violins, presumably for the educator interested in involving students from his or her string program.

The 1962 "Dial 'B' for Beauty" is very different from the 1953 version, just one chorus with a four-measure introduction and an eight-measure coda, taken at a languid tempo, slow enough that the whole performance takes almost three minutes. The interpolation of "Kayepyn" is omitted, with the focus on the tune itself and the beautiful playing of trumpeter Joe Wilder, whom Dameron requested specifically for this recording.[12] Wilder was one of the very finest trumpeters on the scene at that time (perhaps at any time), and his command of the instrument made him welcome in both Count Basie's band and symphony orchestras. His purity of tone, lyrical temperament, and ability to really "sing" his part must have been clearly in Dameron's mind as he wrote this arrangement. Tadd pulls out all the stops here, making the most of the flutes and the French horn, having Bill Evans play harp-like obligati softly in the background and taking full advantage of the conductor's prerogative to shape the dynamics and the tempo.

The brand-new "Bevan's Birthday" is another feature for Joe Wilder. This jaunty ABAC-form melody alternates in time-feel between rhumba and swing and is played by flutes alternating with the French horn–led trombones. Throughout this production Dameron explores several orchestrating possibilities, avoiding a routine or formula. Here, the saxophones support Wilder's solo chorus. Then, after a brass interlude, the flutes play a soli over the first A of the form, with Wilder coming back for the B before the ensemble reprises the second half of the melody. The last two measures of the form are replaced with a tag ending that concludes with Wilder improvising a cadenza over the last three chords.

The next session, on March 9, brought back the same band, with Charlie Shavers in for Joe Wilder and Ron Carter in for George Duvivier. This time they recorded "On a Misty Night," "Swift as the Wind," and "Fontainebleau." This last piece, as discussed earlier, was also scored for Goodman and published by BVC. That there were only three tunes recorded at each of the bigger band sessions was the result of the time needed for Dameron's meticulous rehearsing. Tadd may also have been fine-tuning his arrangements, since these were his first for this exact instrumentation. In the notes to the album, Dameron is reported to have asked (of these gentlemen, no less), "Does everyone have a pencil?" suggesting that there were going to be clarifications and adjustments. Joe Goldberg, who wrote the notes, indicated that there were at least a dozen takes of "Swift as the Wind" alone.

"On a Misty Night" is taken at a brighter tempo than the original, where the mood suggested by the title holds sway. There is another aspect to this melody, an almost giddy joyfulness that comes out when it is played at a faster tempo, and this arrangement explores this quality to great effect. In keeping with this, Dameron makes it a feature for Johnny Griffin, who obliges with cheerful improvisations in and around the ebullient ensembles and backgrounds. This arrangement of "On a Misty Night" is also the basis of the one Dameron wrote for Benny Goodman's Soviet tour band. The only differences are slight: the instrumentation (four trumpets and three trombones, versus three trumpets, French horn, and two trombones) and the assignment of solos. Where the middle, solo chorus, and the solo spots in the out-going chorus were all given to Griffin's tenor sax, the Goodman version has a tenor-sax solo in the middle, and Goodman is featured in the final chorus. It is not clear if this arrangement was ever performed.

"Swift as the Wind" was presented in all three forms related to this project. The up-tempo melody is in AABA form, and it is yet another of Dameron's variations on the "rhythm changes" A/common bridge harmonic formula. The arrangement's general design is similar to that of "On a Misty Night," with an eight-bar introduction, the opening chorus, and an eight-bar interlude. Where there was a middle solo chorus in "Misty Night," there are two in "Swift." The first is split between piano and trumpet, the second for a soloist with only rhythm-section accompaniment. In the *Magic Touch* and Bregman, Vocco and Conn versions, the trumpet (Clark Terry on *The Magic Touch*) continues to play in the second solo chorus. In the Goodman version Benny takes this solo, opening it up to three choruses. In both versions, the final chorus has a percussive sixteen-bar ensemble shout (probably inspired by the playing of Philly Joe Jones), and then the trumpet, or clarinet, comes back in the bridge with a background. The last A has a tag with a long cadenza from the trumpet or clarinet on the next-to-last chord.

The final session for *The Magic Touch*, on April 16, used a nonet of trumpet, trombone, alto sax (doubling flute), two tenor saxes (one doubling flute), baritone sax, piano, bass, and drums: Clark Terry, Jimmy Cleveland, Jerry Dodgion, Jerome Richardson, Johnny Griffin, Tate Houston, Bill Evans, Ron Carter, and Philly Joe Jones, respectively. There was also a singer, Ellington alumna Barbara Winfield, who sang something old ("If You Could See Me Now"), and something new ("You're a Joy"). The two instrumentals were relatively recent compositions, "Look, Stop and Listen" and "Just Plain Talkin'," a blues that may have been brand-new, but could just as well have been written during Tadd's time at Lexington, when he was writing for the big band there.

While the arrangement of "If You Could See Me Now" paraphrases the introduction to the 1946 version—with trombonist Jimmy Cleveland playing the role of Freddie Webster—it is really quite different: not only is the instrumentation very different, but the lines behind Barbara Winfield are mostly new, with the exception of the melody that leads into the bridge. The bridge is sung with only the rhythm section, and the final eight measures of the song and the coda are also unique to this arrangement. Still, while Winfield tries to put her own stamp on the song in her phrasing, the 1946 Sarah Vaughan performance is so iconic as to be inescapable. What is remarkable here—and in the other nonet selections as well—is the fullness of the ensemble. One has to listen carefully to notice that it is not the big band, and with Dameron drawing our attention to the singer and the lyric, it is easy to be fooled into thinking that there is a larger orchestra.

The new ballad "You're a Joy," with an attractive lyric by Bernie Hanighen, has started to attract the interest of some singers in recent years. While it is a beautiful song, its unusual form and harmonic restlessness make it challenging to perform, which may explain why there are few performances beyond the original with Barbara Winfield. The form could be described as ABAC, but the A sections are only four measures long. Section B is the same as A, only a minor third higher, and the flow of the melody suggests that it could be better understood as ABCAD, with all but the final D section four measures in length. The song is in F but moves first to A♭ (yet another exploration of this relationship) and then works its way slowly back to F for the repeat of the opening melodic line. In the final section it returns to A♭, but only for a measure, before again meandering back to F in the final cadence.

A:

F | Gmi7 C7 | F Ami7 | B♭mi7 E♭7 |

B:

A♭ | B♭mi7 E7| A♭ Cmi7 | D♭mi7 G♭7|

C:

Ami7 D7 | G7 C7 | E♭9 D9 | D♭9 C7 |

A:

F | Gmi7 C7 | F Ami7 | B♭mi7 E7 |

D:

A♭ | Ami7 D7 | Gmi7 C7 | Ami7 D7 | Gmi7 | C7 | F | F ||

As mentioned earlier, "Look, Stop and Listen" was first composed for the Stan Kenton Orchestra in 1958, but that arrangement and this one are very different. The melody is in ABAC form, and it is pretty clear that the Kenton version was intended to be a reasonably up-tempo "burner." We say reasonably because a couple of the figures in the trombone parts in particular would put an upper limit on the tempo of about 180 beats per minute, even with Kenton's players. The whole chart comprises more than seven choruses, with one-chorus solos from the second tenor sax and the fourth trombone and two choruses from the first tenor sax. Therefore, one would not want to go much slower than 160. There is an unusual ensemble passage between the first tenor's solo and the out-going chorus. In it Dameron constructs an ABA form from elements of the introduction, the B section, and the interlude that sets up the first solo. In addition, the last A of this section is ten measures long, upsetting the regular cycle of thirty-two-bar choruses that has been established and heightening the dramatic return of the opening theme.

The arrangement of "Look, Stop and Listen" on *The Magic Touch* is a feature for Philly Joe Jones and recalls "Philly J. J." in some regards, representing a complete rethinking of the earlier version. The tune is only heard in its entirety at the beginning, after an eight-bar setup from Philly Joe. The arrangement is fairly complex and could be thought of as a conversation between the ensemble and the drummer. The ensemble segments of this conversation are based on figures that Jones would regularly play in his solos—the second one beginning with a the same eight-note figure that was used to set up the band after Jones's open solo in the 1953 recording of "Philly J. J." Some time later Jones told arranger and trumpeter Don Sickler that Dameron would take his drum solos and base arrangements on them, and this chart is a perfect example.[13]

There are also solos by Jerome Richardson and Clark Terry. Unlike the solos in the Kenton chart, which use the chords of the tune itself, these solos are based on "rhythm changes." This was probably a practical consideration. The chord changes for "Look, Stop and Listen" are not only unique to this melody but highly chromatic and mostly two-to-a-bar. At the tempo of 240 beats per minute, this would mean an unfamiliar chord change almost every half second. Even improvisers of the caliber of Richardson and Terry would find this awkwardly challenging without preparation, which, given their busy schedules, was probably out of the question for this session.

Another of the 1962 tunes, the blues "Just Plain Talkin'," is shared by *The Magic Touch* and the Benny Goodman bands, but this time the arrangements are substantially different, even though they share introductions and opening melodies. The backgrounds for the most part are different, and there is a two-chorus ensemble that exists only in the Goodman arrangement. Also, the respective sizes of the ensemble affect the character of each treatment. The nonet is more intimate in its sound, although there is still the illusion of a larger group. With seven brass and five reeds, the tutti ensembles in the Goodman version would have a much bigger, bolder sound, especially because of the way the parts are voiced.[14]

Goodman's Soviet tour started on Wednesday, May 30, and continued for the next six weeks, ending on Sunday, July 8. The invitation from the Soviets to Goodman was extraordinary. Jazz had long been vilified by Soviet officialdom, which derided it as an expression of Western decadence and vigorously discouraged local enthusiasts. The tour was part of the beginning of a long and difficult effort to ease some of the tensions of the Cold War, an effort that would suffer a severe setback just a few months later in October, with the confrontation over missiles placed on the island of Cuba.

As one would expect from Benny Goodman, the band personnel included some of the finest musicians of the time: trumpeters Joe Newman, Joe Wilder, Jimmy Maxwell, and John Frosk; trombonists Wayne Andre, Willie Dennis, and Jimmy Knepper; saxophonists Phil Woods, Jerry Dodgion, Zoot Sims, Tommy Newsom, and Gene Allen; pianist John Bunch; guitarist Turk Van Lake; bassist Bill Crow; and drummer Mel Lewis. Pianist Teddy Wilson and vibraphonist Victor Feldman were also on board for the combo segments of the concerts, and Joya Sherill was the vocalist. In addition to Dameron's charts, new arrangements were contributed by John Bunch, Mel Lewis, Joe Lipman, Tommy Newsom, and Bob Prince.[15]

Of course, there were many of Goodman's classics in the book as well, and it seems that Benny was a reluctant to program the newer material. As of the middle of June, Tadd was getting word from the younger players in the band that Benny had not called anything new. Dameron's impression was that due to frustration over this, among several issues, they were all planning to leave the band upon its return to the United States.[16] However, by the last leg of the tour, at least "Fontainebleau" and "Swift as the Wind" were played and recorded.[17]

The fifth arrangement for Goodman's Russian tour was an odd piece titled "Moon from the East," a long, minor-key melody with a time-feel that can only be described as "faux Egyptian." In this, the only known version, the tune is presented as a complete composition, without improvised solos, very much like "Lyonia." The basic melody is in AABA form, but seventy-six measures long, with twenty-bar A sections and a sixteen-bar bridge. There is a ten-bar intro-duction, the melody—with an extra two measures inserted at the end of the first A, where Goodman's clarinet reprises the introductory motif, and a long double-tempo coda. All in all, the total performance time would not likely ex-ceed two minutes, which seems rather short. Since it was never recorded—and may not even have been performed—we cannot know Dameron's intention here, and it is hard to imagine just how this piece would have been programmed in concert.

Dameron's return to the scene in 1961 brought his name back into the press to a degree. In the October 12 issue of *DownBeat*, a George Hoefer article dis-cussed the contributions of Dameron and trombonist Fred Beckett to the 1940 Harlan Leonard recordings, which was especially edifying since these record-ings were long out of print and would not be rereleased on LP for another five years. The February 15, 1962, issue of the same magazine ran a profile by Bill Coss titled "Tadd Is Back," based on the first interview with Dameron in a dozen years. There was also an article in the April issue of the British *Jazz Monthly* on the Jazzland release of an LP of Royal Roost air-checks titled *Fats Navarro Featured with the Tadd Dameron Band*. However, these were not enough to create excitement for *The Magic Touch*, which was released by Riverside Records sometime in the summer, probably early July. Sales were not helped by the rather sour review by John S. Wilson in the September 27, 1962, *DownBeat* or the mention by Martin Williams in *Saturday Review*, which, while more favorable in regard to the music, complained of poor balance and muffled sound. Williams said the recorded sound suggested "a band of midgets playing in a cotton-lined packing case."[18] Sound quality was very important to the audiophile community, which included a significant portion of jazz fans. However, while the recording is not the very best example of the recording technology of the time, it is not unpleasant to listen to, and the music is superb. It is hard to understand why the reviewers were so negative. Still, the history of music criticism shows that this is far from a unique situation. Orrin Keepnews, the album's producer and an astute judge of music in general, opined years later that the music in *The Magic Touch* was very good but that "talent has no correlation with success,"[19] and of course, no one had any idea that this would be Dameron's last album.

One of the new pieces on *The Magic Touch*, the song "You're a Joy," introduced a new collaborator, Bernie Hanighen. Unlike most of Dameron's earlier lyricists—Jack Reynolds, Ann Greer, Shirley Jones, and Albert Carlo—Hanighen is known for other work as well, most notably his lyric for Thelonious Monk's "Round Midnight." He also collaborated with Neal Hefti on at least one occasion and wrote the music for "Bob White," for which Johnny Mercer wrote the lyric. He provided lyrics for five of Dameron's late songs, including "What Ever Possessed Me," which would be recorded in 1964 by Chet Baker. Dameron also worked with two other lyricists in these last years, Irving Reid and Maely Dufty, the latter writing under the name of Maely Daniele. With the exception of the two songs mentioned above, none of these were recorded during Dameron's lifetime. Tadd's interest in vocal music goes back to the beginning of his career, and the number of songs he composed in his final years is notable—there are least seventeen vocal compositions that date from the 1961–63 period.

490 West End Avenue

The spring of 1962 brought some other significant events. For one, Tadd and

Maely moved into a nice apartment at 490 West End Avenue, where he would soon get a telephone in his own name, his first since getting out of Lexington. Another was the beginning of his health problems, which would become quite serious in the next year. There was also the beginning of his friendship with Edgar "Egg" Blakeney, the art director of *FM Listeners Guide*, and Blakeney's wife, Barbara. The couple were his friends and confidants during the collapse of his relationship with Maely. They also introduced him to the British writer and photographer Valerie Wilmer. The Blakeneys first met Dameron at Birdland, where they had gone one evening to hear Count Basie. Tadd, with his pleasant memories of his stay in London, had a fondness for the English, and as Val Wilmer put it, "Egg and Barbara were what we used to call 'ravers' ['party animals']. They had not been long in Manhattan but already knew people all over the Village,"[20] including record producer Don Schlitten and jazz journalists Ira Gitler and Dan Morgenstern. Tadd, Egg, and Barbara hit it off right away.

Sometime in May, Val Wilmer came to New York for a visit and met the Blakeneys through the drummer Herbie Lovell, a mutual friend. She ended up going to visit Tadd and Maely with the Blakeneys and came back the next day to interview Dameron and take some pictures of him. These photographs have graced articles and recordings, particularly in the UK, and the interview formed the basis for a brief profile in the British magazine *Jazz News*.[21] The article gives us some of Dameron's thoughts on his career and the work of other musicians, as well as a few of Dameron's characteristically questionable assertions. Tadd reportedly told Wilmer that he would never record as an instrumentalist again and, as he remarked to Ira Gitler and Bill Coss around the same time, that he wanted to focus on composing above all. He went on to say that his favorite arrangers at the time were "Duke and Strayhorn (of course), and Gerry Mulligan, Gil Evans and Marty Paich—he sure writes good." On the other hand, he also articulated some of his complaints regarding the current jazz scene: "They play longer, but Charlie Parker would never have thought of playing more than two or three choruses. Coltrane made a record with me and he played beautifully, but now he's going into this thing, playing twelve or fourteen choruses—he plays for a whole set on one tune!" Dameron also expressed his hopes for success with *The Magic Touch* and his ambitions to tour internationally, as some of his close friends were doing at the time. As for the questionable assertions, he also mistakenly claimed that he had written for Ted Heath for over a year, when he had done so for only a couple of weeks, and that he had gone to Liberia for a couple of months, which is unlikely to the point of impossibility.[22]

After Wilmer returned to England, her friends would bring her up to date on Dameron. In a letter from Barbara Blakeney dated June 19, we find that

Tadd and Maely had come to visit a few days before with the test pressing of *The Magic Touch*. Also, on the next Saturday, June 23, they would be having a party, and Miles Davis, Gil Evans, and others would probably be there. From the Blakeneys we find that Tadd's circle of friends includes not only Miles and Gil but the singers Blossom Dearie and Yolande Bavan, who had replaced Annie Ross in the vocalist group Lambert, Hendricks and Ross. Of course, Dameron was also in contact with his old friends Thelonious Monk and Philly Joe Jones, and Joe Goldberg's notes to *The Magic Touch* tell us that Tadd and Dizzy were still friends, although it seems that Lorraine Gillespie was not terribly fond of Tadd.[23]

Another visitor to Dameron's new apartment was the saxophonist Dexter Gordon, who had worked with Dameron in the 1940s. Like Dameron, Gordon had recently emerged from his own dark days. He had been released on parole from his second imprisonment for heroin possession in 1960, roughly a year before Dameron. Gordon was now well on his way to the successful career he deserved, given his skills as a performer and his role in the evolution of jazz. Dexter later recalled visiting Tadd in 1962:

> I had a tune—really rather simple, but the way it lays, the only conceivable thing that I could think of [was that] it was like a cha-cha. I was trying to pick it out on the piano, showing it to Tadd. Then he started playing it—working on it, polishing it, the changes. And when he got through with it, he made that thing sound so beautiful.[24]

The tune is undoubtedly "Le Coiffeur," which was copyrighted by Tadd Dameron Music, Inc. on August 29, 1962,[25] and recorded on Gordon's Blue Note LP *Gettin' Around* in 1965. Dameron's influence is evident in some subtle harmonic touches, such as the turn-around in the seventh and eight bars of the tune, where an E♭mi7 chord replaces the usual Ami7 in the standard |C Ami7| Dmi7 G7| formula. The bridge of the tune is also notable in the unusual way it remains in the relative minor for most of its eight-measure length, another subtle harmonic surprise.

Dameron was already having heart trouble at this time and was said to have his good days and bad days in this regard. The week before Barbara Blakeney's June 19 letter to Val Wilmer, Tadd had gone to visit Gil Evans. It seems, from Barbara's explanation, that Maely went everywhere with Tadd. While Maely's watchfulness and possessiveness were beginning to irritate Tadd, more than a few of his friends at the time believed that she was making sure he ate well and followed his doctor's orders. On this day, however, Maely was not feeling well, and Tadd went out alone. He and Gil spent the afternoon drinking, which Tadd's doctors had advised him against. Then Dameron dropped in on the Blakeneys. He seemed generally well, but his hands were swollen (a sign, given his heart condition, that he had been drinking); the implication in Barbara's letter to Wilmer is that Dameron, upon questioning, admitted that he had had a few drinks. After visiting for a couple of hours, "he was off to the Jazz Gallery to see Yolande [Bavan]! As he left we warned him not to drink any more and to go easy—a silly thing to say to him!" It seemed clear to Barbara that Tadd was in a mood to drink and visit friends and that her advice, no matter how wise, was falling on deaf ears. When Tadd and Maely visited the Blakeneys together a few days later, Maely said that Tadd had not gotten home until 10:30 the next morning, wet and muddy. He had collapsed in the street and at some point the next day had been unconscious for four or five hours, partly paralyzed, and had had to be hospitalized.

The year after Dameron's release from Lexington had been his most productive since the late 1940s, but this would not last. His health and his domestic situation were about to go into a serious decline. Tadd's stays in the hospital would become longer and more frequent, his relationship with Maely would unravel slowly and painfully, and Richard Carpenter was waiting in the wings to collect what he felt was owed to him.

12

The Final Sessions

Dameron's health was not his only concern at this point. It seems his relationship with Maely was never an easy one. They were both stubborn by nature, and while Maely's watchfulness was, no doubt, good for Tadd's health, he found it increasingly irritating. The couple's quarrels, already a matter of concern to their friends, would come to a head in the course of the latter part of 1962 and 1963. Nevertheless, Tadd was still busy with various projects at the beginning of the summer of 1962. The most significant of these were two recording sessions, one for Milt Jackson and another for Sonny Stitt. This Jackson session was for Riverside. Its connection, if any, with the January date for Atlantic seems only to be that it was another collaboration between the two musicians. Dameron split the arranging chores with Ernie Wilkins, Tadd contributing five ballad arrangements. Using a band with the same instrumentation as the larger of his *Magic Touch* ensembles (and several of the same players), he gives Jackson a warm and sympathetic accompaniment for his interpretations and improvisations. Dameron directed the band himself on either Tuesday, June 19, or Wednesday, June 20, only a week or so after his collapse in the rain. Pianist Hank Jones, who played on that session, recalled that Dameron was quite ill and had to be brought to the session from the hospital.[1] The Dameron arrangements recorded that day were of Monk's "'Round Midnight" and two of his own compositions, "If You Could See Me Now" and the new "The Dream Is You."

"The Dream Is You" is a contrafact of "Out of Nowhere." Although the model is audible, Dameron's mastery of melodic construction is evident in the entirely different shape of this melody, with stop-time in the first and fifth measures of the A sections. In contrast to those for Blue Mitchell, Dameron's arrangements for this project feature Jackson in the statement of the melody and give him more soloing space. While these arrangements are striking in their lush beauty, they are less assertive than the *Smooth as the Wind* charts. If the author's speculation about Dameron's pent-up creative energy needing an outlet in the earlier recording is correct, this would make sense, since *Big Bags*,[2] as the LP is titled, was produced soon after Dameron's own *Magic Touch*.

Still, Dameron presents something with the weight of a symphonic movement in his treatment of Thelonious Monk's "'Round Midnight." It is like the slow movement of a concerto, relatively simple in its structure but deep and complex emotionally. At about 52 beats per minute, the two choruses, plus the introduction and coda, take the better part of seven minutes to unfold. The eight-bar introduction grows out of the long pick-up to the coda that Dizzy Gillespie probably composed for the tune but develops into a different melody. A solo alto sax leads the way in the first four measures and returns at key points in the piece, as if it were a narrator setting the scene for Jackson's soliloquy. Jackson elaborates on the famous melody from the beginning of the first chorus. The ensemble background is finely detailed, with shifting instrumental colors and little fragments of melody in various instruments. The alto sax returns to lead the ensemble in a four-bar interlude that introduces the second chorus. Here Jackson solos over the rhythm section in double-time feel, up through the bridge. For the last A of the chorus, the ensemble returns with a Dameron-invented melody over the tune's chord progression. It begins with the lead alto over the rest of the sax section, recalling the introduction in color and mood. There is a two-measure phrase, the beginning of which is repeated sequentially, up a fourth. This second phrase blossoms out into the full ensemble, with a trumpet taking the lead midway. The paraphrase of Monk's melody continues to its conclusion, leading into a six-bar cadenza from Jackson. The alto sax, along with the rest of the section, returns with the two-measure phrase that began this last ensemble passage, resolving into a final tonic chord with a French horn flourish and final comment from Jackson.

The arrangement of "If You Could See Me Now" from this set is quite different from the previous vocal arrangements and makes no reference to the original, in spite of the prominent presence of the flutes in the introduction. The background line supporting the first four measures of the melody is strong enough to be the beginning of a contrafact of the original, in spite of its simplicity. Although not on the same grand scale as "Midnight," this arrangement shares the same general plan, as do the remaining three ballads: an introduction, the opening chorus featuring the soloist with some melody passages written for the ensemble, a solo with double-time feel, and an abbreviated ensemble passage to close the arrangement. Nevertheless, between Dameron's skill in approaching each tune on its own terms and the brilliant playing of Milt Jackson, each piece tells its own story. Even when listening to all five ballads in succession, it is not the similarity of this general design that stands out, but rather the lyrical beauty of the music and the balance between arrangement and improvisation.

The remaining two ballads, Milt Jackson's "Echoes" and Ranger and Robin's "If I Should Lose You," were recorded on July 5, 1962, along with two of the up-tempo numbers arranged by Ernie Wilkins. The band has Dameron's instrumentation,[3] and although the credits claim only "If I Should Lose You" as his arrangement, the commentary implies that "Echoes" is his work as well. "If I Should Lose You" breaks with the format described above in that there is no introduction, but it does start with the sax section alone for the first phrase, which has an effect here similar to an introduction. The French horn plays a counterline in the second phrase, and Jackson makes his entrance in the third, carrying the melody from that point. The ensemble background is full of little solo and ensemble contrapuntal lines. "Echoes" is another variation on Dameron's arrangement format for the ballads, different from the others in detail but following the same general plan. The lines and the voicings are clearly his, and in spite of the credit assignation, there can be little question, if any, that this is his arrangement.

A couple of weeks later, on July 16 and 17, Dameron was in Atlantic Studios to conduct the last recording he would be part of, a Sonny Stitt session with a mid-sized band that is essentially the brass section of the post-Lexington Dameron orchestra—three trumpets, French horn, two trombones—and rhythm section. At one of the sessions Hammond organ replaces the piano in the rhythm section. Even though Jimmy Mundy arranged four of the nine tunes—and one, titled "Sttisie," was a spontaneous quintet arrangement—the configuration of the ensemble suggests that Tadd largely determined the instrumentation.[4]

Noted jazz journalist Martin Williams was present at one of the sessions. That day, he reported, Jimmy Mundy conducted his arrangements first, while Dameron sat off to the side with a couple of friends, waiting his turn. Williams gives a vivid description of Dameron the conductor at work, bringing out the nuances in the music:

Meanwhile, Tadd Dameron, a keen, sharp-eyed man, had been distributing his own music around the room. His first piece had been given the hasty, last-minute title of "The 490," after Dameron's street address. Once he had signaled the tempo and got the musicians started, Dameron sat quietly facing them, listening to the results with sober face and piercing look. Only once did he raise his hands, to quiet the brass behind Stitt's first entrance. The room had taken on a new life.

At the end, Dameron was exhorting the trumpets to, "Sing it! Sing it! Everybody!" He started them again, this time knowing what to listen for and conducting them modestly with one hand. "Hold it! Hold it!," he stopped them, turning to the trumpeters. "Play it this way, boo-ob-de-*wahhh*."

They tried "The 490" onto tape. Dameron smiled at Philly Joe's exciting and propelling delayed entrance. Gradually, the composer had begun to do more active conducting. But he was not keeping time for them so much as he was signaling dynamics and encouraging feeling, and he frequently sang along silently with the brass as Stitt effectively juxtaposed passionate slow blues improvising against the more sedate ballad-blues writing.

As others have noted, Dameron liked to use a slower tempo in rehearsal to get the musicians to focus on the details:

Dameron began to work with the players on the next piece, "On A Misty Night." Again he was calm and strictly business, and again the musicians were quietly enthusiastic.

"More legato. Make it slurred more right there. Good. Thank you," he said interrupting them and singing the passage for them twice.

Dameron increased the tempo each time they ran the piece through, and a huge, but decidedly lyric, brass sound gradually emerged. For one crescendo he raised himself to his full height, moved forward and conducted the semicircle with both arms.

"Trumpets, it's supposed to go do-*wah*. You're playing do-*dah*, dig?"

In a peak in the coda, Sonny lifted his left foot abruptly behind him, and Dameron held his finger to his lips for the last big chord from the brass. Stitt's coda was of a length dictated by his own inspiration, and Dameron had to bring the brass in under him for the ending when he intuited that Stitt was ready. Each time Stitt made a different ending, and each time Dameron knew when to signal the group to re-enter.[5]

The recording is noteworthy not only because it is the only collaboration between Dameron and Stitt but because it is one of the very few recordings of this saxophonist with large ensemble backing. Like Milt Jackson, Sonny Stitt was an exceptionally inventive improviser, and Dameron gives him plenty of room, while still setting the tone and dimensions of each arrangement. He presented only one new tune on this project, the eight-bar blues "The 490," referred to above. It is a simple tune and only stated once at the beginning—at least according to the copyright lead sheet, which does not appear to be written by

Dameron. However, after the brass ensemble states the registered tune, Sonny Stitt plays an eight-bar passage over an accompanying background, which may be a second-chorus extension of the melody. We have seen other instances when Dameron registered an incomplete statement of the whole melody. After this the organist, Perri Lee, takes a two-chorus solo. Then Stitt returns for four more choruses. After the first chorus, accompanied by just the rhythm section, the brass return, supporting the final three choruses. The last two choruses have the same background, with the final one ending in a coda. In spite of the simple premise of "The 490," Dameron is still very aware of the structure and proportions of the arrangement as a whole. As a result, there is an overall logic to the piece that allows Stitt to channel his creative energy to great effect.

Dameron revisits "On a Misty Night" one more time in this set. As in the *Magic Touch* arrangement, the mood is upbeat, although this one lacks some of the elegance of its predecessor, perhaps because of the absence of the contrasting color of the reeds or the awkwardness of the Hammond organ (or its player) in the ensemble. As in the *Magic Touch* version, the bridge is the one derived from the composer's 1956 piano solo, not the one registered with the Copyright Office. The arrangement has a brief four-bar introduction, and Stitt plays the A sections, with the trumpets playing the bridge. The next chorus starts Sonny Stitt's solo, with just the rhythm section. Then there are two more choruses with ensemble backgrounds. These are written in the first two or four measures of the sections of the form. In most instances, these would be played as a call and response, but Stitt plays over them. Since Dameron is conducting the session, it is clear that he approves, most likely because Sonny Stitt is so deeply engaged with the tune. Still, it is a striking departure from Dameron's usual design.

Dameron's simple, somewhat informal take on the twelve-bar blues "See See Rider"[6] is successful because of its casual nature. Dameron lets the players and the tradition work their magic by setting up the appropriate "props." There is a four-bar introduction, the theme of which continues as part of an accompanying background under Stitt's statement of the theme. Then the saxophonist takes three choruses, the last of which gets support from the brass. Trombonists Jimmy Cleveland and Matthew Gee exchange four-bar solos for two choruses, and pianist Duke Jordan takes a chorus that sets up Stitt's return. He plays two more choruses, one with just the rhythm section and the last with a simple brass background. While Tadd Dameron is not generally associated with the blues, his treatment of the form, as we have seen throughout his work, is always authoritative.

The remaining Tadd Dameron arrangement in the set is "Hey Pam!," a Stitt original. The chart is concise, three choruses with an eight-bar introduction

and four-bar interlude and coda. There is a background for the bridge of this
first chorus. For the out-going chorus the ensemble does a four-bar call-and-
response, with Stitt on alto for the first two A sections. This is more in keeping
with Dameron's general practice, as discussed above. The last half of the chorus
is reprised from the middle of the opening one, and the interlude passage returns as the coda.

Projects and Problems

In a letter from the Blakeneys to Val Wilmer, written at the end of July or beginning of August, Edgar reports that *The Magic Touch* had been released. Barbara
tells of running into Maely while shopping: "[Maely] says Tadd is just 'out of his
mind' for the past week. He has been heavily on the 'booze' again." Maely had
invited the Blakeneys to come visit and try to "bring Tadd to his senses." To Val,
Barbara expressed her reluctance to go; she had grown weary of the quarreling
between Tadd and Maely. A few days later Tadd called from the phone he had
just had installed.[7] Through these various reports a picture begins to emerge
of a man very much conflicted in his home situation. On the one hand, he has
moved with Maely and Bevan into a rather classy apartment, subscribed to telephone service there, and started a business with Maely. On the other hand, he
does not seem to be able to get along with Maely, and it is likely that the stress
of this relationship is at least partly responsible for his excessive drinking—
drinking that runs contrary to the advice of his doctors.[8]

Not long after this letter was sent, Dameron may have made a trip to the
West Coast—at least that is what he told the Blakeneys. While the purpose of
this journey is not known, he may have gone there to explore the possibility of
doing some film or television scoring. Tadd had friends who were already active
in the West Coast studio scene. Gil Fuller, for one, had opened a studio in the
Los Angeles area in 1957.[9] Of course, Gerald Wilson had been out there pretty
much since he got out of the navy at the end of World War II, but he does not
recall Dameron coming out to Los Angeles—then or ever. The "trip to the West
Coast" may also have just been a cover story for a trip back to Cleveland for a
break from his domestic situation.

The Blakeneys reported again in the middle of September. There was some
good news when Tadd returned to New York: *FM Listeners Guide* had made
The Magic Touch the record of the month. There was also work waiting for Tadd
when he returned to New York. First came a call from Charles Mingus. Mingus
was already taking a very big chance in staging a concert with an unusually large

jazz orchestra, of thirty-two players. Then, for some reason, the concert date was bumped up five weeks, from November 15 to October 12. Mingus was calling frantically around town to everyone and anyone who would be able to help him, including Dameron, Hall Overton,[10] Pepper Adams, Bob Hammer, Melba Liston, and Gene Roland.[11]

In her September letter, Barbara also told Val that Dameron was writing for Sarah Vaughan again. Whatever happened to these arrangements is not known, but they may have gotten lost in the chaos of Sarah's personal life at the time. Of course, Tadd and Sarah had a friendship that dated back to 1944 and the Billy Eckstine band, but there was also a new connection through Maely, who was running a booking agency with Sarah's husband, C. B. Atkins. Unfortunately, Sarah's marriage to C. B. was just about to collapse in a very ugly divorce.

Billy Eckstine, too, was talking with Dameron about arrangements, but this assignment did not materialize.[12] Arrangements for the singer Tony Bennett have also been mentioned. Bennett remembers talking with Dameron but cannot be sure if he ever performed any of his arrangements. Too much time has passed, and Bennett has lost track of all the different writers who provided him with scores. This is not surprising, given the frequency with which he was recording in the early 1960s.[13]

A major work attributed to Dameron from this period that is also sometimes mentioned is a ballet score for a Mexican dance company. For example, in *Jazz Masters of the 40s*, Ira Gitler, part of Dameron's social circle at the time, mentions this piece.[14] We do not know if it was performed or where the score is located. However, Dan Morgenstern recalled visiting Tadd at the time the piece was written. When asked about it, Morganstern said, "It did exist. I did visit a couple of times when Tadd and Maely were living together—Tadd was already in poor health—and this particular time I know that he was writing, or had already written, a score for a Mexican ballet company. I don't know what happened with the score, but I know that he was very pleased with that."[15]

It was also most likely in the fall of 1962 that Tadd Dameron started addressing the educational market for arrangements. By February 4, 1963, the Copyright Office had registered the first three of four Dameron arrangements that would be published that year by Bregman, Vocco and Conn. As discussed before, the pieces were "Good Bait," "Fontainebleau," "Our Delight," and "Swift as the Wind," which was registered later in the year. We have no record of how well these sold, but they are known to have still been available as many as ten years later.[16] There are indications that Tadd planned at least six more arrangements for the educational market, but these have yet to surface.

In December, Dameron called the Blakeneys from Gil Evans's place to say he had taken an apartment of his own on the West Side. More likely this was a room at a hotel, like the Almac, where he lived for a short time a year later. Edgar thought that Tadd had finally split from Maely, but the unhappy couple would limp on well into the next year before their final separation. Dameron was still sneaking out and getting drunk, a behavior that was taking its toll, and he was hospitalized occasionally. In a letter dated February 9, 1963, Edgar told Val that Tadd "has been in the hospital once more, but is supposedly better now." He also reported that Lucky Thompson "has been going 'round to Tadd's but is getting tired of the Maely scene—so are we." Nevertheless, the couple was still trying to carry on as business partners.

The year 1963 saw the formation of Tadmal Music. In papers filed with the Copyright Office and signed on March 18, 1963, Tadmal Music Publishing Company took over the rights to the holdings of Tadd Dameron Music, Inc., which had been formed and controlled by Bill Grauer and Riverside Records, ostensibly to help Dameron protect his rights. Most of the melodies composed by Dameron and recorded by Riverside were held by this company, along with the four recorded by Atlantic in the lost Milt Jackson session and two titles by Dexter Gordon.[17] At the same time, Tadmal assigned Dameron's "Swift as the Wind" to Bregman, Vocco and Conn, presumably for the stage-band arrangement mentioned above. On May 13, Tadmal assigned three of the four tunes that Tadd had scored for the Atlantic Milt Jackson set to Cromwell Music, which helps us to put an approximate date on the next document we have regarding Tadmal Music Publishing Company. Sometime after these papers were filed, Tadmal put together a list of the Dameron compositions it claimed and, presumably, could provide music for. The titles assigned to others are not on this list. Of the more than forty pieces listed, only ten were registered with the Copyright Office at the time, and only a handful more have surfaced in the years since Dameron's death.

Three of these late pieces—"Come Close" (which is not mentioned in the Tadmal list), "At Christmastime," and "That's Just the Way It Goes"—were registered in the form of piano arrangements, in a folio, on either January 18 or March 5, 1962[18] along with those from the lost Milt Jackson session. "Come Close" is an ABAC--form ballad with a couple of interesting harmonic details. In the B section, the key moves from F to D (another movement of key by a third) and then works its way back to F. In the second half of the second A section there is an interesting chord progression with an implied rising bass line: Ami7 | B♭Ma7 | Cmi6 | D7 ||. In the piano arrangement the Cmi6 has the 6th or A in the bass, but it is easy to hear a bass line continuing upward to the D, and the effect of this with the melody line is quite striking, bright yet melancholy at the same time. "At Christmastime" is appropriately simple and straightforward; a thirty-two-bar AABA form with an eight-bar introduction. It is harmonically conventional, but it does have its own unique progression, and the bridge, although simple, is not constructed on one of the usual formulas. A lyric was added by Maely Dufty, under the name Maely Daniele, but a lead sheet for this has not come to light. Another lyric was added recently by Chris Caswell, with the title "Each New Christmas." "That's Just the Way It Goes," the title piece of the folio, is another straightforward melody that, by the sound of it, could have been written at almost any time in Dameron's career.

Another suite or folio of pieces was received by the Copyright Office on August 13, 1962, under the title "Moon from the East." In addition to the title composition, it contained "Bevan's Birthday," "Just Pain Talkin'," "Swift as the Wind," and the unrecorded "Milés" or "Miles"[19] (the deposit lead sheet shows the first title, but the cover page for the folio shows the second). "Milés" is a twenty-four-bar melody with an unusual structure, an ABAC form with eight-bar A sections but only four-bar B and C sections. The harmonic sequence could be best characterized as restless. That it was included with these other compositions raises the possibility of another recording project that may have been in the planning stage but had to be abandoned due to Dameron's deteriorating health.

"Sweet Life" was submitted under a separate registration on the same day as the "Moon from the East" set. The melody, with a lyric by Bernie Hanighen, is reminiscent of the songs Dameron wrote while working for Lunceford in the early 1940s. A pleasant, conventional tune seasoned with a few chromatic harmonies, it is basically in AABA form. Interestingly, however, the melody of the last A is a quite noticeable variation on the first two.

There are also several documented titles for which we have no music, as yet.[20] Of these, forty-seven are most likely song-form pieces by Dameron alone. Three more have lyrics by Irving Reid, and one has a lyric by Maely Daniele (Dufty). The Tadmal list also mentions "The Sermon on the Mount," an oratorio with lyrics by Irving Reid and Ira Kosloff. While some of these, such as one titled "Boydstown," were undoubtedly written in earlier periods, we can be reasonably sure that many of them date from the early 1960s. Add to these the pieces that surfaced after Dameron's death (see chap. 13), and it is clear that, until his poor health became a constant and depressing distraction, Tadd Dameron was very productive in his last years.

By June 1963, it appears, things had come to a head between Tadd and Maely. On June 7, Tadd Dameron and Bregman, Vocco and Conn, Inc., filed assignment papers covering forty titles. Most of these were compositions that had been formally copyrighted by BVC.[21] The assignment was probably made primarily to continue these copyrights, but it is intriguing to note that Dameron gave his address as 10524 Eglin Avenue, Cleveland, his brother Caesar's house. Willie Smith recalled Tadd complaining to him that Maely "was trying to muscle in on his royalties." Smith went on to paint an unhappy picture of his friend's life in the spring of 1963: "He got really depressed. This Maely, she was runnin' him through the mill, so that was why he would split and come here. He would stay with Caesar, his brother, because he don't want to be bothered with this babe. Then he started staying with this other broad that he married—he had a wife here."[22]

While Smith speaks of strife over Tadd's business dealings with Maely, in the end it seems that they managed to carry on the publishing company's operation after their personal separation.[23] Nevertheless, there are no other documents related to Tadmal Music after the catalog of available works, at least not during what remained of Tadd Dameron's lifetime.

Mia

There is little hard information regarding the next four or five months of Dameron's life. We know that he wrote some music for Merv Griffin's television show, and Willie Smith said that he wrote several arrangements for Harry James. According to pianist Cliff Smalls, Dameron also wrote a complete nightclub show for Brook Benton.[24]

As Tadd confessed to his wife Mia later, some time in the late spring or early summer, he and Maely had an argument that ended with his hitting her.[25] With this, Maely put Tadd out of their home at 490 West End Avenue, and he probably moved into a room at the Belleclaire Hotel, the address he used when he assigned all of his Bregman, Vocco and Conn compositions to Richard Carpenter's Music Royalty Corporation on November 30, 1963.[26] Dameron was, no doubt, rather desperate at this time. He had mounting medical bills, not to mention the inevitable anxiety that comes with serious health problems. His relationship with Maely, with whom he shared a home, was coming unglued. Finally, there was always that debt he seemed to owe Richard Carpenter. That day, November 30, in a separate document, he also signed over his rights to several other compositions to Carpenter.

In addition to his personal problems, Tadd's health continued to deteriorate. In her Christmas card to Val Wilmer, dated December 17, 1963, Barbara Blakeney reported, "Tadd's been in hospital again for 6 weeks. Pretty ill. Came out Saturday and dropped round to see us last night with a nurse he's going out with from the hospital!! An English girl, too, from Eastbourne. He looks pretty fit now. Laughed at your card and sends regards."

The nurse was Mable Soper.[27] Tadd was not particularly fond of the name Mable, although he was quite fond of her, so she "borrowed" the name Mia from a friend. That is how she has been known ever since. Mia liked to listen to Billy Taylor's radio show and heard him mention that Tadd was in Roosevelt Hospital, where she worked. Taylor suggested that fans send Dameron get-well cards, but Mia decided to visit instead. When she got to his room, Tadd was holding court with several visitors. Mia was shy about going in, but an orderly on the floor said he was well enough to receive another visitor. Dameron was touched that a stranger should come to wish him well, and when the other visitors left, Mia stayed. She would come back often during Tadd's stay in the hospital, even bringing him a hot rum toddy or two. "It was a freezing cold night," she recalled. "I guess I should have known better, being a nurse, but I felt it wouldn't do any harm."

In the days after Dameron discharged himself from the hospital, Mia had been invited to a series of pre-Christmas parties and was not home to receive his calls. Tadd persisted, sending her a telegram with his phone number at the Hotel Almac and an invitation to visit him. When she called, he asked her to bring some pots and pans. She recalled later that she never went back to her East Village apartment again, except to get her three cats.

For the next several weeks Mia, Tadd, and her cats lived at the Hotel Almac, and on January 29, 1964, Tadd and Mia married. "I don't know whether to curse or bless Richard Carpenter," said Mia, since it was at his very strong urging that they married. From what is known of both Tadd and Mia, they were free spirits and may not have married if Carpenter had not set everything up for them, including getting the minister. Carpenter, who had been involved with Dameron since at least the second half of 1956, had a commercial interest here. He could see that Tadd might not live much longer. Perhaps he hoped that Tadd's widow would provide him access to at least part of his estate. Given the assignments made while Dameron was in the hospital, it would seem Carpenter hoped to control all of Tadd's royalties. On the other hand, with a nurse for a wife, Tadd might survive for a while and write some more music. Either way, Carpenter stood to benefit from this marriage. On January 31, Carpenter got Tadd and Mia to sign over their rights to the royalties due on fifty-nine titles. Several of these were copyrights that Carpenter already held; others were part of the holdings of Bregman, Vocco and Conn—these would be disputed later. Still others were among those songs copyrighted by Groove Music, and there are also three previously unknown titles that have yet to surface in either manuscript or recording. Dameron further signed over all of his artist royalties from his Prestige recordings. A week later Carpenter had Dameron sign over his interest in Tadmal Music. Given that Tadmal had likely been formed to protect Tadd's current and future work from Carpenter's control, this must have been a bitter pill to swallow, in spite of whatever remuneration Tadd received.

Due to his poor health, Dameron had not performed much, if at all, since his release from Lexington. However, on January 27, just before marrying Mia, Tadd quietly put in an appearance at a club in Harlem. The occasion was a benefit staged to raise money to buy a proper headstone for the grave of the great blues singer Mamie Smith. At the height of her career Smith had employed musicians of the stature of trumpeter Bubber Miley (an important voice in Duke Ellington's early bands), the great stride pianist Willie "The Lion" Smith, and saxophonist Coleman Hawkins. She had been buried in 1946 in an unmarked grave on Staten Island. As Martin Williams reported in *Down Beat*, "At the bar several heads turned to note the somewhat unexpected presence of composer-pianist Tadd Dameron." Before the night was over, he took his turn at the piano to accompany the singer Lillyn Brown and probably some others.[28]

After they were married, Tadd and Mia moved into a very nice apartment at 247 West Seventy-second Street. Louis McKay, Billie Holiday's last husband, was moving, and he had arranged for the newlyweds to move into the apartment. Unfortunately, it was too expensive for them, and sometime after April they resettled in a smaller place on Central Park West. At both of these homes they received many visitors, among them the writers Dan Morgenstern and Ira Gitler; the pianist Bill Evans, along with the current members of his trio, Teddy Kotick and Paul Motien; and the trumpeter/singer Chet Baker. Baker would even be a houseguest, but it was not a very cheerful visit. Baker had just been deported from Germany for various violations of drug laws, only to find that he could not do a gig that had been booked at the Village Vanguard because he had been denied a cabaret card—a license required for work in New York City nightclubs. An arrest record, especially for drugs, was sufficient reason to deny an entertainer a card. All too often, the city used its licensing authority as a means to punish jazz musicians even after they had paid their debt to society. However, in the case of Baker, one could understand the authorities' concern. In addition to being an unapologetic junkie, he was, at the time, the subject of investigations by Interpol and the FBI. For six weeks he stayed with the Damerons, during which time the two musicians sat around complaining about the sad state of jazz and medicating themselves with drink and drugs.[29]

Another visitor around this time may have been the lyricist Irving Reid, whose best-known song is "A Man Ain't Suposed to Cry" (cowritten with

Frankie Laine and Norman Gimbel). Reid also collaborated with Ray An-
thony and Johnny Richards, among many others. As noted, nine of Dameron's
songs with words by Reid are mentioned in one document or another, but only
five exist in either written or recorded form: "The Happy Heart," "I'm Never
Happy Any More," "Love Took the 7:10," "Never Been in Love," and "Weekend."
The other four songs and the nine-part suite "Sermon on the Mount" remain
lost.

It is not clear just when Reid and Dameron collaborated in these last years
of Dameron's life. We do know that during Dameron's final fourteen or fifteen
months, Tadd and Maely's business relationship continued, and Mia and Maely
got to know each other.[30] In addition, Tadmal claimed all of the Dameron/
Reid songs, along with "Sermon on the Mount." Between the number of pieces
and the complications of both Tadd's health and his relationship with Maely, it
seems most likely that the two men's collaboration started in 1963 and continued
into 1964.

Cancer

Sometime in the late spring or early summer of 1964, Dameron was diagnosed
with cancer. He would be in and out of the hospital seeking treatment until his
death. Apparently, Jack Bregman, of Bregman, Vocco and Conn, managed to get
some assistance from ASCAP, of which Dameron was a member, to help with
the hospital bills. In October of 1964, Tadd was admitted to Roosevelt Hospital for an extended stay. On November 8, Babs Gonzales, another of Tadd's
regular visitors, arranged for a benefit concert for his old friend. Tadd's doctors
gave permission for him to attend the affair, which took place at the Five Spot
Café. Dameron played his own "The Squirrel," "If You Could See Me Now," and
"Good Bait" in a group rounded out by tenor saxophonist Clifford Jordan, bassist Ernie Shepard, and drummer Al Drears. Other performers at the tribute
included pianists Hank Jones, Duke Pearson, and Al Dailey; alto saxophonist Bobby Brown; bassists Nelson Boyd and Ray McKinney; drummers Max
Roach and Frankie Dunlop; singer Abbey Lincoln; and of course Babs Gonz-
laes, who sang and served as master of ceremonies.[31]

Dan Morgenstern attended the event and recalls that it was very sad and
that for anyone who did not know Dameron, it would have been very depressing indeed. "You could tell that he was very, very ill," Morgenstern remembered,
"and the whole thing did not have a very upbeat quality to it. Anyway, all these
people did come and play for Tadd, and it was very moving."[32] Tadd returned

to the hospital after the concert, but it was clear that there was not much that could be done. Since his wife was a licensed nurse, he was released into her care and returned home where he could be more comfortable.

In a letter dated December 2, 1964, Dameron wrote his old friend Mary Lou Williams to thank her for a grant provided by her Bel Canto Foundation. The brief letter tells of his predicament at the time:

Dear Mary Lou:

I am writing to thank you for the very timely gift which we both appreciate so much.

As you know, I have been sick for some time now; trouble with my spine. I'm at Roosevelt Hospital, receiving radiation (cobalt) treatment.

The $50 sent by you will go as a down payment for a special bed, which the doctors say I will need.

We had to leave our apartment; Mia is looking for a new one now. Meanwhile our address is:

Hotel Chalfonte
200 West 70 St.
New York 23, N.Y.

Once again, many thanks for thinking of us. We hope to see you at the Hickory House just as soon as I'm feeling well enough to make the rounds again.

Sincerely,
Tadd Dameron

The letter is typewritten, and Tadd's signature at the bottom is very shaky. In a thank you note from Mia to Mary Lou, she reports that the couple found an apartment at 784 Columbus Street, near Ninety-seventh Street.

Although quite ill, Tadd remained alert, gracious, and even cheerful in the eyes of some of those who visited him in his last few weeks. Everything that was needed for Mia to care for him was brought over from the hospital. However, Barbara Blakeney remembered that Mia had arranged the room so that Tadd could not see himself, or so it seemed. By now he had a large lump on his head as a result of a brain tumor he had developed.[33] Dan Morgenstern, Ira Gitler, and Don Schlitten would go to try to cheer him up as well. "We would talk about music and stuff, and to the very end he had his wits about him," remembered Morgenstern. However, the very last time we came he was already not fully alert, he was so heavily medicated. I'll never forget it, he was lying in bed and we were sitting next to him and Mia said, "Talk, he won't be able to respond very well, but he will hear you." He was almost skeletal, completely sunken cheeks and everything. The one thing that was still there was his hands, and because he was so thin, his hands looked very big on the blanket there. And throughout the time we were there his hands were constantly moving as if he were playing the music in his head at the piano.[34]

Early in the morning of March 8, 1965, just past his forty-eighth birthday, Tadley Ewing Dameron died in his home in the company of his wife.

13

"Le Fôret"—The Legacy of Tadd Dameron

Like so much else about his life, only a portion of Tadd Dameron's work remains known to us today. Over the years, much of his music has been lost. Still, there is reason to hope that, in time, some of it might be recovered. There have been fortuitous recent discoveries, such as "Zakat"—which had not been heard in decades—and "Mary Lou," which had never been performed. Neither of these works is mentioned in any of the copyright documents. Conversely, there are titles listed in those documents for which we have no music.

There can be no doubt that there was much more music that Dameron wrote than we know about, in terms of both arrangements and original compositions. For instance, when interviewed for this book, jazz historian Donald Meade recalled a Dameron tune titled "In Depth," which he said was a contrafact of "Fine and Dandy." Unfortunately, there is no trace of it anywhere but in Meade's memory.[1]

There are also the arrangements of "How about You" and, coincidentally, "Fine and Dandy," which Gerald Wilson mentioned to Eddy Determeyer[2] in the course of Determeyer's research into the life and work of Jimmie Lunceford. "How about You" appears to be lost, but "Fine and Dandy," discussed earlier in this book, can be found at the Smithsonian Institution. In addition, the number of Dameron's melodies copyrighted by New Era Music would lead us to believe there are probably more of his arrangements for Lunceford that are either lost or yet to be discovered.

In 1945 Count Basie recorded an arrangement of a tune titled "San José" for

V-Disc (see chap. 4). The arranger is not credited. However, the voicings and quotes from other Dameron arrangements, as well as the melodic character of the transitions and other ensembles, give ample reason to believe it is one of his charts. There were other arrangements that Dameron must have made for Basie in the 1940s. In the 1960s, Frank Foster remembers Dameron coming to a Basie rehearsal and running down some charts that Basie, for reasons known only to himself, rejected.[3] Add to this the evidence—some but not all of it anecdotal—of arrangements for Pearl Bailey, Brook Benton, Ray Charles, Tommy Dorsey, Ella Fitzgerald, Woody Herman, Illinois Jacquet, Harry James, Stan Kenton, Lucky Millinder, Vido Musso, Boyd Raeburn, Cootie Williams, and others—including lesser-known regional bands—and it becomes quite probable that Tadd Dameron arranged and/or composed perhaps as much as three times the work we have discussed here.

However, if it were only the quantity of his work that distinguished Tadd Dameron, this book would not exist. It is his place in the evolution of jazz that is his greatest legacy. Although Dameron has, for the most part, slipped into obscurity, he is one of the key figures in the formation of modern jazz. Along with Dizzy Gillespie, Charlie Parker, Kenny Clarke, and Thelonious Monk,[4] he laid the foundation for jazz in the post–World War II era. Not only was he present at the birth of the bebop movement; he was one of its prime movers. By the time he went to work for Harlan Leonard in the spring of 1940, Dameron was already well into the evolution of the chromatic harmony associated with jazz in the mid-1940s. Not only are there the indications of it in the recorded work from that year; it can also be seen in the unrecorded composition "Conversation." Further, there are the subtle suggestions of "bebop" harmony in his early work for Jimmie Lunceford, particularly the arrangement of "Bewildered." Anecdotes from several different people have attested to the strikingly advanced nature of his work in the period before and during the first recording ban.

Cleveland saxophonist Andy Anderson recalled that when he first heard Tadd in 1935, he was using chords, progressions, and voicings that the older musicians were not used to hearing. Others have recalled hearing Dameron himself, or his arrangements at performances by various local and regional bands during that time, and realizing later that they were hearing the beginnings of bebop.

Wherever the new approach to jazz was taking shape, Tadd Dameron was there. He and Charlie Parker were jamming privately in Kansas City in 1940. We have Kenny Clarke's recollections of hearing Dameron play chords with flatted fifths and "playing eighth-note sequences in the new legato manner" in the early 1940s at Minton's. Then there are Stan Levy's comments on the way

Dameron showed Al Haig, in 1945, how to accompany in the new style. While Tadd Dameron never enjoyed the ease of soloing at faster tempos that distinguished pianists such as Haig and Bud Powell, he was one of the first to employ the modern block-chord style of soloing.

Tadd Dameron is an influential collaborator in several defining bebop recordings with Fats Navarro, Babs Gonzales, and Dexter Gordon. Of course, he is the leader on several more under his own name. In his recordings he set the stage for the particular integration of arrangement and improvisation that is found in a significant portion of the small-group jazz of the following decades, especially in the work of those associated with the stylistic category of "hard bop," such as Horace Silver, Benny Golson, and Gigi Gryce, among others.

Of course, Dameron was a key player in the development of the progressive big bands of the 1940s. He was instrumental in setting the tone of the Eckstine band in 1944, both in his original compositions, such as "Our Delight," and in his arrangements of ballads. He also wrote for the modernist bands of Georgie Auld, Boyd Raeburn, and Buddy Rich. The recollections of trumpeter Dave Burns place Dameron with the Dizzy Gillespie Orchestra in June of 1946, much earlier than had been previously understood, at least by those of us too young to have been there. This means that although Dameron had not yet written new material for the second Gillespie big band at that point, he was helping to rehearse this influential band in its formative stage.

While Dameron is often described as one of the first arrangers to write for big bands in the bop style, one must remember that the evolution of jazz in the 1940s is evident in the work of a handful of big-band arrangers, Dameron among them. Budd Johnson, Jimmy Mundy, Gil Fuller, Gill Evans, and Eddie Sauter were all developing ideas in the early 1940s that would contribute to the "modern" sound emerging after World War II. Indeed, one always needs to be careful in tracing major developments in the arts. Those innovations that we so often attribute to one person, or to a very small group, are widely accepted because they are "in the air," waiting for clear definition. Still, in this regard Tadd Dameron was outstanding in his ability to clearly define these innovations. As such, he pointed the way for many writers who emerged soon after him. Benny Golson and Gigi Gryce are probably the composer/arrangers who most readily come to mind as having been inspired and influenced by Dameron. However, others have expressed his importance to them personally.

"I met Tadd Dameron in the early fifties," Frank Foster said, "but by the late forties I was influenced by his writing for ten-piece groups. What I admired about Tadd was not his unconventionality but the fact the he wrote so pretty. His voicings were very beautiful."[5] Foster has also said that the arranging concepts heard in those smaller-band arrangements are part of the foundation of his own work.

Jerome Richardson recalled that during his tenure with Lionel Hampton, Quincy Jones "was experimenting with that 'birth of the cool sound' that Tadd Dameron and Gil Evans were writing." Jones has acknowledged elsewhere that Dameron was an "idol of mine."[6]

In the 1950s, Jimmy Heath used to visit with Dameron at the home of drummer Harold "Doc" West and discuss music.[7] Tadd Dameron was very highly regarded in the late 1940s, and, even though they may not have stated it in print, one can hear his influence on several other arrangers who emerged after him, as well.

As became clear during his travels overseas, Dameron's influence extended to European jazz musicians, as well. Even before Dameron arrived on the Continent, George Shearing had written an arrangement of his "Ladybyrd" [sic] for Ted Heath's band. In the fall of 1949, James Moody recorded with a small band of progressive musicians from Sweden. Some of the arrangements they used, particularly one of David Raksin's "Laura"—recorded under Arne Domnerus's name—reflect Dameron's influence.[8]

In 1955, before leaving for the United States, the young English jazz prodigy Victor Feldman recorded four of his compositions for big band, including one titled "Elegy." While Feldman's writing on this session reveals several influences, "Elegy" sounds particularly inspired by Dameron's Capitol recordings, as well as the 1953 A Study in Dameronia. As late as 1985, Norwegian composer and arranger Per Husby paid tribute to Tadd Dameron in his award-winning release Dedications. One can, of course, find more examples Dameron's influence on European musicians.

Dameron's ability to capture what was "in the air" was not limited solely to the bebop movement. In his non-song-form compositions "Nearness" and "Soulphony in Three Hearts" he boldly anticipated the "third-stream" developments of the 1950s. In these works, as well as some of the music in the Studies in Dameronia set, Dameron drew on both jazz and European art-music influences and techniques in an effort to expand his compositional pallet. While the influence of Ellington and Gershwin is unmistakably present,[9] Dameron clearly brings his own sensibility to this process. Most notable is his use of subtle motivic development. While it is difficult to know the extent to which—either by example or in conversation—he shared these concepts with his colleagues, we can see in his work a continuum that predates the "third stream" and resonates today in the work of jazz composers such as Bob Brookmeyer and Maria Schneider. Perhaps some of his later extended works, such as the lost ballet or "The Sermon on the

Mount," will eventually be found, allowing us to hear the continuation of this aspect of his compositional practice, a line that ends, for now, with "Fontainebleau."

As Frank Foster noted, it was the beauty—the lyricism and elegant proportions—of Tadd Dameron's writing that left the deepest impression. This was, of course, his stated intention. In his music, Tadd never uses any harmonic or formal device, however innovative, just for its novelty. Even when Dameron does something startling, it still works. Take, for example, the coda to the arrangement of "You're Not the Kind," written for Sarah Vaughan in 1946. Vaughan found that daring ending, which ends in a distant key, so effective that she that she used it throughout her career.

On the other hand, whenever Tadd Dameron determined that simplicity was appropriate, as in "The Chase" or "At Christmas Time," he wrote simply. It is no coincidence that as a pianist, his greatest strengths were his touch and harmonic grace. He always sounds his very best on ballads and when accompanying a soloist. While Frank Foster credits Dameron's harmonic voicings as the thing that really caught his ear, the source of those beguiling harmonies is Tadd's melodic genius.

Dexter Gordon, who played Dameron's charts while in the Billy Eckstine Orchestra, observed, "Several things always impressed me about his writing. One was that the parts he writes are so melodic in themselves. It's almost as if every part was a lead, in that sense. . . . With Tadd, his parts were always beautiful. A lot of times I'd play the [second tenor sax] parts, and they were beautiful."[10]

"Les Cygnes"—Melodic Technique

There is a saying among musicians that most songwriters—and lesser composers—have only a couple of songs, and they spend their careers just writing variations on these.[11] That is, while some details of rhythm pattern and contour may change, their overall melodic designs remain the same. It is a crude observation, but there is a certain amount of truth in it. One can hear this readily in recordings of many singer/songwriters who insist on singing only their own work. However, like his idol Duke Ellington and other serious composers, Tadd Dameron was an exceptionally thoughtful and creative craftsman. While there are certain things that show up frequently in Dameron's writing—signature rhythmic and harmonic patterns, such as the "common bridge"—there is a fascinating range of melodies and formal designs in the catalog of his compositions. This is all the more remarkable when one realizes that—again like Ellington—

practically everything he wrote is in a major key and 4/4 time.

There are his twelve-bar blues tunes, often with only the parallel movement of I-ii-iii-biii in the seventh and eighth measures to signify their harmonic modernity. There are tunes written on straightforward harmonic sequences, like those found in the two tunes mentioned above. There are others, like the waltz "This Night of Stars," that have a beguiling lyricism but employ sophisticated harmonies. There are the contrafacts, or songs written on the progressions of other melodies. Some of them stay very close to the model. "A Be Bop Carroll" is a good example of this, even to the point of almost quoting the first two measures of the model's melody. Others, such as "On a Misty Night," have embellishments on the model's harmonic sequence that are essential to Dameron's new melody. Still others of his tunes, such as "The Scene Is Clean" and the never-released "Sando Latino," have original and very intricate progressions that offer a serious challenge to the improviser. The common thread with all of these is a concern for the melody and how the harmonic progression reflects and supports the melody.

It takes both inspiration and skill to consistently craft fine melodies. As composer and educator Leon Dallin wrote,

> Of all the aspects of musical composition, the ability to write effective melodies is the most elusive, the most dependent upon natural gifts, and the most difficult to teach. But if one must rely upon natural gifts for the original conception of a melody, he can employ technique to put it in its most effective form and make the best use of it.[12]

In studying Dameron's melodies—in both copyright deposits and recorded performances—and comparing multiple arrangements of various pieces, it has become evident that he had both "natural gifts" and technical skill. A somewhat casual examination of the melodic design and dynamics of six of his most popular compositions should make this clear, in that it reveals great variety of melodic technique. These are "Good Bait," "Lady Bird," "If You Could See Me Now," "On a Misty Night," "Soultrane," and "Hot House." In the case of these six pieces, all but one of them is in thirty-two-bar AABA form, and all of them are written within "square" forms: built in four-, eight-, and sixteen-measure sections. Within these constraints of mode, meter, and form, Dameron composes seven very different melodies, each with its own internal logic.

The economical "Good Bait" is based on one eight-bar idea, since the bridge is just the A melody repeated up a fourth (when it is not left open for improvisation). Still, there is something so compelling about its melody that this is probably Dameron's second-most-recorded work, after "If You Could See Me Now." Musicians as diverse as Count Basie, Albert Ayler, Nina Simone, and Warne Marsh have recorded it. The core eight-measure melody is spun out of a four-note motif. First it is preceded by an eighth-note pick-up, and then it is repeated up a fifth, but with a long scalar pick-up of seven eighth notes. The second half of this melody is a four-bar phrase incorporating the motif two more times. One should also note the lack of syncopation in the melody and the rhythmic resemblance of the motif to the little figure played by drummers in 4/4 swing time, the one they most often play on the ride cymbal. Additionally, the two shorter phrases end on the third beat of bars one and three, while the final long phrase, with its chromaticism that balances the essential diatonic nature of the other phrases, ends on the first beat of the final bar. The rhythm alone "tells a story" not unlike the rhythmic scheme in a poem or a skillfully written joke.[13]

If, as we have good reason to believe, "Good Bait" was written in 1939, it is definitely forward looking, in spite of its simplicity. This is also true of "Lady Bird," which has been recorded almost as many times as "Good Bait" and most likely dates from the same early period of Dameron's writing. However, it has a very different melody. For one thing it is a single sixteen-bar statement, without sectional repeats, and it does not have a final cadence. The melody is designed to continually turn back on itself until a final extra measure, or a coda of some sort, is added. Where the melody of "Good Bait" begins with a simple, almost unassuming one-bar phrase, which then grows in meaning through the addition of the longer pick-up and transposition to other pitch levels, "Lady Bird" opens with a grand four-bar phrase[14] that is repeated, but with a different ending. This is followed by a two-bar phrase that is repeated a half step higher and a final four-bar phrase. The result is a sophisticated composition in miniature.[15]

In "If You Could See Me Now" we find yet another melodic design. Dameron sets up a kind of gently rocking energy in the first four measures of the A, section with two identical pairs of one-bar phrases. This is answered by a long four-bar phrase. In the first statement this answering phrase rises chromatically from the dominant note, B♭, heading for the tonic, E♭, but finally comes to rest on G, to make a half cadence. In the second A, it arrives at its target E♭ to make the full cadence. The bridge starts off in the distant and brighter key of G major (a major third above the home key), before it works its way back to E♭. The final A is the same as the second one. The design of this melody is developed around the lyric. For instance, the departure to the distant, brighter key in the bridge sets words that describe a chance meeting with the lost lover. The return to the original key expresses the singer's inability to hide the pain in her or his heart.

The phrase structure of "Misty Night" is yet another design. In the A sections there are two essentially four-bar phrases, with the last four notes of the first phrase repeated as the beginning of the second. In the preferred bridge there is a one-bar phrase followed by a three-bar phrase. The first phrase is repeated in a sequence a half step lower to begin the second phrase. All this is repeated up a whole step in the second half of the bridge, with the second phrase getting a different ending.

"Soultrane" has not achieved the popularity of the other six, but it has been recorded by several artists over the years. It is in the key of E♭, and like "If You Could See Me Now,"[16] it opens with an ascending E♭Maj7 arpeggio. Still, because the rhythm pattern is different and because the melody proceeds in a very different manner, one would not make the connection between the two pieces just by listening to them. Actually without the pick-up note, D, the first measures of "If You Could See" and "Soultrane" have the very same pitches, but the first phrase of "Soultrane" finishes by dropping dramatically by a major seventh, from C to D♭. This dropping motif is repeated in the next two one-bar phrases. In the second four measures of the A section, the rising arpeggio becomes a motif, heard as a C♭Maj7 played over the progression A♭min7-D♭7, which begins a long four-bar phrase. A Gmin arpeggio (starting on D) with the same rhythm pattern as the other two arpeggios begins the bridge, which is constructed in four two-bar phrases.

"Hot House," one of the defining melodies of bebop, has already been described to some extent in chapter 4. The chord changes, taken from Cole Porter's "What Is This Thing Called Love," are in AABA form, but the melody is ABCA. It is noticeably different from the other six melodies in this discussion, not only in its phrase structure but in its expressive character and the treatment of dissonances. Whereas the dissonant notes in the other tunes mentioned here are presented in what could be termed a lyrical way, they are presented quite boldly in "Hot House."

"L'Adieu"—The Man and His Tragedy

At the beginning of the research for this book, and even well into the writing of it, Tadd Dameron seemed inscrutable, enigmatic, and mysterious. At the end of this project he is only slightly less so. He was secretive almost to the point of paranoia; of the several musical associates interviewed for this book, only one was able to answer questions about his personal life, and then only in the vaguest terms. "We only talked about music," was the most frequent response of those who considered Tadd Dameron a good friend. Then there are the legends he invented himself, especially the story about medical school and the 1950 article in Cleveland's *Call and Post*, in which he conveyed an account of his activities totally divorced from reality. Because of these, it took a great deal of research to be able to come to the conclusion that most of the time Dameron was telling the truth about his life. Yet why did he indulge in these stories? There are probably a few reasons for the medical school story. For one thing, African Americans, especially those in the arts, were not used to being taken seriously when Dameron first told this tale. The story of shifting his career from medicine to music asserts his sense of himself as part of the middle class. For another thing, among his friends Tadd was known to enjoy the art of the "put-on." What harm could possibly come from pulling Barry Ulanov's leg?

The fictions in the *Call and Post* are most likely an indication of just how desperate Dameron was in the summer of 1950. As explained earlier, by this time he was thoroughly addicted to heroin, and his relationship with his lover, Margo, was likely coming to an end, if it had not collapsed already. He was, and still is, well respected as a Clevelander who had gone out in the world and achieved distinction. It is not surprising that he may have wanted to bring home some good news. However, it is sad that he could not think of a positive spin on his situation that was closer to the truth.

Like his friend Thelonious Monk, Tadd Dameron was private and individualistic. Both men are key players in the developments in jazz in the 1940s, yet they stand a little off to the side, as it were, even among the other highly individualistic musicians who were the originators of the new style. The characteristically "boppish" harmonic and melodic complexity in Dameron's work, combined with his romantic lyricism and his interest in larger, fully composed pieces, serves as a metaphor for his complexity as a human being. Dameron is at once a musician with an essentially middle-class vision of a modern idiom (one that is both accessible and intellectually satisfying) and the quintessential underground hipster. He is dignified, gracious, and proud on the one hand, secretive and self-destructive on the other.

Dan Morgenstern was impressed with Tadd Dameron's courtesy and consideration the first time he met him in 1948, and later in the 1960s, when they developed a friendship, Morgenstern's initial impression was confirmed. Pianist Patti Bown got to know Dameron in the 1960s and spent some time with him discussing music and sharing ideas at the piano. She recalled, "He was very impressive. He seemed a peaceful man, very intelligent and he had a beautiful smile. We had a lot of laughs together."[17] Jimmy and Jeannie Cheatham would also visit Dameron around this time and have warm memories of the man.

On the other hand, we have seen how he could be mischievous, and "A," the unnamed fellow inmate at Lexington, quoted earlier, recalled instances when Dameron could exhibit a cruelly sharp tongue. There is also the one reported instance of him acting with violence, but that seems to be an isolated event at a time of considerable stress.

The drummer Herbie Lovelle, who seems to be a psychologically perceptive man, met Dameron socially and shared his observations with Val Wilmer. Lovelle had the distinct impression that "Tadd showed me the Tadd he wanted me to see. He was a man of many layers, and I only got to see one of them." Lovelle felt that Dameron's complexity was a defense mechanism and that different people who knew him might well have known a very different man. Lovelle also sensed that beneath the charming surface of Dameron there was a man who should not be crossed.[18] This characterization has resonance with the image of the young man who could whip the Harlan Leonard Rockets into shape, even though he was younger than several of the key members of the band and no older than the youngest of them.

Tadd Dameron was an enormously gifted man with a very high degree of musical aptitude. Five years after graduating from high school he was writing arrangements that hold their own with the work of some of the best veteran writers of the day. He did this with very little, if any, formal musical education. He had studied on his own, with help from his brother and Louis Bolden. Like all of the finest composers, he was motivated by the beauty he heard in the work of others and the glimmers of it that he could hear in his own mind. His musical memory was remarkable. Various people, saxophonist and composer Sam Rivers among them, saw him write out arrangements from many years earlier without referring to recordings. Some of these were his; some were the work of others. Tadd Dameron knew what he was hearing without the aid of a piano or other instrument—he himself was the instrument. Philly Joe Jones, with whom he roomed at times, remembered Dameron lying on the floor writing arrangements and only occasionally going to the piano to check something. Then there is the arrangement of his own "Look, Stop and Listen" for Kenton, which we have good reason to believe was written while he was held at Rikers Island, the city prison of New York.

At various times in the 1950s, Dameron was well positioned to take advantage of promising new opportunities, but his involvement with heroin always got in the way. He had the show in Atlantic City that, by all accounts, he had scored brilliantly. He had a plan for taking a similar show to England and quite possibly elsewhere. Just how close he was to realizing this plan we will probably never know. However, he was well respected, and he had good connections, so this was, in all likelihood, more than a mere pipe dream. But when he fled Atlantic City to avoid the raid that he had been warned of, he decided to lay low. As Benny Golson recalled later, "the police were looking for him and he had to get out of town."[19] He managed to weather that setback and became very active again in 1956, releasing a well-received LP, *Fontainebleau*, and arranging for Tommy Dorsey and Carmen McRae. He was probably also writing for others, who would have been happy that he was back in action. Once again, his addiction got in the way, this time with an arrest. He then compounded the arrest by entering into a kind of "deal with the devil" with the notorious Richard Carpenter. This decision would haunt him to the grave and beyond. Even then, after he had paid a heavy price to get out of the jam created by this arrest, he could not, as several of his friends had done, shake the habit. By the time he managed to break the addiction and pay his "debt to society," not only was he saddled with his arrangement with Carpenter, but his health was deteriorating, in all likelihood as a result of his drug use.

The quality of the music we have examined shows what a tragedy this was. One of the "fathers" of modern jazz, Dameron worked almost exclusively with the very best of musicians. When he went to work for Vido Musso in 1939, the tenor saxophonist had already become a star in the bands of Benny Goodman and Gene Krupa. The Harlan Leonard band was one of the best to come out of the Southwest. The trumpeters with whom he associated are a who's-who of the modern lineage: starting with his high school buddy Freddie Webster, the list includes Dizzy Gillespie, Miles Davis, Fats Navarro, Clifford Brown, Kenny Dorham, Clark Terry, Donald Byrd, and other masters. Saxophonists Charlie Parker, Illinois Jacquet, Charlie Rouse (who made his first recordings with Dameron), Dexter Gordon, James Moody, Cecil Payne, and Benny Golson were among his sidemen or clients. The deservedly very well-known trombonists J. J. Johnson and Kai Winding both played in his bands, and later Jimmy Cleveland, Curtis Fuller, Urbie Green, and Britt Woodman recorded with him. The bassists who played with him included Curly Russell, Nelson Boyd, and John Simmons, who may not be household names but had impressive careers; on Dameron's later recordings one finds Percy Heath, George Duvivier, Paul Chambers, and Ron Carter. Then there are the drummers, Kenny Clarke, Art Blakey, Shadow Wilson, and Philly Joe Jones chief among them. When he chose not to play piano on a project, one finds Bill Evans, Tommy Flanagan, Hank Jones, or Duke Jordan in the piano chair.

While Tadd Dameron was only one of many jazz musicians whose lives were diminished by heroin addiction in the 1950s, his life is one of the most tragic. Many of heroin's victims managed to free themselves and live to enjoy a proper appreciation of their talent and contributions. Then there were those who died young, such as Freddie Webster, Fats Navarro, and the brilliant pianist Dick Twardzik, leaving us to wonder what they would have done with a full life. Tadd Dameron died a slow death, starting in the early 1950s. He was like a man who had fallen down a well from which he could not be rescued, but whose voice could still be heard in the distance. In his struggle to cling to his creative life he produced some of his best work, but given his exceptional ability, there is far less of his music than there could, or should, have been.

After his death Tadd Dameron was grieved in the music press but given only a short obituary in the *New York Times*, where his name was misspelled. The *Times* coverage of Dameron's funeral was better, but it still could not get his name right. "The Benny Golson Quintet played 'The Squirrel' yesterday at the Advent Lutheran Church at Broadway and 93rd Street. It was one of the late Tadd Dameron's favorites and his friends said that he would have loved it. Tadley G. [*sic*] Dameron died on Monday of bone cancer at the age of 48," George Dugan wrote in the Friday, March 12, 1965, edition. Still, the funeral was well attended. Around 150 well-known musicians were in attendance. For those in the jazz world, especially those who knew Tadd personally, his death was heartbreaking.

The clergyman who presided at Dameron's funeral had recently become a friend of his, as well. Over the years, Lutheran pastor John Gensel had become friendly with several jazz musicians, and one of them, Max Roach, explained to Gensel that there were many in the jazz community who believed in God but did not belong to any church. This inspired Gensel to ask church authorities to let him minister to the jazz community as well as his own congregation, which they consented to let him do. Reverend Gensel recalled later that "Tadd was in Roosevelt Hospital in New York City, and I used to visit him. He lived not too far away from where I lived on the West Side of Manhattan. I would visit him at his home and we'd talk. What an incredible musician!" Dameron's was one of the first funeral services for a jazz musician Reverend Gensel conducted.[20]

In the years immediately following Dameron's death in 1965, jazz entered a difficult period. Over the next few years rock and roll would be getting most of the attention of the record-buying public. Many of the finest jazz musicians would go into exile in Europe. Others would retreat into the steady employment available in Las Vegas shows or ride out the last years of abundant studio work. Others would just throw in the towel.

In some ways Dameron's death coincides with the so-called death of jazz itself. Of course, jazz has never really died. Dameron's music would surface here and there in the next few years, and he did receive some well-deserved attention in the 1980s. First there came the historical reissues. In fact, some of these began appearing even earlier. In 1961, just as Dameron was rejoining the active musical world, his radio broadcasts from the Royal Roost were released on the Jazzland label. However, Fats Navarro was given top billing on these, even though it was Tadd's gig, and most of the music was Tadd's. In 1966, a year or so after his death, RCA Victor reissued the 1940 recordings of Harlan Leonard, including most of the takes that had never been released, such as "Dameron Stomp." In 1971 Capitol reissued the Big Ten recordings, and Prestige reissued the sessions with Clifford Brown. In 1975 Prestige put out a two-disc set of recordings it had made of Gil Evans and Tadd Dameron. Also around this time pianist Barry Harris recorded an entire album of Dameron's music for the Xanadu label. Admittedly, these were aimed at a small audience, but at least the music was available again.

Posthumous Releases

In April or May of 1964, Chet Baker recorded five Dameron tunes for an album released later that year by Colpix, under the pretentious title *The Most Important Jazz Album of 1964/65*. The melody of "Aloof Spoof," now with a lyric by Bernie Hanighen, becomes "Whatever Possess'd Me," a convincing ballad that Baker would record again later. The other titles, "Soultrane," "Tadd's Delight," "Gnid," and "Mating Call," had all been released before. The band is only a quintet, but the modest arraignments are all credited, with Dameron treating three of his tunes, as well as the blues "Walkin.'"[21] According to the notes, "Soultrane" and "Gnid" were arranged by Jimmy Mundy. The arrangements consist of an occasional introduction, as well as harmonizations and guide-tone lines for the "heads." Those credited to Dameron do sound like his work, although "Mating Call" could be just an adaptation of the original from 1956.[22]

After Dameron's death in 1965 a few previously unknown songs were recorded, and words were added to some of his known tunes by a singer who had taken a fancy to them. In October 1974, vocalist Muriel Winston and bassist Bill Lee recorded six of Dameron's compositions, including four that had never been released before, as part of an album on Strata East titled *A Fresh Viewpoint and Muriel Winston*. One of these is a wordless performance of "Soultrane." Another, "Love Took the 7:10," is "I Think I'll Go Away," from 1947, with a new set of words by Irving Reid. In fact, the remaining previously unrecorded four songs from the set on this recording all have lyrics by Reid. "The Happy Heart" is a well-crafted, if rather conventional song in AABA form. The same could be said for the attractive "Weekend," a recasting of one of his pieces for the 1953

Fig. 13.1. Dameron's "Never Been in Love" © 1978, Twenty-Eighth Street Music.

Paradise Club show, and the ballad "I'm Never Happy Anymore," which gets a playfully ironic treatment on this record as a samba.

The ballad "Never Been In Love" (fig. 13.1) has a more elaborate form than the other songs in this set and is worth examining from the standpoint of melodic construction. First there is a short, six-bar verse (not shown in the example), a rarity in Dameron's output. The chorus could be described as A, A1, B, A1, C, and the way the opening motif is developed is an example of brilliantly economical melody writing. In the A section, the opening motive (1.) is repeated three times, with rhythmic alterations, and the section is concluded with a second, rising motive (2.), coming to rest by falling a minor sixth, from A to C. This repeats in A1, except the line keeps rising through C and D♭ to D.

The B section presents motive 1 up a fourth and then in sequence down a step from there—incidentally the same harmonic sequence found in the B section of "Never Happy." The first three notes of motive 2 (2a.) begin the next phrase. At letter C, motive 1 returns, again harmonized by a B♭Ma7 chord, but this time it starts on a D, a fourth higher than it had before. It descends sequentially in whole steps, forming a melodic chain, this time returning to the tonic. The next phrase (2b.) can be seen as a further development of the second motive, and motive 1 returns once more, developed into a final cadence. Here it starts on F instead of E, so that the opening interval is a major third instead of a minor third.

In March of 1982, pianist Hod O'Brien recorded "Lovely One in the Window" as part of a medley with "Heaven's Doors Are Open Wide." There is an eight-bar verse to the song, followed by an attractive AABA chorus. Although a copyright deposit of "Lovely One" does not exist, the title is mentioned in the June 7, 1963, catalog of titles assigned (or reassigned) to Bregman, Vocco and Conn. O'Brien recalled that he learned the song from drummer Al Leavitt, who had recorded it earlier as part of a project that was never released.[23] There is a lyric for the song, but the author is unknown at the time of this writing.

In 1986, Norwegian arranger and bandleader Per Husby released a recording titled *Dedications*. Three previously unrecorded Dameron tunes were included, "That's the Way It Goes," "Take a Chance on Spring," and "Accentuate the Bass." Husby also recorded his take of "I'm Never Happy Anymore" and a medley of "Good Bait" and "Lady Bird." "That's the Way It Goes" is a retitling of "That's Just the Way It Goes," the piano arrangement filed by Tadd Dameron Music, Inc., in 1962, with a lyric by English vocalist Georgie Fame.[24] Fame makes some very slight changes to the melody, in order to accommodate the words, and may have added the verse that is sung here, since it is not part of either the original piano arrangement or the second lead sheet supplied to the author by Cromwell Music, Inc., the current copyright holder. There is also supposed to be another lyric for this melody by Irving Reid under the title "That's How It Goes," but it has yet to come to light.

"Take a Chance on Spring," with lyrics by Maely Daniele (Dufty), contains only the third known verse that is, without a doubt, Tadd Dameron's. Composing verses for his songs seems to have been a late development in his songwriting practice. The verse is twenty measures long, and the appropriately sprightly chorus is thirty-two measures, in ABAC form. The song was first mentioned in a list of songs and compositions issued by Tadmal Music Publishing Company, the company set up by Dameron and Dufty, in the spring of 1963. Like "That's the Way It Goes," "Accentuate the Bass"—a classic Dameron ABAC bop tune with a twist—was originally a piano arrangement, to which Georgie Fame added lyrics. Here Dameron explores the relationship between the keys of F and A♭ again, so that harmonically the melody is ABCB. The contour and rhythm of the A-section melody are maintained at C, but the progression moves to the key of A♭.

In the years after Tadd Dameron's death, his very close friend and colleague Philly Joe Jones held on to the hope that someday he could make people aware of Dameron's music. As Don Sickler, who would help him do something about this, put it, "Philly Joe felt that Tadd was one of the most ignored real geniuses. Joe was determined to do something for Tadd." Through the persistent effort of Eloise Wood Jones, Joe's wife, he received a grant from the National Endowment for the Arts in 1981. This gave him the money to have arrangements of many of the pieces he had recorded with Dameron transcribed and new arrangements written to develop a working book. After much careful consideration with trumpeter and general musical handyman Sickler, with whom Jones had been discussing the idea of this project for several years, they settled on a nine-piece band like the one on 1953's *A Study in Dameronia* LP. The band would cut down to just eight pieces for the material from the *Fontainebleau* album, which would free Sickler to conduct when necessary. Sickler did most of the transcribing and arranging, some of it with the help of Woody Herman's pianist John Oddo.

Next there came the task of picking the musicians. Bassist Larry Ridley and saxophonist Charles Davis had been working with Jones on something of a regular basis. Baritone saxophonist Cecil Payne, who went back with Dameron to the days of the Dizzy Gillespie Orchestra, and trumpeter Johnny Coles, who worked and recorded with Dameron in 1953, were obviously perfect choices. Needless to say, they were delighted to be in the band. Rounding out the ensemble were saxophonist Frank Wess, who had played Dameron's arrangements as a member of the Billy Eckstine Orchestra, trombonist Britt Woodman, and pianist Walter Davis Jr., all among the finest musicians on the scene at that time, or at any other time for that matter. Cecil Payne proved particularly important to the sound of the music.

When Sickler first began hiring some musicians to run through his transcriptions, everything sounded correct, but he felt something was missing—something he could not quite identify. Sickler recalled finding the answer: "I remember we had our first rehearsal with all of the guys—Frank Wess, Charles Davis, Cecil Payne, Johnny Coles, myself, and Britt Woodman—and once we started the rehearsal, my question of what was missing was answered. Once I heard Cecil Payne play the baritone parts with his soft approach [to tone], and the way he would slide into the notes, it made all the sense in the world to me."[25]

The band played first in Philadelphia, where Jones was living, and then in the first week of April 1982, they played a four-night stand at Lush Life in New York. The management began to worry that the band, which was unavoidably expensive, might not draw: Dameron, after all, had been gone for eighteen years, and Philly Joe, great as he was, was better known as a sideman. Hoping to drum up interest, they got jazz critic Robert Palmer to write a preview article for the show in the Sunday *New York Times*.

On the day of the opening, a freak snowstorm almost shut the city down, but Dameronia, as the band was called, packed the house anyway. By the last night of the stand people were lined up outside the club waiting to get in, proving what Jones had long believed—if people could just hear how beautiful Dameron's music was, they would respond with enthusiasm.

So successful were the performances that the band would continue to work for the next three years, until Jones's death in the middle of 1985 (and even a bit beyond, with Kenny Washington in the drum chair), playing, among other venues, New York's Philharmonic Hall and European jazz festivals, all the while bringing Dameron's music to a wider audience.

Since that time many of Dameron's recordings have remained in print on compact disc, and others have recorded tributes to him on occasion, right up to the present. Most recently a series of concerts by vocalist Vanessa Rubin featured Dameron's songs, all arranged for a characteristically Dameronian octet by some of the best arrangers in jazz (all Dameronians), including Frank Foster, Jimmy Heath, and Benny Golson. These have been recorded, and it is hoped they will be released soon.

Additionally, Jamie Abersold, well known for his educational materials, has released a play-along recording that features well-known Dameron pieces, as well as some that should be better known, for the benefit of a whole new generation of musicians. There is also the well-received CD set of Tadd's tunes performed by pianist Tardo Hammer, which was released in 2007.

In June of 2008, the American Society of Composers, Authors and Publishers, of which Dameron was a member, finally inducted him into their "Wall of Fame," a hopeful sign that Tadd Dameron's spirit will remain with us for a long time to come.

Notes

Chapter 1

1. This is not the Willie Smith who played with Lunceford and Ellington. Willie Smith of Cleveland was also an alto saxophonist and arranged for Lionel Hampton and Motown Records, among others.

2. For more on Cleveland jazz history read Joe Mosbrook, *Cleveland Jazz History* (Cleveland, Northeast Ohio Jazz Society, 2003) and Mosbrook's articles posted under the heading "Jazzed in Cleveland" at http://www.cleveland.oh.us. As of this writing, the complete list of Mosbrook's articles can be accessed from the home page. The method of navigating the site changes from time to time.

3. From the certificate for Ruth's marriage to Adolphus Dameron, which says "Koscinska." There is no such place, and only two letters differ between this likely misspelling and the spelling of the known town. Ruth's mother's maiden name is also misspelled on this document as "Padley."

4. According to his marriage certificate, Silas would also have been born in 1893. This a deduction made from his and Ruth's given ages on the dates of their respective marriage certificates. If correct, it would seem they were born in quick succession.

5. It was not until 1951 that civil marriage licenses were required for all cases in Cuyahoga County, OH.

6. Tadley Dameron did not start spelling his nickname with two *d*'s until the late 1940s. In this book, however, his name will be spelled with two *d*'s unless a source is being quoted where it is spelled otherwise.

7. The directory ending in Aug. 1916 shows Caesar Harris to be the householder of 2201 East Thirtieth Street and Isaiah Peake to be a resident.

8. W. J. Zoul was a "longtime justice of the peace in Cleveland," according to Joe Mosbrook. In 1918 he presided over the civil marriage of Sidney Bechet to Norma Hale. It could have been the case that second marriages were not performed at St. Paul's or that doing so would have been embarrassing to the founder of the church.

9. Langston Hughes, *The Big Sea* (New York: Hill and Wang, 1964), 27. Between 1910 and 1920 the black population of Cleveland rose from 8,448 to 34,451, and by

1930 it would grow to 71,899. According to Carol Poh Miller and Robert A. Wheeler, "Central Avenue [basically one block south of Cedar] became a hotbed of gambling, prostitution, and crime; law enforcement was lax in the 'Roaring Third,' as whites called the area." See *Cleveland, A Concise History, 1796–1996* (Bloomington and Indianapolis: Indiana University Press, 1997), 121–23.

10. Information on local adoption procedures in the 1920s is courtesy of staff at the Cuyahoga County, OH, Probate Court Adoption Department.

11. Tadd Dameron and Benny Golson, interview with Harry Frost, Mid Town Hotel, St Louis, MO, spring 1952; *The Dave Cliff/Geoff Simkins 5 "Play the Music of Tadd Dameron"* (Spotlite Records, SPJ-(CD) 560, 1997), track 12.

12. Denise Dameron (Tadd's niece), interview with the author, Aug. 10, 2004.

13. Bill Coss, "Tadd's Back," *Down Beat,* Feb. 15, 1962, 18.

14. Myron Styles, interview with the author, Inner-City Yacht Club, Cleveland, OH, July 22, 2000. All further quotations of and references to Styles and his friend Buddy Crewe come from this interview.

15. Ira Gitler, *Jazz Masters of the 40s* (New York: Da Capo Press, 1983), 264. The quotations at the end of this paragraph and the one in the next paragraph come from the same source.

16. Dameron and Golson, interview with Frost, spring 1952.

17. Dameron and Golson, interview with Frost, spring 1952.

18. Joe Mosbrook, interview with the author, Aug. 10, 2004.

19. Gitler, *Jazz Masters of the 40s,* 263.

20. Jimmy Williams, interview with the author, Aug. 10, 2004.

21. Ian MacDonald, *Tadd, the Life and Legacy of Tadley Ewing Dameron* (Sheffield, England: Jahbero Press, 1998), 74.

22. Barry Ulanov, "Tad Dameron, Second in a Series on the Leading Beboppers," *Metronome,* Aug. 1947, 24, +35. The medical school reference is also found in Ulanov's *History of Jazz in America* (New York: Viking Press, 1952), 278. Later, Max Jones reported that he "was originally intended for the medical profession. But after six years' study he gave up medicine for music" ("And Next We Come to Soulphony," *Melody Maker,* June 4, 1949, 4). Tadd also related another version of this story to Bill Coss, which appeared in Coss's 1962 *Down Beat* profile ("Tadd's Back," 18–19). Because Dameron was the source of this rumor, it was not contested. Inquiries at Oberlin, made by this author and others, revealed that Dameron never attended the school or at the very best enrolled for a course but never finished it. Near the end of his life he also admitted to his wife Mia that he had made up the story (MacDonald, *Tadd,* 25).

23. Val's-in-the-Alley was often host to the pianist Art Tatum, both before and after he achieved fame.

24. Caesar A. Dameron (1914–77) was an important figure in his community. Well regarded by many as a fine musician, he was also the subject of controversy for both his illegal business operations and his role in the merger of the black American Federation of Musicians (AFM) local 550 with the white local 4.

25. Albert McCarthy, *Big Band Jazz* (New York: G. P. Putnam's Sons, 1974), 33.

26. Leonard Feather, *The Encyclopedia of Jazz* (New York: Horizon Press, 1960), 246. See also John Chilton, *Who's Who of Jazz, Storyville to Swing Street* (Philadelphia: Chilton Book Co., Time-Life Records Special Edition, 1978), 136.

27. Jimmy Scott, interview with the author, May 29, 2003. Cab would recall a later possible encounter with Tadd in the company of Dizzy Gillespie in the 1940s and may have known Tadd for some time. On the other hand, Mr. Scott's memory of this may not be correct.

28. McCarthy, *Big Band Jazz*, 162–63. More on Whyte can be found under "Further Details" in the appendix, at http://www.press.umich.edu/22963/dameronia.

29. *Down Beat*, Jan. 1937, p. 20.

30. Gitler, *Jazz Masters of the 40s*, 263.

31. Dameron and Golson, interview with Frost, spring 1952.

32. George Hoefer, "Hoefer's Hot Box," *Down Beat*, Oct. 12, 1961. There is a photo of Tad Dameron in the Aug. 1, 1940, edition of *Down Beat*, discussed in chap. 2, that mentions these submissions.

33. Joe Mosbrook, "Jazzed in Cleveland, Part 21—Some Historic Cleveland Jazz Clubs," WMV Web News Cleveland, http://www.cleveland.oh.us/, Apr. 3, 1997.

34. Stanley Dance, *The World of Earl Hines* (New York: Scribner, 1977), 297, citing *Down Beat*. He was playing with Erskine Hawkins as well that year (Chilton, *Who's Who of Jazz*, 346).

35. Ira Gitler, *Swing to Bop* (Oxford, New York, and Toronto: Oxford University Press, 1985), 96.

36. Gitler, *Swing to Bop*, 147. It is interesting to note that Trummy Young played on the first recorded performance of "Good Bait."

37. Gerald Wilson, interview with the author, May 7, 2001.

38. Myra Taylor, interview with the author, Aug. 7, 2001.

39. Will Lee, in *Artistry In Rhythm* (Los Angeles: Creative Press of Los Angeles, 1980), 79, suggests that Stan Kenton shared the piano chair in this band, and if so, this would be the beginning of an association between the two that would last into the 1950s.

40. *Down Beat*, Jan. 1, 1940, 1.

41. Gitler, *Jazz Masters of the 40s*, 264.

42. Tadd Dameron (ghost written by Orin Keepnews), "The Case for Modern Music," *Record Changer*, Feb. 1948, 5, +16. According to Keepnews, he interviewed Dameron but decided, with Tadd's approval or even encouragement, to present Dameron's thoughts as an article, authored by the man himself.

Chapter 2

1. More on the Kansas City Rockets can be found under "Further Details" in the appendix: http://www.press.umich.edu/22963/dameronia.

2. Leonard Feather, program notes to *Harlan Leonard and His Rockets* (RCA Victor, LPV-531). Leonard probably knew of Dameron already, possibly from Andy Anderson, who played in Kansas City with Buster Smith's band in 1937–38, or from other musicians, like Leroy "Snake" White, who had connections in both Cleveland and Kansas City.

3. Myra Taylor, interview with the author, Feb. 5, 2001. The remaining information in this paragraph is from Chuck Haddix's unpublished notes on Dameron for *Kansas City Jazz*, written with Frank Driggs (New York: Oxford University Press, 2005), supplied as a courtesy to the author.

4. Gitler, *Jazz Masters of the 40s*, 20. Dameron also said, "This was in 1941. This was when war was declared—I remember it definitely." His memory must have failed him here because he was with Lunceford in New York when the United States entered World War II. Also curious is the statement that "I never knew he played alto." Parker was playing with Jay McShann, one of the top bands in Kansas City, at the time. If we are to take Dameron at his word here, this would imply that they met very early in his residency in Kansas City.

Dameron also recounted a story of this meeting to pianist George Ziskind, who recalled some further details regarding the playing of "Lady Be Good" at the jam session: "On the last four bars of the bridge, Bird played two beats each of | Emi9 A9 | Dmi9 G9 | and then on the final two bars, the usual bar of Gmi7 and then a bar of C7. Tadd, at the piano, was comping exactly the same thing." See George Ziskind, "I Remember Tadd," Jazz Institute of Chicago, 1999, http://www.jazzinstituteofchicago.org/educates/journal/i-remember-tadd.

5. Max Jones, *Jazz Talking: Profiles, Interviews and Other Riffs on Jazz Musicians* (New York: Macmillan Press, 1987; reprint, New York: Da Capo Press, 2000), 193.

6. The Mary Lou Williams Collection is in the Institute of Jazz Studies, Dana Library, Rutgers University.

7. Stanley Dance, *The World of Count Basie* (New York: Charles Scribner's Sons, 1980), 252.

8. Driggs and Haddix, *Kansas City Jazz*, 194–95.

9. Danny Barker, *A Life In Jazz*, ed. Alyn Shipton (New York: Oxford University Press, 1986), 164. Dizzy Gillespie was also with Calloway and probably met Charlie Parker for the first time while the band was in town. There is no indication that he met Dameron at this time, although it cannot be ruled out entirely.

10. Chicago, July 15, 1940. The notes to the CD *Harlan Leonard and His Rockets—1940* (Classics 670) indicate tenor saxophonist Henry Bridges doubling clarinet and Leonard doubling clarinet and baritone sax, but Dameron seems not to have used these doubles, and the few photographs of the band at work do not indicate their presence, although it is possible that in one of them the clarinets are obscured by the music stands. Certainly no baritone is present in the photographs of the band in performance.

11. Gunther Schuller, *The Swing Era* (New York: Oxford University Press, 1989), 792–93.

12. Ron Javorsky, interview with the author, Jan. 6, 2005.

13. Gitler: *Jazz Masters of the 40s,* 266.

14. Myra Taylor, interview with the author, Feb. 5, 2001.

15. Most of the recorded work of the Rockets can be heard on Classics CD 670, and selections that were released on 78-rpm discs may be found at http://www.jazz-on-line.com.

16. Durham (1906–87) and Smith (1904–91) were two pioneering arrangers from the Southwest. Both arranged for Basie early on and helped create the "Kansas City Sound."

17. Mosbrook, *Cleveland Jazz History,* 106.

18. See a replica of the piano part and further discussion of the harmonies under "Further Details" in the appendix: http://www.press.umich.edu/22963/dameronia.

19. If, as we have very good reason to believe, "Lady Bird" was written in 1939, we see that Dameron had already extended the relationship of the dominant to the note a half-step above to key relationships. In that tune, whose home key is C, the melody moves to A♭ and then to G before returning to C.

20. One could make an argument that Ellington's ability to continually vary, and thereby develop, his material is also an inspiration for Dameron. However, the general results of this variation are closer to the other arrangers mentioned.

21. See "Further Details" in the appendix: http://www.press.umich.edu/22963/dameronia.

22. See "Further Details" in the appendix: http://www.press.umich.edu/22963/dameronia.

23. Since there are two William Smiths in the band, it is not clear which is the composer. This information may be available from Library of Congress records of copyright registrations. The author regrets that he did not make note of this when researching these documents. The expense of correcting this and the tangential nature of the exact citation preclude supplying the name of the particular Smith in question.

24. This is according to the discographer Walter Bruyninckx.

25. Myra Taylor, interview with the author, Feb. 5, 2001 (original emphasis).

26. This chord can also be interpreted as a Gmi7(♭5).

27. A commercially recorded performance of this tune is planned and may be available by the time this book is released.

28. BVC's copyrights are now held by its successor, Warner Bros. Music.

29. Uncredited photo and caption, *Down Beat,* Aug. 1, 1940, 21.

30. Driggs and Haddix explain other factors contributing to the Rockets' decline, involving changes at MCA and the ASCAP radio boycott (*Kansas City Jazz,* 194–97).

31. Dameron, "The Case for Modern Music."

32. Gitler: *Jazz Masters of the 40s,* 265.

33. The AFM recording ban was a strike by the union against the recording companies over pay and royalties for recording sessions.

34. The author has also heard rumors of a letter from Ruth Dameron to the Selective Service begging for an exemption for Tadd as sole support for her after the death of Adolphus.

Chapter 3

1. Gerald Wilson, interview with the author, spring 2001; Gerald Wilson, interview with Kirk Silsbee, "Master Roots, Gerald Wilson Goes Time Traveling . . . ," *Down Beat*, Jan. 2006, 50. The Lunceford Band played the Palace in Cleveland for a week, starting on Oct. 17, 1941 (*Down Beat*, Oct. 15, 1941). They returned to New York the next week.

2. Dameron, "Case for Modern Music," 5+.

3. Gitler, *Jazz Masters of the 40s*, 265.

4. By Herb Waters, Ted Choate, and Mary Schaeffer. Rust and Bruyninckx cite Dameron, Ruppli includes him as one of three arrangers for the session; Eddy Determeyer cites Richard Segure; see *Rhythm Is Our Business*, 1st ed. (Ann Arbor: University of Michigan Press, 2006). This recording, along with those of "It Had to Be You" and "I Dream a Lot about You," has become very rare. The most recent reissue of all three of the arrangements recorded by Lunceford and discussed here is on Classics CD 862, now out of print.

5. It is possible that the written keys are D♭ and E♭ respectively, due to inconsistencies in transport speed during recording or transfer from one medium to another. Still, the author thinks this unlikely because of the difference in tempo that would result.

6. A "finding aid" is a catalog of items completed by the curator of the collection.

7. It has been suggested that some time after Lunceford's death Ed Wilcox and Joe Thomas, who co-led the band for a while, split the book between them. It is understood that the works in the Driggs collection came from Wilcox. In their present form they were orchestrated for three trumpets, three trombones, and five saxes—AATTB. The exact instrumental makeup of Lunceford's band varied considerably over the period when Dameron was writing for Lunceford, suggesting that they were reorchestrated as the band's instrumentation changed. The location of Thomas's share of the arrangements is unknown at this time.

8. This incomplete score is for two trumpets and trombone, alto, tenor, and baritone saxophones, rather than the six brass and five reeds of the other arrangements.

9. Determeyer, *Rhythm Is Our Business*, 197. The finding aid credits the arrangement to Ed Wilcox, most likely because the parts appear to have been written by him. Gerald Wilson also recalled a Dameron arrangement of "How about You."

10. The address given by the composers is not the same as the address Dameron wrote on the piano part for "Rock and Ride," which leads the author to suspect that the song was filed by Reynolds, possibly after Dameron had left Kansas City.

11. This was most likely the saxophonist Charles White, whose picture appears on the same page as Dameron's in the Aug. 1, 1940, issue of *Down Beat* and who was reputed to be a friend of Charlie Parker's.

12. The chord progression is not indicated in the lead sheet; however, it is quite clear to the author's ear. A variety of musicians have performed this tune with the author and agree with him.

13. The piano part is stamped with Dameron's union "bug," the AFM seal, and the

words "Tadley E. Dameron, A & C No. 6, Local #550—1942." "A & C" stands for "arranger and composer," and local 550 was the black local in Cleveland. Even though he was working out of a New York office, he kept his Cleveland local membership.

14. Analysis continues under "Further Details" in the appendix: http://www.press.umich.edu/22963/dameronia.

15. Jones, *Jazz Talking*, 199. Mason's Farm, previously known as the Cedar Country Club, was a popular retreat for black Clevelanders. Coincidentally, Myra Taylor performed there in 1939, roughly a year before she met Tadd Dameron.

16. One of the longest-running clubs in Cleveland, Lindsay's Sky Bar opened in 1934 and presented jazz until its owner, Phil Bash, died in 1952.

17. Ira Gitler, *Swing to Bop*, 97.

18. Linda Dahl, *Morning Glory* (Berkley and Los Angeles: University of California Press, 1999), 126. Dahl does not cite her source for this.

19. Dahl, *Morning Glory*, 128.

20. Gitler, *Jazz Masters of the 40s*, 265.

21. Benny Carter, interview with the author, Boston, 1995 or 1996.

22. "Poor Little Plaything," "Good Bait," and "Stay On It." There is a fourth likely Dameron chart for Basie, "San Jose," discussed further on.

23. Dameron, "Case for Modern Music."

24. Willie Smith, interview with the author, July 23, 2000.

25. Leonard Feather, *Inside Jazz* (New York: J. J. Robbins, 1949; reprint, New York: Da Capo Press, 1977, 1980), 8 (originally titled *Inside Bebop*). Clarke actually said 1940, but he was probably mistaken about this date since he only took over the house band at Minton's at the end of 1940 or the beginning of 1941. Before that the jam sessions were not geared toward the young modern players, and Clarke was engaged with other work.

26. Charles Parham, interview with Bob Rusch, *Cadence*, Dec. 1987, 20–21.

27. Feather, *Encyclopedia of Jazz*, 224.

28. Quoted in MacDonald, *Tadd*, 31. Gaskin is not speaking precisely here, as is often the case in conversation. Monroe's was in Harlem, and Gaskin worked there. He jammed at the clubs in midtown on Fifty-second Street as well and saw Tadd there, too.

29. Dameron, "Case for Modern Music."

30. Dizzy Gillespie, with Al Frazier, *To Be or Not To Bop* (New York: Doubleday, 1979), 217. Johnson recalls this taking place around the time Gillespie went with the William Morris Agency and began his association with Billy Shaw.

31. Gitler, *Jazz Masters of the 40s*, 265. Given the personnel and the location, this would have happened sometime between late Dec. 1943, when Wallington became the regular pianist with the Pettiford/Gillespie band, and the end of Jan. 1944, when Budd Johnson replaced Don Byas. Later, in a 1962 interview with Bill Coss, Tadd recounted the Onyx story in basically the same way, except that he stated that it was Byas who put him on the spot.

Chapter 4

1. Warren, another Ohioan, had possibly known Tadd for some time, since he was a member of the Marion Sears band around the time Tadd was beginning to come to the attention of Cleveland musicians. This turned out to be the Basie band's last commercial recording with Lester Young, who takes beautiful solos on both takes of "Plaything." Two recent reissues of the master take can be found on *The Lester Young Story* (Proper Box 8) and *Blue Lester: The One and Only Lester Young* (Savoy Jazz CD 17549). Other Savoy reissues of Young's recordings have this quality as well; see the discography at http://www.press.umich.edu/22963/dameronia.

2. MacDonald's discography indicates that Dameron also directed this recording; however, the author has not been able to confirm this in any other source.

3. There is a suggestion of this the arrangement of "My Dream," for Harlan Leonard. The trumpets are muted, but the edginess of the cup-mute sound and the dissonance of the diminished-scale line make them stand out in sharp contrast to Darwin Jones's smooth singing.

4. More on Sabby Lewis may be found under "Further Details" in the appendix: http://www.press.umich.edu/22963/dameronia.

5. To the author's knowledge this is only available on a very rare LP, Phoenix LP9.

6. Dameron, "Case for Modern Music," 5. Dameron also said that he joined Auld before Eckstine, but this seems unlikely, as explained further on.

7. Hines himself was one of the most progressive musicians of his generation, and key elements of modern jazz piano style can be traced directly back to his playing as recorded as early as the 1920s.

8. Barbara J. Kukla, *Swing City: Newark Nightlife, 1925–50* (Philadelphia: Temple University Press, 1991), 235.

9. Or so it is said. If Wilson was drafted, then he was rejected rather quickly, which is altogether possible, for he joined Basie in the fall, after the band's return from the West Coast.

10. According to Eckstine himself, "I went . . . to the Lincoln Hotel and . . . Basie . . . said, 'I understand you're gonna start a band,' and I said, 'Yeah, man, I ain't got no music.' So he turns around to Henry Snodgrass [Basie's road manager] and told him, 'Give him the key.' I went in . . . the music trunk and just took scores of Basie's music to help me be able to play a dance." See Gitler, *Swing to Bop*, 125. Earlier, in 1936 or '37, Henry Snodgrass had worked for Fletcher Henderson and was on hand to help Basie by giving him some of the Henderson Band's arrangements.

11. Robert Reisner, ed., *Bird: The Legend of Charlie Parker* (New York: Citadel Press, 1962; reprint, New York: Da Capo Press, 1977), 50–51. The owners of the Plantation had a solid reputation as tough gangsters. Gil Fuller told the author about leaving St. Louis in the middle of the night, without collecting his pay, because he feared for his life after a dispute with them. Note too that while Blakey listed Billie Holiday as the band's

singer, his memory is faulty here; Holiday did not travel or even perform with this band at any other time, as far as we know. Sarah Vaughan was the other singer with the band.

12. While the song shares its opening phrases with Schaeffer and Levnenson's "Living from Day to Day," it is sufficiently unique to stand the test of being a separate work. Indeed, Levenson never saw fit to contest Eckstine's authorship of "I Want to Talk about You," and in spite of some speculation that Dameron had a hand in writing this song, the fact that Tadd never made any claim regarding it leads us to accept Eckstine as the sole author. The arrangement of another song recorded at the same Dec. 5, 1945, session, "I'll Wait and Pray," has been credited to Dameron in some discographies, but it was written by Gerry Valentine. Valentine was one of the chief arrangers for the band, and it seems unlikely that he would not have arranged this song as well. Further, the arrangement in question does not sound at all like Dameron's work from this or any other period.

13. The movie version from the summer of 1946 is even slower.

14. There are recent reissues of the original Delux recording: Savoy Jazz 17286 and Proper 2068.

15. Jones, *Jazz Talking*, 240.

16. A recent reissue is Savoy Jazz 17607.

17. This is the author's assumption, given that both Dameron and Vaughan were working with the Eckstine band at the same time. They also left the band at about the same time. Recent reissues of both songs, plus "I Want to Talk about You," from the same date, can be found on *President* (CD 545); "Don't Blame Me" can only be found on Proper Box 27.

18. At the time of this writing only the Gillespie studio recording is currently available.

19. See the band itineraries, *Down Beat*, Dec. 1, 15, 1944, 14. Eckstine closed at the Downtown Theater in Chicago on Dec. 14, and Cootie Williams's band played the Paradise in Detroit from Dec. 1 through Dec. 7.

20. Gitler, *Swing to Bop*, 97–98.

21. Jack McKinney, liner notes, *Boyd Raeburn—Jewells* (Arista Records, Savoy SJL 2250).

22. Bruce Raeburn, liner notes, *Boyd Raeburn and His Orchestra—More 1944–1945* (Circle Records, CCD-113).

23. Gitler, *Swing to Bop*, 207.

24. "Tadd Dameron Returns to Paris after Month Here," *Melody Maker*, June 28, 1949.

25. Burt Korall, *Drummin' Men: The Bebop Years* (New York: Oxford University Press, 2002): McKusick, 189, Lewis, 238.

26. There was an arrangement made for Eckstine that was never recorded and may be different from the one recorded many times by Gillespie. In Ira Gitler's *Jazz Masters of the 40s* (267), Dexter Gordon is reported to have recalled that Dameron transcribed a Charlie Parker solo for the sax section in the Eckstine arrangement.

27. In some of the broadcast transcriptions, trumpeter Fats Navarro plays the melody, while in others he improvises. This would suggest that the choice was Navarro's. Gillespie, too, sometimes opts for a statement of the melody in the bridge. One could split hairs here, but it does not change the basic point about Dameron's use of brief improvisations as compositional elements.

28. There has been speculation that this shout line is Dizzy's creation, but the way Dameron uses and reuses the elements that make up this melody strongly suggests that it was part of his larger concept of the piece from the beginning.

29. Thomas Stewart, conversations with the author, various occasions.

30. Stan Levey, interview with the author, July 29, 2004.

31. Korall, *Drummin' Men*, 116.

32. Stan Levey, interview with the author, July 29, 2004.

33. By Haven Gillespie, Seymour Simons, and Richard Whiting. All five Dameron charts can be heard on Classics CD 1351; "Honey" and "Just You Just Me" are on on Mucicraft CD 62/Discovery CD 70062.

34. Coss, "Tadd's Back," 19.

35. Dahl, *Morning Glory*, 186.

36. Although the guitarist DeArango was from Cleveland himself and knew Caesar Dameron, he was introduced to Tadd by Gillespie around the same time as this recording session. See MacDonald, *Tadd*, 33.

37. Neither the ASCAP database nor the BMI database has any information on this title, and no composer is given on any of the issued recordings.

38. Some have speculated that this was because Nat Jaffe could not cut the part. However, Jaffe was more than capable of playing on this tune. He was one of the most employed pianists on Fifty-second Street and considered one of the most advanced pianists of the time. Jaffe remains largely unknown today because he died at age twenty-six or twenty-seven, only two months after this session.

39. Richard S. Sears, *V-Discs: A History and Discography* (Westport and London: Greenwood Press, 1980), 57. There is no record of current ownership of this title. At the time of this writing, the V-Disc recording is available for listening at http://www.jazz-on-line.com.

40. Dameron, "Case for Modern Music."

41. Deposited by Charing Music Corp. with the Copyright Office on Jan. 27, 1946, with Herman listed as coauthor. There is no record of it ever being used by Woody or by Wildroot, and Tadd recycled it a little later as "Do-Bla-Bli" (see chap. 6).

42. Both have been rereleased on Musiccraft CD 56 and Discovery CD 70056.

43. Budd Johnson, interview with Jeff Sultanof (Johnson's student assistant at Queens College), City University of New York, circa 1976–77.

44. These pieces may have been heard after Lunceford's death, since these charts came to the Smithsonian from Frank Driggs, who got them from Ed Wilcox. Wilcox, Lunceford's pianist, kept the band going for a while, co-leading it with saxophonist Joe

Thomas. At some point the two men split the book and continued to find work with it when they could.

45. Determeyer, *Rhythm Is Our Business*, 197.

46. Dameron and Golson, interview, spring 1952.

47. *Zakat* means "alms" in Arabic, and there is Arabic writing on the front of the second sax (first tenor sax) part. Many African American musicians were looking into and converting to Islam in the mid-1940s. However, the significance of all of this is not clear at this time.

48. The massive sound of this chord is further enhanced by having the baritone and second tenor saxes play their lowest notes. There is a possibility that there were originally four trumpets and four trombones; even so, the fourth trumpet would almost certainly have played an A♭ (second space) and the fourth trombone a D♭ (third line). We would still have the same characteristic voicing with perfect intervals on the outside and close, even cluster, voicing in the middle.

49. *Esquire's 1946 Jazz Book* (New York, Smith & Durrell, 1946), 44, 47–48.

50. Doug Meriwether, with discography by Clarence C. Hintze, *Mister, I Am the Band! Buddy Rich, His Life and Travels* (North Bellmore, NY: National Drum Assoc., 1998), 268.

51. The Rich version has been released on Hep CD 56, the Auld on Classics 1351, Musicraft CD 62, and Discovery CD 70062.

52. Hep CD 12.

53. Rereleased on Classics 958, Mosaic MD6-187, and Proper Box 27. HRS was a specialty label founded by a "group of jazz partisans that included George Frazier, John Hammond, Charles E. Smith, Steve Smith and Marshall Stearns, who were initially concerned with preserving great recordings and then went on to produce several very interesting sessions based purely on the quality of the musicians and the music and without any commercial consideration." See Mosaic Records Brochure 40, Nov. 2001, 6.

54. The details of Tadd's involvement with this date are not known, but in addition to his friendship with Sarah, he had connections with Budd Johnson, the Basie veteran Wells, and Jimmy Crawford, who was still in the Lunceford band when Tadd was on staff.

55. Gillespie, *To Be or Not To Bop*, 254.

56. Dave Burns, interview with the author, Nov. 21, 1991.

57. Cecil Payne, interview with the author, July 25, 1991.

58. According to the notes in the boxed set *The Complete Count Basie, vol. 11 to 20, 1941–1961* (CBS 66102), it was recorded in the same session with "Hob Nail Boogie," "Danny Boy," and "Mutton Leg," but it was not assigned a matrix number and was never previously released.

59. With the possible exception of the first "For Europeans Only" chart, which was recorded by both Don Redman and Louis Bellson. However, the Bellson recording has parts added by Redman, who was working with Bellson's wife, Pearl Bailey, at the time of the recording.

60. Gitler, *Jazz Masters of the 40s*, 264.

61. There is yet another angle on the "Stay On It" story that must be considered, the possibility that the chart came to Gillespie from Eckstine. More than one mention has been made of an arrangement of "Stay On It" being in the Eckstine book, but if there was, it might have been different from the Basie/Gillespie one. In 1962 Caesar Dameron claimed to Thomas Stewart that Tadd originally wrote the tune in 1939 and that he had it in his book.

62. Most sources are vague about the date, but the available research suggests the first week of July as the most likely time for the filming.

63. Mark Cantor, "Rhythm in a Riff," *IAJRC Journal* 34 (Winter 2001). The page reference is not known since the author's source is text transmitted to him via an email from Mr. Cantor. DVDs that include the scenes with the Dameron charts are included in the discography: see http://www.press.umich.edu/22963/dameronia.

Chapter 5

1. Count Basie, as told to Albert Murray, *Good Morning Blues* (New York: Random House, 1985), 282. Basie says, "Willard Alexander got in touch with me about a new Club in Chicago [the Brass Rail] for about a month. . . . So that's how I happened to come back to work during the first part of that next year, leading a six-piece combo." In the same book there is a picture of the band at the Brass Rail, but there are seven musicians.

2. Thomas Stewart, a trumpeter, arranger, and educator from Birmingham, AL, told the author (Mar. 14, 2006) that members of Millender's band in the late 1940s recalled that Dameron wrote many charts for the band in 1947–48. There is also the possibility that some of them were performed in the movie *Boarding House Blues*, which stared Jackie "Moms" Mabley and featured the Millender band.

3. There is also speculation that Tadd contributed to a Jacquet session for RCA Victor on Dec. 19, 1947, but these arrangements do not sound at all like his work. However, two charts, "Blue Satin" and "Stay Away," recorded by Jacquet on Dec. 14, 1949, also for Victor, are almost definitely Dameron's (see chap. 11). Further, in later years Jacquet told trumpeter and publisher Don Sickler that Dameron had "written a lot" for him (Don Sicker, interview with the author, spring 2006).

4. The most recent reissue is Steplechase CD 36020.

5. Marked letter E in the score. The score is in the Don Redman collection in the Special Collections Department of the Schomburg Center for Research in Black Culture of the New York Public Library.

6. The lead sheet is titled "Lady Byrd."

7. The copyright deposit, probably written by Gil Fuller, shows just the melody without chords, with two endings, indicating a thirty-two-bar form.

8. Other examples include Eddie Vinson's "Tune Up," Gigi Gryce's "Minority,"

Horace Silver's "Silver Serenade," Sam River's "Beatrice," and Wayne Shorter's "Night Dreamer," to name just a few.

9. More on this arrangement can be found under "Further Details" in the appendix: http://www.press.umich.edu/22963/dameronia.

10. Inclusion of a written quote of "The Squirrel" was planned, but complications regarding permission made this impossible. Please refer to one of the recordings (see the foreword).

11. The Carnegie Hall concert was recently released on Back Up CD 73106.

12. Max Jones, "And Next We Come to Soulphony," *Melody Maker*, May 14, 1949, 4.

13. Some would use the word *classical* here. There is a trend toward adopting the term *concert music* for the European art-music tradition, however, and the author prefers this term.

14. Bill Milkowski, *Swing It! An Annotated History of Jive* (New York: Billboard Books, 2001), 124.

15. Babs Gonzales, *Be-Bop Dictionary, and History of Its Famous Stars* (New York: Arlain Publishing Co., 1948[?]), 5.

16. Bob Bach, "Babs' Three Bips and a Bop," *Metronome*, May 1947, 26. The graphics accompanying the article imply that Gonzales, Tinney, and Phipps are the "Bips" and Dameron is the "Bop."

17. Bach, "Babs' Three Bips and a Bop."

18. Valerie Wilmer, *Jazz People* (London: Allison & Busby, 1977), 97.

19. The bridge melody in the "Do-Bla-Bli" deposit, unlike the one in "Charlie," may not even be Dameron's. The deposit is not in Dameron's handwriting, and it would not work with the voices, since it goes out of their range.

20. Gitler, *Jazz Masters of the 40s*: 266.

21. Babs Gonzales, *I Paid My Dues, Good Times—No Bread* (East Orange, NJ: Expubidence Publishing Corp., 1967), 40. Later, in Wilmer, *Jazz People*, 96, Gonzales recalled that Dameron followed Tucker in the piano chair. However, Tucker himself has been quite clear that he took the chair after Dameron (Bobby Tucker, interview with the author, April 17, 2004).

22. Donald Clarke, *Wishing on the Moon: The Life and Times of Billie Holiday* (London: Penguin Books, 1994), 261.

23. There may be an AFRS recording of this broadcast, but the author has not been able to locate a copy.

24. "Also during that time [1945–48] I managed Fats Navarro, and got Fats on Savoy; I did all those be-bop boys, did all the guys for Savoy" (Gil Fuller, interview with the author, Aug. 19, 1991).

25. These "holes" are not shown in the copyright deposit, which is also inaccurate in other aspects and appears to be a sloppy transcription made by someone working for Savoy owner Herman Lubinsky, who was also the publisher.

26. Gitler, *Jazz Masters of the 40s*, 266.

27. William P. Gottlieb to the author, June 18, 2001.

28. One of the photos appeared on page 2 of the Aug. 27, 1947, issue of *Down Beat.* Links to some of these photographs can be found at "Further Details" in the appendix; see http://www.press.umich.edu/22963/dameronia.

29. Gitler, *Jazz Masters of the 40s,* 269.

30. Yusef Lateef, interview with the author, Jan. 13, 2001.

31. Terry Gibbs, interview with the author, Jan. 10, 2003.

32. Links to photographs of this session by Gottlieb are at under "Further Details" in the appendix: http://www.press.umich.edu/22963/dameronia.

33. Monk recorded "Well You Needn't" for the first time on Oct. 24, 1947, for Blue Note (BN543). Dameron quotes "Well, You Needn't" in his solo on the Oct. 9, 1948, broadcast transcription from the Royal Roost.

34. Pianist and educator Paul Verrette, professor emeritus of music at the University of New Hampshire, recalled playing "The Chase" often on gigs in the New Hampshire seacoast area in the 1950s. However, he did not know who wrote it, which suggests that the tune had passed into general usage aurally by that time. Paul Verrette, interview with the author, Feb. 22, 2005.

35. "'Debts Shutter Swing Spot': Troubadour closed after O'Day's first week. Joe Marsala and Nat King Cole is definitely cancelled. At Press time the original owner of the Troubadour, Freddie Lamb, decided to re-open as club 18 with Tadd Dameron's group as attraction. Troubadour closed September 24." (See *Down Beat,* Oct. 8, 1947, 3.)

36. Charlie Rouse, interview with the author, Oct. 2, 1987.

37. For more on "Half-Step Down, Please," see "Further Details" in the appendix: http://www.press.umich.edu/22963/dameronia.

38. At least that is what we infer from the credits on the CDs Savoy 17161 and Savoy Jazz SVY-17027. This is also the understanding of Dan Morgenstern, who wrote the notes for SVY-17027.

39. Gerun Moore, "Unlucky? Maybe Your Name Is Spelled Wrong," *Down Beat,* Oct. 15, 1939, 4. Wingy Manone (*ne* Mannone) and Geroge Brunis (*ne* Brunies) both were reported to have changed the spelling of their names on Moore's advice.

Chapter 6

1. The program, which was produced by Ray Pino under the banner "Variations In Modern Music," included Art Blakely and His Messengers (with Bennie Harris on trumpet and Thelonius Monk on piano), Babs Gonzales's Three Bips and a Bop, and Herb Jeffries.

2. Roy Porter, *There and Back* (Baton Rouge: Louisiana State University Press, 1991), 68–69.

3. Pianist Roy Testamark, guitarist Tiger Hawes, and bassist Bill Pollard.

4. Arnold Shaw, *52nd St.—The Street of Jaz,* (New York: Coward, McCann &

Geoghegan, 1971; reprint, New York: Da Capo, 1977), 272. Kay's quote is from Gitler, *Jazz Masters of the 40s*, 269.

5. "Customers Outbop The Boppers; Roost Doesn't Have To Toss In Towel," *Down Beat*, Aug. 25, 1948, 3.

6. More on the personnel of Dameron's Royal Roost bands can be found under "Further Details" in the appendix: http://www.press.umich.edu/22963/dameronia.

7. "About Town," *New Yorker*, May 8, 1948.

8. Dan Morgenstern, interview with the author, Jan. 6, 2003. As stated before, Dameron probably heard the arrangement in rehearsal, but he had never heard it performed publicly.

9. Recorded Oct. 26, 1956, and first released on Prestige 7166.

10. Recorded May 3, 1957, and first released on Columbia CS8109.

11. Lewis Porter, *John Coltrane, His Life and Music* (Ann Arbor: University of Michigan Press, 1998), 128–31, + 145.

12. There are, of course, variations on this. In one all the chords are major sevenths, Cmaj7-E♭maj7-A♭maj7-D♭maj7. In another, the one of importance in regard to Coltrane's work, the major sevenths alternate with sevenths, Cmaj7-E♭7-A♭maj7-D♭7. The choice of ♭5 versus #11 is largely one of taste, as are alterations to the seventh chords.

13. More on this song can be found under "Further Details" in the appendix: http://www.press.umich.edu/22963/dameronia.

14. See the Mary Lou Williams Collection. The music is in the folder titled "Keepin' Out of Mischief."

15. On the Oct. 9 broadcast they presented an all-Dameron program, with "Lady Bird," "Our Delight," "Good Bait," "Stay On It," and "Cool Breeze." They also played an arrangement of "The Squirrel" on Oct. 2, 1948.

16. Bill Cole, *Miles Davis: The Early Years* (New York: William Morrow & Co., 1974; reprint, New York: Da Capo Press, 1994), 52.

17. This can be heard as early as Mar. 1949 on an Oscar Pettiford date recorded on Mar. 10 and rereleased most recently on Mosaic MD4–147, *The Complete Serge Chaloff Session*. The arrangers for this date were Shorty Rogers, Leonard Feather, and quite possibly Al Cohn.

18. Jeff Sultanof. Kentonia discussion group, Yahoo.com, Sun., Dec. 8, 2002.

19. The musicians on this date were Fats Navarro, trumpet; Kai Winding, trombone; Sahib Shihab, alto sax; Dexter Gordon, tenor sax; Cecil Payne, baritone sax; Tadd Dameron, piano; Curly Russell, bass; Kenny Clarke, drums; Diego Ibarra, bongos; Vidal Bolado, conga; Rae Pearl, vocal.

20. Oddly, this piece was not copyrighted until 1961. The deposit lead sheet, which appears to be written by Dameron, is titled "Tadd's Delight," probably because it was better known by that title by then.

21. Jeannie Cheatham, interview with the author, July 24, 2004. Pennsylvania also

had blue laws, but some residents of Sharon have indicated that the local officials were willing to look the other way, most likely if there was some sort of compensation.

22. There are several titles from the 1960s for which we have no music, and it is possible that he may have done just this. However, until such a song is discovered we cannot assume that it exists.

23. "Tadd Dameron Arrives in London," *Melody Maker*, May 28, 1949. Although there is no mention of this in the write-up of the concert in the *Pittsburgh Courier*, one gets the impression that there may well have been more awards given out than those referred to in the article.

Chapter 7

1. Mike Hennessey, *Klook: The Story of Kenny Clarke* (London: Quartet Books, Ltd., 1990; reprint, 1994, Pittsburgh: University of Pittsburgh Press), 79.

2. An item in *Melody Maker* (May 14, 1949, 1) suggested Dameron would write for Lewis, but no further evidence of this has surfaced.

3. "Tadd To France," *Down Beat*, Dec. 17, 1947, 7.

4. Max Jones, "Post-Festival Paris," *Melody Maker*, July 30, 1949, 9: "Proteau has two or three Dameron numbers in the books."

5. Steve Race, "Paris Jazz Festival" (review of the opening concert), *Musical Express*, May 13, 1949.

6. André Hodier, "Le Festival 1949," *La Musique de Jazz Hot*, June 1949, 7.

7. The most recent reissue of this material is Japanese Sony CD SRCS5695, *The Miles Davis/Tadd Dameron Quintet in Paris Festival International de Jazz*.

8. This and all further quotes from Mr. Mairants are taken from an interview conducted on the author's behalf by Val Wilmer in the fall of 1991.

9. St. Denis Preston, "Backstage with Bechet and Bop," *Melody Maker*, Aug. 27, 1949, 3.

10. Ray Brown, interview with the author, May 14, 1991; James Moody, interview with the author, May 17, 1991.

11. The interest in Dameron's arrival in the UK was not limited to the British musical press. In a letter from Hot Lips Page to British pianist Gerry Moore, he expresses his regret that he would not be able to come to England after the festival and goes on to write, "I know that Tad will enjoy his trip there." Oran Page to Gerry and Josie Moore, May 31, 1949 (courtesy of Gill Moore, Gerry's widow, and Val Wilmer).

12. "Never seen a suit like that": at this time England was still recovering economically from World War II, and there was very little available in men's fashion other than blue serge suits and traditional tweeds.

13. "Tadd Dameron Returns to Paris after Month Here," *Melody Maker*, June 28, 1949 (copied source supplied by correspondent).

14. Moira Heath, interview with Val Wilmer, Jan. 1992. Moira Heath wrote the lyric to "That Lovely Weekend," one of the Heath band's most successful recordings.

15. Maurice Pratt, interview with Val Wilmer, Apr. 17, 1992.

16. Max Jones, interview with Val Wilmer. In all the press notices where she is mentioned, Margo is identified as Tadd's wife.

17. Some have speculated that the title "Lyonia" may well be a reference to this place, but Dameron said, "We had to go to Lyon, France, and while we were on the train . . . it gave a little pattern. I made this tune and called it Lyonia" (Dameron and Golson, interview, spring 1952). See Dave Cliff/Geoff Simkins 5, *Play the Music of Tadd Dameron* (Spotlite SPJ-[CD] 560), track 12.

18. Roy Carr, interview with Val Wilmer, Nov. 11, 1990.

19. "Tadd Dameron," *Music Fare*, July 1949, 14

20. "Tadd Looks In on Tito's Decca Session," *Melody Maker*, June 11, 1949, 1.

21. Scott was in New York, visiting Harlem and Fifty-second Street, on a few occasions in 1947 and may have met Dameron first at that time.

22. Lennie Breslaw, interview with Val Wilmer, Feb. 22, 1996.

23. Wendie Gray, letter to the editor, *Guardian*, Dec. 31, 1996. Gray was responding to Ronnie Scotts's obituary in the Dec. 27 issue.

24. Roy Carr, interview with Val Wilmer, Nov. 11, 1990.

25. Aubrey Frank, interview with Val Wilmer, May 2, 1991.

26. "Tadd Dameron Returns to Paris after Month Here," *Melody Maker*, June 28, 1949, 1.

27. This letter is courtesy of Ivor Mairaints. Jim Davidson, who was in charge of "light music" for the BBC, told Ivor Mairants, "Well you can't get a permit just like that. He'll have to leave the country first, then he can write to us and we'll send him a permit which he will show the Ministry of Labor to say that we haven't got an arranger like this here."

28. Max Jones, "Tadd Dameron Returns to States," *Melody Maker*, July 23, 1949, 7.

29. Frisco was an expatriate black American entertainer.

30. Hennessey, *Klook*, 76.

31. James Moody, interview with the author, May 17, 1991.

32. As with "Half-Step Down, Please," Hawkins is given cowriter credit, probably in return for recording the composition.

33. Max Jones, "Tadd Dameron Returns to States," *Melody Maker*, July 23, 1949, 7.

34. "Dameron, Davis Woodshedding a 'Dream Band,'" *Down Beat*, Sept. 23, 1949, 1.

35. Tadd Dameron, "Fred's Delight" (Artie Shaw Collection, University of Arizona Library, Tuscon, box 22, item 105). It is interesting to note that this band continues the interracial makeup of both Tadd's and Miles's recent bands. While it is beyond the scope of this book, there was a trend at the end of the 1940s toward crossing the "color line" in jazz that would fade in the 1950s and only return in the later 1970s.

36. Sonny Rollins to the author, June 20, 2005.

37. The three Dameron scores written for Artie Shaw are located in the Shaw Collection, University of Arizona Library.

38. This is discussed further under "Further Details" in the appendix: http://www.press.umich.edu/22963/dameronia.

39. Michael Sparke, "Stan Kenton—Innovations In Modern Music," http://www .tiare.com/innovations.htm, © 1997, 1998 Michael Sparke; complete essay originally submitted as liner notes for the two-CD Capitol set *The Innovations Orchestra* (CDP7243 8 59965 2 8) but cut by over half because of the restrictions envisaged by an eight-page booklet.

40. Milt Bernhart to Anne Kuebler, email, summer 2000.

41. These can be found on the Mosaic set *The Complete Illinois Jacquet Sessions 1945–50* (MD 4–164).

42. Don Sickler, interview with the author, spring 2006.

43. Don Manning, interview with the author, Mar. 1, 2006.

44. Ken Vail, *Miles' Diary* (London: Sanctuary Publishing, 1996), 31.

45. "Shu Unit in Brooklyn," *Down Beat*, Nov. 4, 1949, 12.

46. Ronnie Scott, interview with Val Wilmer, July 12, 1991. Although Dameron usually lived on the Upper West Side or in Harlem, the English musicians probably visited him in Greenwich Village; the 1950 New York telephone directory lists Tadd Dameron at 9 Charlton Street, at the corner of Sixth Avenue, a few blocks south of Houston Street.

47. Leonard Feather, "Dameron Likes Dixie and Bird," *Metronome*, May 1950, 23 + 35–36.

48. Item with photograph, *Pittsburgh Courier*, Oct. 15, 1949; *Baltimore Afro-American*, Oct. 22, 1949.

49. "Former Clevelander, Exponent of Modern Music, Here from Europe," *Cleveland Call and Post*, July 1, 1950.

50. "Tad [*sic*] Dameron, 'Shep' Stars in Trio Now Playing Popular Amvets Post," *Cleveland Call and Post*, Sept. 30, 1950. There is also an advertisement for this engagement on the same page.

Chapter 8

1. Dance, *World of Count Basie*, 274.

2. MacDonald, *Tadd*, 48. The author recalls Keepnews using this term in his interview with him as well.

3. Stan Levy, interview with the author, July 29, 2004.

4. This interview subject has requested anonymity in this matter.

5. Val Wilmer to the author, Nov. 18, 1993: "Finally, a friend of mine told me that Denis Rose told him." Cocaine use is reported to have been fairly common, in certain circles, in the UK at the time.

6. MacDonald, *Tadd*, 48.

7. Ronnie Scott, interview with Val Wilmer, July 12, 1991.

8. Miles Davis, with Quincy Troupe, *Miles* (New York: Simon and Schuster, 1990), 129.

9. Venus Irving-Prescott, interview with the author, Oct. 22, 1991.

10. Charlie Rouse, interview with the author, Oct. 2, 1987.

11. Buddy Crew and Myron Styles, interview with the author, Inner-City Yacht Club, Cleveland, July 22, 2000.

12. Donald Meade, interview with the author, Jan. 11, 2002.

13. Willie Smith, interview with the author, May 9, 2003.

14. Billy Paul, interview with the author, Jan. 30, 2005.

15. Ron Javorsky, interview with the author, Jan. 6, 2005.

16. Donald Kennedy, interview with the author, spring 2002.

17. Don Sickler, interview with the author, fall 2002.

18. Willie Smith, interview with the author, July 23, 2000.

19. Mosbrook, *Cleveland Jazz History*, 54.

20. Rereleased on *Merry Christmas Baby* (King KCD-5018), *Bull Moose Jackson Greatest Hits* (King KSCD-1409), and *Bull Moose Jackson Sings His All-Time Hits* (Audio Lab AL1524), respectively. There is only vague documentation of Dameron's arranging credit for these, but based on the features described, and failing contrary information, the author feels confident in making this assertion.

21. All three are on *Bull Moose Jackson Greatest Hits* (King KSCD-1409).

22. Benny Golson, interview with the author, Apr. 29, 1991.

23. Benny Golson, interview with Steve Voce, early 1980s, available at the Jazz Institute of Chicago Web site: http://www.jazzinstituteofchicago.org/index.asp?target=/jazzgram/people/golson-voce.asp.

24. Jim Merod, "Forward Motion: An Interview with Benny Golson," *boundary* 2 23, no. 2 (1995): 53–93, reprinted in Robert G. O'Meally, *The Jazz Cadence of American Culture* (New York: Columbia University Press, 1998), 42.

25. Although Dameron was a studio guest on Symphony Sid's show on at least two different occasions, no transcriptions of those broadcasts have surfaced. There is also a recording of Dameron introducing his band at the Royal Roost, recorded by Boris Rose but never released.

26. The exact instrumentation of the Bull Moose Jackson band on the road is not known. The instrumentation of his recording bands in the early 1950s varied, and an ad for the opening of the Ebony Club in Cleveland mentions a septet. See *Cleveland Call and Post*, May 15, 1951.

27. The author spent several hours both at the Boston Public Library and on the Internet looking for references to the jahbero but could only find it mentioned as the title to Dameron's composition. Some time in 1948, Art Blakey visited West Africa, not North Africa, but he could have told Dameron about such a bird, if it exists.

28. Liner notes, Jimmie Lunceford, *Blues in the Night—1938–1942* (MCA Records, MCA-1314). For more on Segure's contribution to "Yard Dog," see Determeyer, *Rhythm Is Our Business*.

29. Gerald Wilson, interview with the author, spring 2001. The author has been told that some members of the Lunceford band maintained that Dameron orchestrated the arrangement of "Yard Dog Mazurka," but without further knowledge of who these mu-

sicians were and some explanation of the timeline, it is difficult to support this. Another claim that falls into this gray area involves the arrangement of Dizzy Gillespie's "Emanon," which Dameron claims to have written in "The Case for Modern Music." The chart is also claimed by Gil Fuller but may have been written by John Lewis. In the case of "Emanon," a loosely arranged blues that definitely sounds like something written "by committee," it is easy to imagine that all three writers had a hand in putting it together.

30. Billy Paul, interview with the author, Jan. 30, 2005.

31. Dr. Willis Kirk, interview with the author, Jan. 12, 2008.

32. "'Mayor of Harlem' Contest Draws to a Close," *Cleveland Call and Post*, Jan. 17, 1953.

33. Terry stayed with the band until 1959, after Dameron had gone to Lexington.

34. The score and a few parts for "Duke Ellington's Opening Theme" are located in the Ruth Ellington Collection, National Museum of American History, Smithsonian Institution, Washington, DC.

35. When asked, Clark Terry could not recall this piece and was, in fact, quite surprised to learn of its existence.

36. At one time the author had a tropical lily that had very large flowers. When it was time for the blossoms to open, the plant would wave back and forth for a minute or so, and then the flower would open suddenly.

37. Further discussion can be found under "Further Details" in the appendix: http://www.press.umich.edu/22963/dameronia.

38. There is confusion here about whether this Apollo appearance was with a Jackson band or a Dameron band. However, Golson is pretty sure it was Jackson's gig.

39. The most recent reissue is *Clifford Brown Memorial* (Original Jazz Classics, OJCCD-017-2).

40. Noal Cohen and Michael Fitzgerald, *Rat Race Blues—the Musical Life of Gigi Gryce* (Berkeley, Berkeley Hills Books, 2002), 84–85.

41. Raymond Horricks, *These Jazzmen of Our Time* (London: Gollancz, 1959), 191.

42. As Golson mentions in the foreword to this book, Dameron was responsible for adding "Philly" to Jones's name.

43. More on the chord changes to "Philly J. J." can be found under "Further Details" in the appendix: http://www.press.umich.edu/22963/dameronia.

44. Copyright of melodies, tunes, or songs can be established in various ways. Titles alone are often registered. However, the most secure process is to provide a reasonably accurate lead sheet, written in musical notation. It is these deposits that have provided many of the insights presented in this book.

45. There is an alternate second take in which Dameron does not take a solo, but the take with his solo was used in the original release.

46. Art Blakey, interview with the author, fall 1988.

47. Nick Catalano, *Clifford Brown: The Life and Art of the Legendary Jazz Trumpeter* (New York: Oxford University Press, 2000), 71.

48. Andy McGee and Jimmie Slyde, interview with the author, May 17, 1991.

49. Cohen and Fitzgerald, *Rat Race Blues*, 87–88.

50. There has been some confusion about Betty Carter's involvement with this review. The song she sang here would not have fit in the show, and the author feels that she was not a regular part of the cast but may have made a few appearances. Benny Golson says that this is where he first met her.

51. Cohen and Fitzgerald, *Rat Race Blues*, 87.

52. By comparing various narratives of events surrounding it, it can be established that the raid most likely took place on July 12 or 19.

53. Cecil Payne, interview with the author, July 25, 1991.

54. "Dameron to Score for Scott?" *New Musical Express*, July 17, 1953, 6.

55. Quincy Jones, *Q: The Autobiography of Quincy Jones* (New York: Doubleday, 2001), 98–99.

56. Gitler, *Jazz Masters of the 40s*, 273.

57. Advertisement, *Cleveland Call and Post*, May 14, 1949.

58. This and the preceding paragraphs: Willie Smith, interview with the author, July 23, 2000.

59. Sam Noto, interview with the author, Aug. 24, 2007.

60. "Max And Clifford Open at Loop," *Cleveland Call and Post*, Feb. 4, 1956.

Chapter 9

1. The title is misleading since it was recorded in a studio, probably Capitol, at 146 West Forty-sixth Street. The band was to have recorded live while playing at Ralph Watkins's club over the Christmas and New Year's weeks. The live recording did not work out, but they named the album for Watkins's establishment just the same.

2. Michel Ruppli and Ed Novitsky, *Mercury Labels, a Discography* (Westport, CT: Greenwood Press, 1993), 541. The notes on the releases from Mercury and its successors indicate Feb. 16, but Ruppli and Novitsky's research used the session logs, so this is almost certainly the correct date.

3. More can be found in the appendix, under "Further Discussion": http://www .press.umich.edu/22963/dameronia.

4. "Moon from the East," written in 1962 for Benny Goodman but apparently never performed, seems to be another (see chap. 11). There have been references to other, later compositions that may have fit this category, but to date they have not surfaced.

5. *Brownie's Eyes* (Philology CD).

6. While Howard Johnson (alto sax) in "Nearness" and Dizzy Gillespie in "Soul-phony" take liberties with their parts in the respective pieces, these are not the same as the open solos over chord changes in most jazz arrangements. They are more akin to the liberties that a featured soloist or singer would take in presenting a theme.

7. *Dameron 1956* (first released on Prestige LP 7037); *Dameron 1962* (first released

on Riverside RLP419); *Goodman 1962* (first released on RCA Victor LSO 6008/LOC 6008).

8. In the 1956 recording, the triplets are played more as glissandi, but the reference is still clear.

9. The clave used here is the one-bar type found in calypso and samba, among other Caribbean and South American folkloric rhythms. *Clave* could more accurately be described as a rhythmic concept that infuses the music of the African diaspora, but a proper discussion of that topic is beyond the scope of this book.

10. More can be found in the appendix, under "Further Discussion": http://www .press.umich.edu/22963/dameronia.

11. Originally released as Decca DL8347; rereleased on CD most recently in 2004 as Decca UCCU-5233.

12. We are reasonably certain that Dameron wrote arrangements for Ella Fitzgerald, but these were never recorded, and it is not clear when they were written.

13. Billy Vera, liner notes, *Carmen McRae—Blue Moon* (Verve 314 543 829–2, 2000).

14. "Jazz Man's Bail 10G in Dope Rap," *New York Daily News,* Apr. 11, 1956.

15. Tenor saxophonist Gene Ammons was put in jail for life because of this law and was only released after receiving a presidential pardon.

16. Former Lexington Federal Hospital inmate, interview with the author, July 20, 1991. This person, who knew Dameron at the hospital, has asked that his name be withheld.

17. "Dameron Narcotics Sentence Suspended," *Down Beat,* Oct. 3, 1956.

18. Willie Smith, interview with the author, July 23, 2000.

19. For a time in the later 1940s Gil Fuller published some of Dameron's compositions, and then he sold his catalog to J. J. Robbins. Companies associated with Savoy Records also had some of Tadd's tunes, as did Atlantic Music Corp. and the somewhat mysterious Tad Music Publishing Corp. The "Tad" is not a reference to Dameron's name. The compositions recorded on Capitol were published by Atlantic Music Corp. (no relation to Atlantic Records).

20. George Vedegis, in conversation with Jeff Sultanoff, ca. 1982–83, as recounted to the author. The one available exception to the good quality of Dameron's musical manuscripts is the 1958 score of "Stop, Look and Listen," most likely written while incarcerated at Riker's prison in 1958 (see chap. 10).

21. Bob Weinstock, interview with Dan Gould, Feb. 2004 (Organissimo Jazz Forums, Tadd Dameron's Mating Call—Who's Missing), 2.

22. Willie Smith, interview with the author, July 23, 2000.

23. Dr. Willis Kirk also remembers hearing Coltraine play in Bull Moose's band.

24. Lewis Porter, ed., *The John Coltrane Reference* (New York: Routledge, 2008), 69–71, 77–78.

25. At the time of this writing, this is available on CD under the original title (Savoy/Atlantic 92981-2). There was also at least one other LP reissue of the original known to the author.

Chapter 10

1. Jackie McLean, interview with the author, fall 1998 or spring 1999.

2. A bright and swinging piece that should be better known, it is on an album, *Woody Herman 1958*, that has yet to be reissued.

3. This is listed in discographies, but it is not on the discs indicated. Just the same, there may be a recording of "Small Crevice" from the live performance that has not been released.

4. George Ziskind, "I Remember Tadd," Jazz Institute of Chicago, 1999, http://www.jazzinstituteofchicago.org/educates/journal/i-remember-tadd.

5. It is possible that the state police had made the earlier arrest. Still, that would make the omission of the earlier offense at a federal trial even more surprising.

6. Dorothy Dameron, interview with the author, Aug. 16, 1991.

7. It usually takes only a couple of weeks to "kick" the habit cold. However, it is known that drugs can make their way into prisons, so Dameron may have maintained his addiction even though he was in jail.

8. MacDonald, *Tadd*, 61–62.

9. Carl Hayse, interview with the author, Jan. 10, 1993.

10. Sam Rivers, interview with the author, Nov. 1998.

11. Orrin Keepnews, liner notes, *Smooth as the Wind—Blue Mitchell with Strings and Brass* (Riverside Records, OJCCD-871-2 [rerelease of RLP-9367]).

12. Gitler, *Jazz Masters of the 40s*, 274–75.

13. It is interesting to note that Benny Golson had a very successful career writing music for television programs and commercials.

14. Orrin Keepnews, interview with Leonard Feather, liner notes, *A Blue Time* (Milestone, 47055).

15. Note also the more open voicings in the 1962 background lines, versus the 1945 arrangement.

16. More can be found under "Further Details" in the appendix: http://www.press.umich.edu/22963/dameronia.

17. Jack Cooke, "Tadd Dameron—An Introduction," *Jazz Monthly*, Mar. 1960, 23–26.

18. Mike Butcher, "Tadd—The Forgotten," *Jazz News*, Apr. 12, 1961, 6.

Chapter 11

1. Barbara Blakeney, interview with the author, Nov. 20, 1990.

2. George Ziskind, interview with the author, July 14, 1991. Maely Dufty was also a close friend of Thelonious and Nellie Monk, as explained in Robin D. G. Kelley, *Thelonious Monk: The Life and Times of an American Original* (New York: Free Press, 2009), 156 and elsewhere.

3. Dan Morgenstern, interview with the author, Jan. 9, 2003.

4. Chris Albertson, interview with the author, Jan. 7, 2008.

5. Blue Note CD 21484, titled *The Lost Sessions.*

6. Michael Cuscuna and Michel Ruppli, *The Blue Note Label: A Discography, Revised and Expanded* (Westport, CT: Greenwood Press, 2001), 131.

7. Ziskind, "I Remember Tadd."

8. Also on Jan. 26, there was a gala benefit concert at the Apollo for the Negro American Labor Council. The event was organized by Maely Dufty, with Tadd and Clark Terry serving as musical directors. Many of the jazz community participated in this concert. See Kelley, *Thelonious Monk,* 319.

9. The other titles were "Come Close," "At Christmastime," and "That's Just the Way It Goes."

10. Claude Schlouch, *The Unforgettable Kenny Dorham: A Discography* (self published, 1999), 33.

11. There are some indications in the correspondence between Barbara Blakeney and Val Wilmer that Dameron was interested in the bossa nova, a rhythm that was becoming popular in the United States in 1962.

12. Joe Wilder, interview with the author, Jan. 11, 2008.

13. Don Sickler, interview with the author, Dec. 15, 2005.

14. More can be found in the appendix, under "Further Discussion": http://www .press.umich.edu/22963/dameronia.

15. George Avakian, liner notes, *Benny Goodman in Moscow* (RCA Victor, LOC-6008/LOC 6008). Some have questioned the contributions of Mel Lewis here, since he is not generally known for arranging. However, Avakian was an experienced producer and A&R man, so his reporting would not likely be careless.

16. Barbara Blakeney to Val Wilmer, June 19, 1962.

17. *Benny Goodman in Moscow.* (RCA Victor LSO 6008/LOC 6008, 1962).

18. Martin Williams, "Mostly Modernists—Included in the Supporting Cast," *Saturday Review,* Sept. 15, 1962, 47.

19. Orrin Keepnews, interview with the author, July 2, 1991.

20. Valerie Wilmer, *Mama Said There'd Be Days like This: My Life in the Jazz World* (London: The Women's Press, 1989), 83.

21. Valerie Wilmer, "Tadd Dameron," *Jazz News,* July 4, 1962, 4.

22. It is possible that Dameron made a short trip to Algeria during the month he was in France in the summer of 1949, but he would have only had a week there at most, since he was busy writing music for various musicians active in Paris.

23. Loraine Gillespie, interview with Melvin Williams on behalf of the author, fall 2001.

24. Gitler, *Jazz Masters of the 40s,* 267.

25. Accounting for the usual delay in registering copyrights, this would mean that it was sent off around the end of May.

Chapter 12

1. Hank Jones, interview with the author, Apr. 15, 2005.

2. The most recent reissue is Riverside Original Jazz Classics 366–2.

3. Ernie Wilkins used the more conventional 4-4-5-3 instrumentation for the session devoted solely to his charts.

4. At the insistence of the producer, Ahmet Ertegun, Hammond organ was used for one session. Piano was used for the other session.

5. Martin Williams, *Jazz in Its Time* (New York: Oxford University Press, 1989), 116–19.

6. This is the traditional "C. C. Rider." The spelling of the title allows Stitt to claim authorship of this particular performance and therefore a composer's royalty.

7. Edgar and Barbara Blakeney to Val Wilmer, Aug. 2, 1962 (postmark).

8. Dameron was not reported to be a heavy drinker, and everyone interviewed regarding the couple opined that they were not well matched. However, it should also be noted that ex-heroin addicts are often known to drink heavily after they have broken the narcotic habit.

9. Gil Fuller, interview with the author, Aug. 19, 1991.

10. Barbara Blakeney to Val Wilmer, Sept. 14, 1962.

11. Brian Priestley, *Mingus: A Critical Biography* (New York: Da Capo Press, 1983), 138.

12. Bobby Tucker, Eckstine's long-time accompanist and music director, said without equivocation that Dameron did not write for Eckstine in that period of time. Bobby Tucker, interview with the author, Apr. 17, 2004.

13. Gray Sargent, interview with the author, June 24, 2005. Sargent is Bennett's guitarist, and he asked him about this on the author's behalf.

14. Gitler, *Jazz Masters of the 40s*, 275.

15. Dan Morgenstern, interview with the author, Jan. 9, 2003.

16. A reissue of these arrangements is in the works as of this writing.

17. There is also one by Ann Patterson and three by Freeman Lee. Riverside producer Orrin Keepnews signed the assignment document.

18. "Sando Latino," "Beautiful Adorned," "Milt's Delight," "Slightly Flighty," "Come Close," "At Christmastime," and "That's Just the Way It Goes" were copyrighted as a suite of pieces, all under the title "That's Just the Way It Goes" (Eu 705540). The cover sheet has the receipt date Mar. 5, 1962; the individual lead sheets are stamped "Jan. 18, 1962."

19. This is not to be confused with the misnamed "Milano," recorded off the air by Boris Rose and discussed earlier in this book.

20. The titles are listed in the appendix under "Further Details" and "Catalog of Titles": http://www.press.umich.edu/22963/dameronia.

21. Seven of the titles had never been registered with the Copyright Office, and only two had been recorded.

22. Willie Smith, interview with the author, July 23, 2000. There has never been any evidence that Dameron actually married this woman. As far as anyone has been able to tell, Mabel "Mia" Soper Dameron was Tadd's only wife.

23. MacDonald, *Tadd*, 72.

24. MacDonald, *Tadd*, 68. This has also been confirmed by Thomas Stewart.

25. Mia Dameron, interview with the author, July 9, 1991.

26. After Dameron died, Carpenter had to sign these compositions back to Bregman, Vocco and Conn.

27. Unless otherwise noted, all further recollections of Mia's come from the July 9, 1991, interview.

28. Williams, *Jazz in Its Time*, 143–44.

29. James Gavin, *Deep in a Dream: The Long Night of Chet Baker* (New York: Alfred A. Knopf, 2002), 197–98.

30. MacDonald, *Tadd*, 71–74.

31. "Nostalgic Afternoon Concert Pays Tribute to Tadd Dameron," *Down Beat*, Dec. 17, 1964, 13.

32. Dan Morgenstern, interview with the author, Jan. 9, 2003.

33. Barbara Blakeney, interview with the author, Nov. 20, 1990.

34. Dan Morgenstern, interview with the author, Jan. 9, 2003.

Chapter 13

1. This being said, Donald Meade is known and respected for his prodigious memory.

2. Determeyer, *Rhythm Is Our Business*.

3. This and all other uncited statements are from Frank Foster, interview with the author, Jan. 25, 2008.

4. Mary Lou Williams and others could arguably be added to this group.

5. Dance, *World of Count Basie*, 193.

6. Jones, *Q*, 77, 86.

7. Jimmy Heath, interview with the author, May 31, 2001.

8. James Moody later credited Gösta Theselius with the arrangements (interview with the author, Jan. 10, 2002). This arrangement may have been written by someone else, given the amount of time passed between the recording and the conversation with Moody. What is important here is that the chart was written by a European.

9. It should also be acknowledged that an argument could be made for the "third stream" actually beginning in the mid-1940s, with the open interaction and appreciation between members of the jazz and classical communities. Stravinsky's "Ebony Concerto" for Woody Herman is a good example of this.

10. Gitler, *Jazz Masters of the 40s*, 267.

11. There is some anecdotal evidence that Dameron claimed to have used the Shillinger Method in his composing. More can be found in the appendix, under "Further Discussion": http://www.press.umich.edu/22963/dameronia.

12. Leon Dallin, *Techniques of Twentieth Century Composition* (Dubuque, IA: Wm. C. Brown Co., 1974), 4.

13. More can be found in the appendix, under "Further Discussion": http://www.press.umich.edu/22963/dameronia.

14. If one listens to the live Gillespie recordings of the big-band arrangement, one can understand that a sense of grandeur was at least one of Dameron's conceptions of this melodic line.

15. More can be found in the appendix, under "Further Discussion": http://www.press.umich.edu/22963/dameronia.

16. Even though Sarah Vaughan sang "If You Could See Me Now" in Ab, it was published in Eb.

17. MacDonald, *Tadd*, 64.

18. Val Wilmer to the author, Nov. 5, 1992 (Wilmer recalled the essence of her conversation with Lovelle in this letter).

19. Gene Lees, *Cats of Any Color* (New York: Oxford University Press, 1995), 133.

20. Joe Mosbrook, "Jazzed In Cleveland: Part Sixteen" Dec. 4, 1996, http://www.cleveland.oh.us.

21. The authorship of this tune is the subject of controversy. Richard Carpenter claimed it, but some maintain that it was written by Lucky Thompson, and others cite Gene Ammons. The author is inclined to agree with the latter assignation but cannot prove it.

22. Baker recorded more of Dameron's music in 1965, and some have speculated that these tunes, too, were arranged by the composer, but there are no arrangements. The tunes are played as on a casual gig with a pick-up rhythm section. Included in these recordings is a tune named "Baby Breeze" that Ian Macdonald has identified as Dameron's (*Tadd*, 10, 68). This tune is not mentioned in any of the copyright information and is officially claimed by Richard Carpenter. Given Carpenter's reputation, he could have stolen it from Dameron. However, there are seventy-five titles listed under Carpenter's name in the BMI database, and without more research, it is difficult to say that he did not write any of them. "Baby Breeze" is an eight-bar blues that sounds more like something written by Hank Mobley.

23. Hod O'Brien, interview with the author, Feb. 2, 2006.

24. He was born Clive Powell. Fame has also provided a lyric for "A Blue Time" under the title "There's No More Blue Time."

25. Don Sickler, interview with the author, Dec. 15, 2005.

Comprehensive Index

Harris, Opal (aunt), 3, 5, 6
Harris, Ruth Olga (mother), 2–3. *See also* Dameron, Ruth Olga
Harris, Silas Caesar (grandfather), 2–3
Harris, Silas, Jr. (uncle), 3, 5, 6, 28
Harris, Sophie Tadley (grandmother), 2
Harris, Tennie (aunt), 3, 5, 6
Hart, Clyde, 8, 41
Hart, Lorenz, 138
Hawkins, Coleman, 58, 81, 104, 111, 185
Hawkins, Erskine, 111
Hawthorn Avenue (Cleveland), 7
Hayse, Carl, 150–51, 153
Haywood, Cedric, 110
Heard, Eugene "Fats," 1
Heath, Jimmy, 192, 205
Heath, Moira, 100
Heath, Percy, 124, 199
Heath, Ted, 81, 99–103, 106–13, 171
Heatwave (Cleveland), 8
"Heaven's Doors Are Open Wide" (arrangement and song), 91, 203
Hefti, Neal, 170
Henderson, Fletcher, 6, 7, 8
Henderson, Ray, 155
Henry, Ernie, 69–70, 77, 79
"Hep-sations" (band and tour), 62, 79
"Hepster's Guide, The" (tune), 35
Herman, Woody, 53, 72, 147, 190, 204
heroin
    Dameron's use of, 83, 114–17, 199–200
        arrests for possession of, 140–46, 148–49
        becomes more visible, 114–17
        beginning of, 83
        disappearance of at Paradise Club raid, 129
        incarcerated for second violation, 149–56
    Holiday's trial for possession of, 74
"Hey Messy!" (song), 33–34, 35
"Hey Pam!" (arrangement), 178–79
Heyman, Edward, 90
Hill, Teddy, 37, 63
Hines, Earl, 10–11, 39, 43, 51, 114
Hite, Les, 58
Hodier, André, 96
Hoefer, George, 10, 169
Holder, T., 36
Holiday, Billie, 74, 157, 185

Hollywood Cafe (Cleveland), 10
"Honey" (arrangement), 51
"Honey Hush" (tune), 159
"Honeysuckle Rose" (song), 21, 23, 24
hospital, Dameron's incarceration in, 149–56
"Hot House" (arrangement and tune)
    analysis of, 69
    BVC registers copyright for, 132
    inclusion on potential Dameron's "greatest hits" album, 142
    melodic technique in, 194, 196
    mentioned, 51, 70, 86
    recordings of, 49–50, 112
Hot Record Society (HRS) (record label), 60–61
Hotel Almac (New York City), 184, *photo section*
Hotel Ambassador (Cleveland), 9
Hotel Chalfonte (New York City), 187
Hotel Du Sable Lounge (Chicago), 83
Hotel Syracuse (New York), 89
Houston, Tate, 163–64, 166
"How about You" (arrangement), 189
"How High the Moon" (arrangement), 63
"How Strange" (arrangement), 81
Howard University (Washington, DC), 120
HRS (Hot Record Society) (record label), 60–61
Hughes, Langston, 4
Husby, Per, 192, 203

"I Can Make You Love Me" (arrangement), 61–62, 119
"I Dream a Lot about You" (arrangement), 29, 30–31
"I Get the Neck of the Chicken" (song), 75
"I Let a Song Go Out of My Heart" (arrangement), 10
"I Love You, Yes I Do" (arrangement), 118–19
"I Never Loved Anyone but You" (arrangement), 119
"I Think I'll Go Away" (arrangement and song), 77, 85, 87, 92, 201
"I Want to Talk about You" (arrangement), 44–45, 64
"I Was Doin' Alright" (arrangement), 139
"Ice Freezes Red" (tune), 75
"I'd Rather Have a Memory Than a Dream" (arrangement), 52, 61
"If I Should Lose You" (arrangement), 176

Musical Works Index

Made in the USA
Las Vegas, NV
06 September 2021